T0271108

ROUTLEDGE LIBRARY EDITIONS:
COMMODITIES

Volume 3

THE MODERN
PLANTATION IN
THE THIRD WORLD

THE MODERN
PLANTATION IN
THE THIRD WORLD

EDGAR GRAHAM
WITH
INGRID FLOERING

Edited and with a Foreword by
DAVID FIELDHOUSE

Routledge
Taylor & Francis Group

LONDON AND NEW YORK

First published in 1984 by Croom Helm Ltd.

This edition first published in 2024
by Routledge
4 Park Square, Milton Park, Abingdon, Oxon OX14 4RN

and by Routledge
605 Third Avenue, New York, NY 10158

Routledge is an imprint of the Taylor & Francis Group, an informa business

British Library Cataloguing in Publication Data
A catalogue record for this book is available from the British Library

ISBN: 978-1-032-69509-9 (Set)
ISBN: 978-1-032-69313-2 (Volume 3) (hbk)
ISBN: 978-1-032-69315-6 (Volume 3) (pbk)
ISBN: 978-1-032-69314-9 (Volume 3) (ebk)

DOI: 10.4324/9781032693149

Publisher's Note
The publisher has gone to great lengths to ensure the quality of this reprint but points out that some imperfections in the original copies may be apparent.

Disclaimer
The publisher has made every effort to trace copyright holders and would welcome correspondence from those they have been unable to trace.

The Modern Plantation in the Third World

EDGAR GRAHAM
with
INGRID FLOERING

Edited and with a foreword by
David Fieldhouse

CROOM HELM
London & Sydney

© 1984 E. Graham and I. Floering
Croom Helm Ltd, Provident House, Burrell Row,
Beckenham, Kent BR3 1AT
Croom Helm Australia Pty Ltd, First Floor, 139 King Street,
Sydney, NSW 2001, Australia

British Library Cataloguing in Publication Data

Graham, Edgar
  The modern plantation in the Third World.
  1. Plantations——Economic aspects
  I. Title
  338.1   HD1471.A3

  ISBN 0-7099-1101-7

Printed and bound in Great Britain

CONTENTS

For Lindsay, Clare and Oliver Graham

LIST OF TABLES AND FIGURES

Tables

Figures

LIST OF ABBREVIATIONS

ACP	African, Caribbean and Pacific signatories of the Sugar Protocol to the Lomé Convention, 1975
BAI	Booker Agriculture International
BET	Basic Export Tonnage (sugar)
CEA	Consejo Estatal del Azucar (Dominican Republic)
CDC	Commonwealth Development Corporation (London)
CFDT	Compagnie Française pour le Développement des Fibres Textiles (Mali/Upper Volta)
CIBC	Commonwealth Institute of Biological Control
EEC	European Economic Community
FAO	Food and Agriculture Organisation
FELDA	Federal Land Development Authority (Malaysia)
FFB	Fresh fruit bunch (oil palm)
G & W	Gulf and Western Industries
HFCS	High fructose corn syrup
IAA	Instituto do Açucar e do Alcool (Brazil)
IMF	International Monetary Fund
INAZUCAR	Dominican Sugar Institute
INESPRE	Government Price Stabilisation Institute (Dominican Republic)
ISA	International Sugar Agreement
ISC	International Sugar Council
ISO	International Sugar Organisation (London)
ISSCT	International Society of Sugar Cane Technologists
KTDA	Kenya Tea Development Authority
LDC	Less developed country
LSC	Lonhro Sugar Corporation
MOC	Mumias Outgrowers' Company (Kenya)
MOD	Ministry of Overseas Development (UK)
MRDC	Malaysian Rubber Development Corporation
MSC	Mumias Sugar Company (Swaziland)
OECD	Organisation for Economic Co-operation and Development
RSSC	Royal Swaziland Sugar Corporation
SIS	Swaziland Irrigation Scheme

SMR	Standard Malaysian Rubber
SSA	Swaziland Sugar Association
SSE	Simunye Sugar Estate (Swaziland)
SUCOMA	Sugar Corporation of Malawi
TCD	Tonnes of cane daily
TCH	Tonnes of cane per hectare
TLE	Tate and Lyle Engineering
TLTS	Tate and Lyle Technical Services
UNCTAD	United Nations Conference on Trade and Development (Geneva)
VIF	Vuvulane Irrigated Farms (Swaziland)

EDITORIAL STATEMENT

This book is the fifth in the Croom Helm Commodity Series. The aim of the Series is to advance the understanding of issues relating to the production and marketing of primary commodities. Most volumes in the Series concentrate on analysing the essential properties, production and trade of a single commodity. Others, such as *Commodity Models for Forecasting and Policy Analysis* by Walter Labys and Peter Pollak, address wider themes. The present volume, however, stands in a class of its own. It is the product of a business rather than an academic career and it offers a new perspective on a subject which is important to the production of many primary commodities, namely the modern plantation estate.

To Edgar Graham, who sadly died in November 1983 just before the book was completed, we owe the debt of the time spent and the attention given to setting down on paper the insight deriving from many years of close involvement with plantation agriculture. He offers a detailed working knowledge of both the strengths and the weaknesses of the plantation; in many ways his analysis poses a challenge to more traditional schools of thought.

Edgar Graham was assisted by the substantial contribution of Ingrid Floering who wrote Chapters 7 to 9 and helped bring the manuscript to its final form. In addition, David Fieldhouse, who had close knowledge of Edgar Graham's thinking on the subject and had agreed to write a foreword, undertook to revise the manuscript and see it through to publication.

Fiona Gordon-Ashworth
Series Editor

FOREWORD

The plantation, plantation estate or estate (the words are used inter-changeably in this book) has played a leading role in the demonology of writers on 'Third World' economic development and 'under-development'. It has been accused of many things: of resulting in over-specialisation in export crops, monoculture and agglomeration of land needed for food production; of employing servile, semi-servile or merely very badly paid labour; of the creation of economic and social enclaves dominated by foreign capital and the consequential transfer of wealth to overseas owners. Such accusations have two main roots. One is past history, stretching from the slave plantations of colonial and nineteenth-century America and the Caribbean to late-nineteenth-century and early twentieth-century plantations in Africa, South East Asia and the Pacific, when the plantation was synonymous with the exploitation of human labour. The other root lies in some of the basic assumptions of many writers on economic development since the 1940s. One very common belief was that there were 'structural' obstacles to proper development in Third World countries, and among these obstacles was the dominance of foreign capital. Since many plantations were owned and run by overseas companies, they formed part of this structural problem and must be abolished. Conversely, very few studies have been made of the realities of plantations in the second half of the twentieth century, when decolonisation and subsequent control by the successor states of all aspects of the economic and social life of less developed countries radically changed conditions in those places where plantations are commonly found: the myths of the past live on. There is therefore an urgent need to reassess the character of the plantation as it exists in the last decades of the century rather than as it was in a different era; to redefine its functions and to assess its potential value to host countries and to the world economy.

This book is an attempt to start such a process of redefinition and evaluation. Indirectly it derives from work I did in a study of *Unilever Overseas* (Croom Helm, London, 1978), which included chapters on two of Unilever's largest plantation enterprises, in Zaire and the Solomons. That book was written in close collaboration with Edgar Graham, then a Director of Unilever and Chairman of its

Overseas Committee, which was closely involved with the company's plantation interests. We discussed many aspects of plantations and influenced each other's attitudes towards them. Edgar
Graham had had long experience of Unilever's plantations in West
Africa, Zaire, Malaysia and the Pacific. Unlike most theoretical
writers on the subject, he had a deep grasp and direct experience of
the economic, social and technical aspects of plantation production;
and he wrote as a pragmatist, working from observed fact. Above
all, he had studied and thought deeply about the changes that he had
seen taking place during the last three decades. His starting-point
was the fact that the 'modern plantation', as he called it, bears very
little resemblance to that of the past, on which most hostile accounts
are still based. In his view two recent changes have altered the very
nature of the issue. First, the modern plantation exists within an
economic environment controlled by independent governments who
are fully aware of the problems it may raise, including that of foreign
ownership and management. They now have the power to regulate
foreign enterprises of all kinds, including the often-used power of
expropriation and the ability to demand a share in their equity.
Moreover, they can and do fix wages and prices, insist on the use of
indigenous managers and control imports and exports. The post-
colonial state can thus determine the character and very existence of
plantation enterprises. If they continue to exist, it is as a result of a
policy decision, not compulsion. Second, there has been a rapid
development in the field of technology which has revolutionised
most aspects of plantation production, from plant research resulting
in vastly improved yields to entomological work on control of pests
and the introduction of new machinery to harvest and process the
product. The result of these two types of change is that the modern
plantation offers host governments the option of using this as possi-
bly the most efficient way of utilising available factors of production
to provide a maximum social return: that this is a genuine possibility
was demonstrated a decade ago by I.M.D. Little and D.G. Tipping's
classic pioneer study, *A Social Cost Benefit Analysis of the Kulai Oil
Palm Estate, West Malaysia* (OECD Development Centre, Paris,
1972). Moreover, Edgar Graham did not restrict his conception of
the plantation to the traditional unitary estate: he took account of
the wide range of 'peasant' options, such as the highly successful
Federal Land Development Authority (FELDA) system in Malaysia
and of other co-operative systems. What is essential to any form of
plantation is efficiency in management, planning and technology,

and this can come in a variety of forms within the concept of a 'modern plantation'.

Sadly, Edgar Graham died suddenly in November 1983. At that point he had undertaken a final revision of his own part of the manuscript and was about to review the revised version of Ingrid Floering's chapters. Since I had been associated with the project from the start, I was asked to act as editor and to help in seeing the book through its final stages. I have gladly done so; but I have kept my part to a minimum. No two academics see a particular issue from the same standpoint or would write the same book, even if they agreed on all essential issues, as in fact Edgar Graham and I did. But in this case the contrast is increased by the fact that he was and thought as a businessman with academic interests, I as an academic who had studied a multinational corporation. His approach and manner of expression were more practical and less orientated to contemporary theoretical debates over (for example) the implications of capitalist investment in underdeveloped countries than mine would have been. There is great value in his practical approach since, ultimately, economic development involves action based on practical experience. I have therefore made no attempt to restructure his book: it stands basically as he left it. My main contribution has been to add occasional paragraphs in order to tidy up arguments and ensure continuity of thought. I am most grateful to Ingrid Floering who, having worked with Edgar Graham and written the chapters on the sugar industry, has also undertaken much of the final donkeywork, such as preparing the bibliography.

The book owes a great deal to the School of Oriental and African Studies, University of London, of which Edgar Graham was a Governor and Honorary Treasurer. After his retirement from Unilever the School provided him with a place to work, made a grant to enable Ingrid Floering to collaborate with him, and allowed Miss Joan Woods to retype the final manuscript. But above all he benefited from the company of the School's many specialists on Africa and Asia, on whom he tried out his ideas and from whom he received much constructive help and advice.

No one book can produce all the answers; but this book is, to my knowledge, the first attempt by someone with direct personal experience and expertise to define and rationalise the character and functions of a plantation in the contemporary world. It presents a case clearly and bluntly. Many will disagree with it; but no one who has to deal with the plantation as a theoretical or practical issue will be able to ignore its central thesis.

D.K. Fieldhouse
December 1983

PREFACE

This book is the result of many visits to developing countries in Africa, Asia and Latin America while working for United Africa and its parent, Unilever, between 1947 and the late 1970s. These visits usually concerned industrial or trade matters, but sometimes touched on food supplies; and each visit began with a look at the economy and general situation of a particular country. A constant and critical theme in all discussions with local political, administrative and business contacts was the problem of the agricultural sector of the economy and supplies of food.

To one whose questions began with manufacturing and distribution, selling and finance, the contrast between official plans for development in these sectors and governmental attitudes to agriculture was striking and puzzling. Development plans for industry were often well researched and realistic. Projects were prepared on a scale and of a character that could be discussed in concrete terms. Foreign partners were often called in by Third World governments and provision made for the application of technology by those who understood it and had applied it elsewhere. The span of managerial responsibility was closely defined. Degrees of efficiency and success varied widely. Some ventures failed but many went ahead, and one project did not carry inevitable consequences for the whole: there could be failure in one area and success in another.

The contrast in official attitudes to the land was striking. In many countries during the early post-Second World War years production from the land did not rate high in the hierarchy of development planning and expenditure. The large landowner and peasant had produced crops from time immemorial and would, presumably, continue to do so in their own way. Bigger and better crops were assumed to come from better weather, more extensive cultivation and marginally improved techniques within the same framework of land ownership and occupation, provided the market gave sufficient incentive. Government planning and investment were thought to be largely unnecessary. In the period of post-war shortages in Europe there were a few attempts by imperial governments at innovation and large-scale planning in some colonies in Africa, notably groundnuts in Tanganyika and eggs in Gambia. Both were disasters and

1

discredited the application of modern mechanised techniques to tropical agriculture. For the rest, government agricultural services encouraged improved methods of peasant production, sometimes with politically disastrous results, as in Kenya. A few specialised organisations and institutions were established. But collective schemes usually depended on the loosest form of agricultural institution, the co-operative.[1]

The surprising thing was that in many Third World countries there had long existed a form of production that brought to agriculture the corpus of skills typical of modern industry. This was the plantation. The efficiency of plantation estates often contrasted very sharply with the inefficiency of the surrounding agricultural economy. Moreover, there was, in the early post-war years, very little adverse criticism of these plantations in overseas countries: they were praised at all levels, from central government to local officials, and by managers and leading members of indigenous communities. There might be arguments about land ownership, rates of pay, prices of their products and distribution. But these were points of detail: there was no questioning the desirability of the plantation for the economy of the host country.

In Europe, however, there was growing criticism and often outright condemnation of the plantation among many development economists and by academics and organs of opinion concerned with the Third World. In time, and particularly after decolonisation in Africa and the East, this hostility was taken up in the Third World itself, leading to government policies which rejected for agriculture the very methods of industrial production that were being proposed or tried in other sectors of the economy. The reasons for this rejection were various. Some could be traced to the past. Large-scale organised agriculture suffered from its association with slavery and the importation of slave or semi-servile labour, with all its connotations for the countries from which the slaves came as well as for those to which they were taken. There were dark areas of labour exploitation after the abolition of slavery and the effects of labour migrations. Specialisation on export commodities for the developed countries and the apparent insulation of plantations within 'enclaves' were anathema to theorists of the Latin American *dependencia* school. Socialists were hostile because many plantations were established, owned and run by foreign capitalists. For the anthropologist and the sociologist there were doubts about change in social patterns and the uprooting of traditional societies.

These concepts and criticisms were widespread. Meantime, the number of newly independent states in the Third World increased rapidly in the two decades after 1950, and with them proliferated international agencies and professional planners and advisers, all concerned with theories of economic development. Many of the early strategists clung to the one man:one smallholding approach and neglected the benefits which could best come through use of managerial technology. International professional opinion was commonly attached to the concept of the peasant smallholder and many new states were from the start committed to the extension of peasant landholding at the expense of large estates. For these and other reasons the potential value of corporate forms of agricultural production received little serious attention and criticisms of the plantation were seldom challenged.

Yet, to anyone who had looked at the issues from within the developing countries, such attitudes seemed narrow and unrealistic. Indeed, they were increasingly rejected by those who held power in the new states. They were fully aware of the political appeal of redistribution of land into smallholdings and of attacks on foreign capitalists. But in practice many governments came to see the economic value of agricultural corporations, once the problem of foreign ownership could be dealt with: leasing and local participation in the equity became common solutions. The managerial system was increasingly seen to be as valuable in agriculture as in industry and other parts of the modern sector. Sometimes the state itself went into the plantation business, as in Malaysia. In the 1970s the World Bank began to plan and encourage plantations as well as smallholder schemes. Even before the 1980s possible alternatives to peasant production were coming to be respectable.

There is today clearly seen to be room for both the peasant and the managerial approach; but as yet there is no widespread understanding of the managerial/institutional system as applied to agriculture. Those who use it with success have not found it necessary to explain or to be apologists for it. The word 'plantation' is commonly used to describe such a system, but the term itself is ill-defined and brings with it connotations from the past which have long been outdated. In particular there have been changes since the Second World War which are fundamental; and developments within the last five to ten years have been rapid and far-reaching.

The aim of this book is to examine the modern managerial institution in agriculture, to define its present nature and to consider what changes are necessary to adapt it for wider use. The starting-point is practical experience. Although the author had much to do with government ministers and civil servants, planners and academics, he was never one of them. It was from this outside standpoint that he had to look at the theories of academic colleagues when invited to join in their discussions and at the policies of international agencies when he worked with them. This book is an attempt to relate their arguments to the facts of the plantation estate as it is today.

Note

1. See, for instance, T. Forrest, 'Agricultural Policies in Nigeria 1900–1978' in J. Heyer, P. Roberts and G. Williams (eds.), *Rural Development in Tropical Africa* (St Martin's Press, New York, 1981), pp. 229–30 and pp. 249–50. For an account of the Groundnut and Gambia Egg Schemes, see D.J. Morgan, *The Official History of Colonial Development*, vol. 2, *Developing British Colonial Resources 1945–1951* (Macmillan, London, 1980), pp. 226 f.

PART ONE: THE PLANTATION AND ITS CHARACTERISTICS: ANALYSIS AND ECONOMIC THEORY

1 THE PLANTATION AS A PRODUCTION SYSTEM

Introduction — Agricultural Problems in the Third World

Though it is said that in his history man has used 3,000 plant species for food, and that at least 150 of them have been commercially cultivated to some extent, the world's population today depends upon about 20 crops — the cereals such as wheat, rice, maize, etc.; root crops such as potato and cassava; legumes such as peas, beans, groundnuts; oilseeds such as coconut and palm oil; sugar cane and sugar beet; and bananas. Today rapidly rising populations and even more rapidly rising expectations have put increased production of all of them at the head of the world's queue of problems. There is at the same time a parallel increase in demand for those raw materials of industry, such as rubber and cotton, that come from the land; and indeed agriculture is now being called upon to supplement and perhaps eventually to replace some of the world's non-renewable assets, with substitutes for present energy sources as a new priority.

This has brought examination by the economist and the social scientist, the agronomist and the historian; they have studied the traditional types of husbandry in many forms and in many countries and have developed theory and practice for new approaches. A wide range of experiments and schemes have been invented and tried — smallholder projects, agricultural extension systems, co-operatives, collective farms and many variations upon them.

Yet, though progress has been made, the results have matched neither expectation nor requirements. The World Food Conference in Rome in 1974 set a world target of 4 per cent growth in food production per annum; but the result for the decade of the 1970s was an increase of only 2.8 per cent per annum.[1] The decade was not typical, for the performance was worse than the 1960s. The oil crisis began in 1973/4 and subsequent years were deeply affected by its consequences. Matters might have been worse: it was possible to offset some of the production shortfall by a rundown of stocks in the late 1970s. But the fact remains that this performance is only just ahead of the growth of world population as a whole: it leaves no room for maldistribution or local variation; within the total some areas have suffered heavily; no ground has been made for the large proportion who still suffer from the whole range of deficiency between malnutrition and starvation. Faster progress is needed; to attain even the modest 4 per cent per annum, the increase in production has to go up by more than a third from the level of the 1970s.

There are, moreover, even more intractable particular difficulties hidden within these general totals. In the developing countries as a whole World Bank figures suggest that GNP *per capita* rose by 2.7 per cent per annum between 1970 and 1980; but in low-income countries the increase was only 1.6 per cent and in low-income Sub-Saharan Africa the income of oil-importing countries fell by 0.4 per cent per annum.[2] These low-income countries are those where the forms of society tend to be the most traditional and the economy most dependent on undeveloped and unchanging forms of agriculture. They are losing ground relatively to the rest of the world, though absolutely in terms of national GNP they may be making slight progress.

The shortfall from the 4 per cent target has not been for want of spending money. If we take the case of food alone among the worst performing group — Sub-Saharan Africa — we can get some general figures which show the size and the nature of the failure. About $5 billion in aid flowed into agricultural projects in these countries between 1973 and 1980, $2.4 billion of which was from the World Bank. Yet, whereas in the 1960s food production as measured by the major crops had risen by about 2 per cent per annum over the whole range of the countries, in the 1970s the rate fell to 1.5 per cent as the general level, while the oil-exporting countries performed much worse; in Nigeria there was hardly any increase except in rice, and groundnuts fell by 14 per cent per annum between 1969 and 1979.[3]

Nigeria is only an extreme case of a general failure; to quote the same World Bank Report, 'this decline occurred over a period when the various government and external sources of finance focused more strongly on food production projects than ever before'. The limitations and dangers of agricultural data are well known; but the general pattern seems established beyond denial.

It is becoming clear that there is a need for a change of approach and the World Bank publication confirms this. What has been started in the co-operatives, the smallholdings and the extension schemes forms the base for improvements; at a minimum what has been done has meant the extension of the areas under cultivation, which in itself has led to greater production; but what is needed now is higher productivity within the new schemes, and this has had much less attention.

Most of the research and writing on the subject of the various new forms of agricultural experiment has dealt almost exclusively with the primary task of setting up the new organisations. This is not surprising. Even the simplest idea of any formal systemisation of agricultural methods was a strange one to many areas of the Third World. Working units for the cultivation of the land have usually depended from earliest times on the individual, the family, or at most the tribe; they have been of a type which demanded individual not collective effort. A series of men or women performed all the tasks and covered all the needs from the clearing of the land through planting and harvesting to distribution. Where the raising of the crops was for the subsistence of those directly concerned — the man and his family or his tribe — it was the same individuals who distributed or marketed as well. Where the goods were grown for sale and consumption some distance away, a different organisation had to take over: the farmer could not usually leave his fields for a long enough period to carry the crops physically to their destination, or remain there long enough to distribute and sell them.

So the middleman, the merchant, came into being. But on the land itself there were no apparent advantages in such a division of duties, and most of those who began to study the subject in the twentieth century started from this assumption. The main principles of most of the new ideas and systems that were suggested lay along the lines of the improvement of the traditional effort of the individual. If he could be induced to use better tools, better seeds, better weed-killers and fertilisers, it was believed that he would produce more while still continuing to work in much the same pattern as he and his ancestors had always done in the past. Where new practices were necessary, advisers and extension officers would teach the individual farmer to adopt them, but he would remain a worker who had to cover the whole range of duties himself. The pattern would remain the same for most of what he did; the new would have to be fitted into the old framework of life and work, of village tradition and family practice and ties.

Yet a setback in a harvest, an unusual spell of weather requiring adjustment of a programme, or a fall in the price obtained for a season's production, was very likely to bring disillusionment. New ideas often required a more disciplined programme of work — perhaps a stricter adherence to dates in a calendar — which was strange in most communities.

Wholesale and immediate change over the whole face of a rural society to fit in forthwith with new methods is clearly impossible. On the other hand, it would seem that, if the needs of rising populations for food alone are to be met, some more rapid progress will have to be achieved than the gradualism of the present approaches. On the demand side, it is in itself the change in the ways of life, caused by the rapid improvement in health and social conditions, and the consequent increase in the number of mouths to feed, that is causing the increase in basic requirements of food; at one remove the same is true of some raw materials. It would be hard to deny that a matching change in agricultural institutions and social patterns must come on the production side as well.

The initial reaction in some cases has been to attempt to reverse the drift of country dwellers to the towns, and to spread ownership of the land more widely, in the hope that this would produce a greater quantity of subsistence crops. But there are very real physical limits to the numbers who can be directly employed in owning and working the land. Desirable though it may be, politically and emotionally, that each family should have his own plot, the most simple piece of arithmetic will show that in most developing countries it is impossible for any high proportion of the population to own a viable patch of ground. Barbara Ward, a convinced believer in the small farm, does not conceal the difficulties:

> In fifty-two of the eighty poorest developing lands, there is less than one hectare of land available for each rural inhabitant. Take India, Pakistan and Bangladesh. The minimum economic holding for Indians and Pakistanis is held to be between three and five hectares. In Bangladesh it is about two hectares. But the land available for each peasant in India is less than 0.5 hectares. In Bangladesh it is as little as 0.2. Even if land were redistributed on the basis of minimum-sized viable holdings, there could remain over 25 million landless families.[4]

In other words, there are large numbers in many countries for whom the social objective of individual land ownership with a rural, traditional way of life cannot be realised, no matter what agricultural developments take place. There is not a great deal more room to move in that direction, nor does it seem at all likely that, with present arrangements and at the present pace, quite apart from questions of ownership, what are basically traditional systems will be able to overcome developing shortages of food and raw materials. The 2.8 per cent per annum increase of the 1970s is admitted not to be enough; an unknown percentage of this comes from an extension in the area of cultivated land, to which again there must be an early limit. Further progress will have to come from increased production through present schemes or the development of new approaches. The World Bank Report on Sub-Saharan Africa, the World Development Report 1982 and much other evidence suggest that the increase will in fact have to come from both.

The ideas that lie behind attempts to improve the performance of the smallholder — the individual farmer working in his long-accustomed fashion on a small plot of land — have centred almost exclusively on the problems and possibilities of one family working on its own and covering the whole range of what has to be done. The idea of breaking the task down into individual parts and seeking improved output by specialisation on the one hand and team-work on the other has received far less study until very recently. This is surprising, for the concepts have been extensively applied in many Third World countries in the field of industrial production.

The difference is clearly seen in the forms of organisation that have been used in tackling agricultural problems, in contrast to those which have appeared in new ventures for manufacturing industry. While the latter have almost universally been created in the form of a corporation with a closely defined aim and responsibility — whether the shareholders and capital are private, government, parastatal or a mixture — the agricultural venture has usually, until recent times, taken a looser form. Co-operatives have been the favourite approach, or a direct network of agricultural extension, led by government officials without a closely defined form of institutional framework, and frequently reporting back through several layers of authority to central government itself. The management corporation style used by industry enjoys shorter lines of delegated authority and communication and a narrower span of control. It can produce ready decisions and quicker progress; individual ventures can prosper or fail on their own local merits, and need not be affected by a range of irrelevant other circumstances brought into consideration because of the many different interests and multiple layers of controlling authority involved.

Given the need for new ideas, it seems reasonable to examine the desirability of applying the industrial approach to agriculture as well. Indeed there is an institution which has already evolved a long way along the lines of specialised management methods and systems of control of production for agriculture, with a well-defined responsibility and close delineation of purpose which has enabled it to concentrate on the primary task of increasing production and applying research and development to that end. It is the plantation estate. Because of its history and the practices with which it has been associated in the past, the name is so overlaid with emotive connotations that it has for a long time not been a respectable subject for serious academic study. Nevertheless its practitioners have now brought it to a point where it is very different from the picture that is usually conjured up by the use of the word 'plantation'. The new form started to evolve not much more than a hundred years ago, when the limited liability corporation was first applied to agricultural production in what is now South East Asia; its management, methods and specialised technology achieved a rapid advance after the Second World War. Now, in the 1980s, it has become a well-established institution.

Yet — in contrast to schemes for the smallholder — there has been little formal analysis of the modern plantation estate and no detailed attempt to describe, assess and improve it. Even less has any effort been made to develop a form of presentation that might make it better understood, better accepted and more used than it is now; so attitudes towards it survive today — as platforms for teaching or a basis for planning and government policy — which have rarely been subjected to critical examination. Yet the plantation in its modern form can be shown to be an effective institution which can help with a basic and central problem. As a result of its earlier history, it is regarded as having undesirable political, economic, social and cultural consequences. If it is to be better used, it needs a survey and justification under all these headings. It is the purpose of this book to define, describe and examine it as it is today, to see where it may need adaptation and to suggest ways in which its systems and the management ideas behind it could be applied in a wider field.

A preliminary comment is, however, necessary on the relevance of the plantation estate and its associated principles to the problem of food shortages in the Third World which, it has been suggested above, constitutes a major challenge to the later twentieth century. Here there is an apparent paradox. Much of the evidence on the operation of plantations presented below does not directly relate to food production; and the case studies revolve around three commodities — palm oil, rubber and sugar — of which only palm oil has strong nutritional properties. Some other plantation products mentioned in this book, notably cotton, make little or no direct contribution to the problem of food shortages. Conversely, there is little evidence on the utility of the plantation as a producer of basic foods, such as cereals and legumes. How, then, can it be claimed that the plantation can make a valuable contribution to the solution of hunger in the Third World?

The main reason why so much of the evidence on plantations derives from a narrow range of products, some of which have no food value, is that the majority of plantations on which detailed information is available are of this type. In particular, Unilever's plantations, of which the author had most direct experience, concentrate mainly on producing palm oil, copra and rubber. This is accidental; but in fact there are two sound reasons for holding that the plantation can make a valuable contribution to the availability of food in Third World countries. These will be developed in more detail later, but can briefly be outlined here.

The first derives from the standard principle of comparative advantage. If a Third World country has a factor endowment that makes it particularly well adapted to the production of non-edible agricultural commodities (e.g. rubber, cotton) for which there is sufficient world demand; and if it can produce these things, using the same quantities of land, labour and capital, more efficiently than it could cereals or legumes, then it should be to its advantage to devote at least part of its resources to their commercial production and export. If the choice of products is properly made, the country can then exchange these commodities for a greater quantity of foodstuffs than it could have produced on its own account with the same resources; and the fact that there are now huge surpluses of various temperate foodstuffs in the developed countries suggests that the barter terms of trade might be favourable. Thus, the first standard argument for adopting the principles of plantation production, as they are defined below, is that by their relative efficiency they should increase the real incomes of Third World countries, earn them foreign exchange and so enable them to increase the total availability of food for domestic consumption. In this sense one may grow fatter from rubber than from sweet potatoes. In addition, if commodity exports earn more foreign exchange than is needed to pay for imports of food, the balance can be used to pay for imported capital and intermediate goods to expand industrial production.

This may be regarded as the indirect contribution that the plantation principle may make to Third World welfare. The point is obvious and is mentioned only to indicate that it has not been ignored. But the plantation can also make a more direct contribution to food supplies. It is suggested below that one main reason why existing plantations tend to concentrate on commodities such as palm oil and rubber is that these products can be cropped throughout much of the year, so that the labour force and equipment can be employed more or less continuously. Even sugar, which has seasonal peaks and troughs, requires substantial work throughout the year. By contrast, most food crops are highly seasonal and do not lend themselves so readily to an industrial system of production. Yet this may be misleading. One central argument of this book is that the essence of the plantation is not found in the obvious features of the conventional estate, but rather in the quality of organisation, management and technical skill that a plantation requires. This characteristic can be applied to many different types of agricultural production by intelligent adaptation, and not least to the production of food. In this sense the modern plantation estate is a laboratory in which methods of increasing agricultural efficiency are developed and tested and some of whose discoveries can be adapted to quite different products and methods of production. Thus, while the early part of this book concentrates on evidence from existing plantations, irrespective of their direct contribution to food production, the later part increasingly examines the potential application of fundamental principles derived from the plantation to the whole range of agricultural production in Third World countries.

Defining the Modern Plantation Estate

P.P. Courtenay is the first writer to carry the study of plantations to the point where in their modern form they can be seen as an industrial institution; indeed he uses the term Industrial Plantation for their latest stages. He has described in broad outline the processes that have gone to produce today's plantation estate, and has written a good and comprehensive history of its development.[5] It is not proposed here to duplicate this examination: none the less, because recent changes have been so fundamental and so fast, there is a need to define more closely what the institution has now become. It will be necessary to look at some definitions from the past and pick out the essential identifying characteristics, at the same time separating out those elements which have become outdated or greatly modified.

Since there has been much recent change — within the last ten and even five years — a full picture of the modern plantation is not very widely known. Detailed examination will be necessary for some of the alterations that have taken place, particularly where there have in the past been unfavourable features that have attracted hostile reaction to the system; it will be necessary to show that they have been modified or have disappeared before any judgement can be made of the suitability of the present institution for use and extension.

One particular caveat is necessary. By far the greatest volume of literature on the subject has been written on the history and development of plantations in the Americas; much of the specialised work has been done by writers of the West Indian school who have used the corpus of these studies to produce a description and theory of plantations which, whatever its validity even 25 years ago, is not generally tenable today.[6] It relates only to the American — largely the West Indian — scene and varies widely from the patterns that are seen in other regions, particularly South East Asia, which is now in the vanguard of modern plantation development.

A First Definition

In the past the word plantation has borne a host of meanings. It has been used widely of many forms of cultivation, and especially trees, whose only common feature has been that they have been set up as a pattern or according to a plan — that they have arisen deliberately rather than haphazardly. A closer definition is needed for what we are examining — the plantation as it is today — at least as a hypothesis, and it will be necessary to test the validity of much of the examination against this hypothesis.

Let us then call our subject 'the modern plantation estate' and give it an initial narrow definition as follows:

An organisation for the large-scale production of commodity crops by a uniform system of planting, cultivation and often on-site processing under a central management and with a trained labour force, sometimes living in estate housing in an environment controlled by the same management. Its foundation is the expert direction and training of its work-force by the use of a technology of detailed routine working and supervision.

The narrowness arises because these are in fact the particular characteristics of the cultivation of a restricted range of crops — mainly rubber, tea and oil and coconut palm though they are more generally applicable with some slight modification to coffee, sugar, bananas and some other crops as well. It may need widening later. But it is used here as the beginning of an attempt to bring out the principles behind the management of plantations. If there is one peculiar feature of a particular crop which does not fit the definition, it will be necessary first to re-examine the theory and then if necessary to widen the definition. It is the management system and concepts which are important; the definition is an attempt to set out the identifying characteristics of a system, not to list categories of crops that can be grown by that system. It is, for instance, likely that some crops at present produced by other methods could be grown under plantation conditions by the plantation system as far as their cultivation and harvesting are concerned, without needing on-site processing. They should not then be excluded from this study, for as long as relevant parts of the management methods can be applied to them they are part of the subject. But if the methods cannot be applied — if for instance there is a marked seasonal peak to harvesting which demands large additions to the labour force for a short period in the year, thus disturbing that regular and continuous employment of a stable work-force on well-understood and carefully allocated tasks which is one of the marks of the management system of the modern plantation — then a fundamental problem for the system and the definition has been identified. The task becomes one of eliminating or modifying the harvesting peaks in order to use the system to its fullest advantage; if this cannot be done, the venture cannot be called a true plantation, for it will not be able to provide regular employment for a large part of its labour force with all the associated advantages that this implies. Too much of a seasonal peak in the growing of a crop would then exclude the project from our definition; it would not be a plantation, because the regular employment of the skilled labour force could not be provided; the detailed management supervision on a daily routine basis would have to be spasmodic, and both labour and management, when not working on the crop, would have to have other employment within the project, or be hired and fired as needed. The growing of the particular crop then becomes only a part of the activity of those engaged in it; they cannot concentrate their efforts or their skills narrowly enough to begin to reap the benefits of specialisation; they must learn a different set of methods for each activity and become generally conversant with many trades rather than expert in one. Such an activity will then tend to be excluded from the plantation category.

On the other hand, the lack of on-site processing does not in any way interfere with the use of systematic method on the agricultural side. Such processing need not then be a universal feature of every plantation; it is not an essential part of the definition, although the synergy that it produces is a highly desirable part of the production process for some crops.

Characteristic Features

Most definitions, even those of the earliest type of plantation, including those which were slave-based, have recognised and identified the element of management and control as the most important constituent element. They have also identified other common features. Thus Eugene D. Genovese quotes a definition from Lewis C. Gray which, though it is specifically describing a slave plantation, begins to identify the elements which, refined and developed, make the modern plantation what it has become today. He says 'a plantation is a capitalistic type of agricultural organisation in which a considerable number of unfree labourers were employed under a unified direction and control in the production of a staple crop'.[7]

Today this is still valid in many respects. It will be argued later that, in a broad sense, a capitalistic type of organisation may be the most effective format; that a large work-force is necessary in that the units of operation are usually large — hence the problems and opportunities of detailed control; that there are economies of scale. The labourers today are not 'unfree', but the development of the argument will have to examine fully the conditions under which they are employed; the 'unified direction and control in the production of a staple crop' has already been singled out as the most characteristic feature.

Beckford, writing in 1972 and concerned with the plantation in its post-Second World War form, with a particular care for the social issues that arise, lays an even greater stress on the management and supervisory aspects when he says:

> [Plantations] differ from other kinds of farm in the way in which the factors of production, primarily management and labour, are combined. The plantation substitutes supervision — supervisory and administrative skills — for skilled adaptive labour,

combining the supervision with labour whose principal skill it is to follow orders.[8]

Though his definition is correct in the stress it lays on supervision, it greatly underestimates the expertise of the 'labour', particularly if the term is to include all those — supervisors and foremen as well as the operators of the actual tools — who carry out the physical tasks. The point is an important one; Baldwin, for instance, from the supposed lack of skills draws conclusions about wage levels, income distribution and consequent patterns of purchasing power which are certainly invalid for the modern plantation today.[9] Nor indeed was it true even in the slave plantation; recent evidence from the southern United States suggests a high degree of skill throughout the range of jobs, from black managers (who were plentiful) right through to the worker amongst the trees and the crops.[10] Today's plantation worker is a skilled individual, a specialist in his trade.

A definition from the International Labour Committee of Work on Plantations (1950) confirms the main features: plantations are

large-scale agricultural units developing certain agricultural resources of tropical countries in accordance with the methods of Western industry . . . The institution is essentially a large-scale enterprise, depending on large capital investment, a large supply of labour, extensive land areas, well-developed management and specialisation in production for the purpose of export.[11]

This adds the further two criteria of 'extensive land areas' and 'export', both emotive issues which will need discussion.

From all these definitions the list of salient features is: a 'capitalist' type of organisation (which will be redefined later as 'corporate'); a large labour force; extensive land areas; skilled management; close supervision for a system of detailed routine; export of the product. On-site processing and its integration with the agricultural side is important but is an essential element of the plantation only for certain crops, and is not a universal feature. Similarly estate housing is not universal, but is an important and indeed difficult part of the management task when it exists; it then becomes a defining part of the plantation.

There is an extended variety of crops for which the plantation system can be used and which in turn influence its working and basic principles. Tea, coffee, coconuts and cocoa are grown in plantations in many countries. Sugar and tobacco are major commodity crops which are grown by methods which are often those of the plantation, and their divergencies can be used to test the definition. Cotton has been the subject of one of the biggest and earliest of modern experiments in the Gezira scheme in the Sudan.

But the best examples to date are rubber and palm oil; indeed most of the characteristic features of the modern plantation, particularly in the management and supervisory structures and the techniques of the training of labour, arise from the methods originally conceived from around the beginning of the twentieth century in the rubber industry and developed and improved continuously since that time.

What then is the management structure and the form of its organisation?

The Organisation and Working of a Plantation

The key feature of a plantation is the use of detailed routine — the methods it employs, the framework that makes it effective and the technology and skills that are thereby deployed.

This detailed routine is, as the definition states, a technology in itself. It is this which makes effective the application of the different sciences and ensures that the best practices are carried through. Its secret lies in continuity and planned repetition in the performance of well-defined and skilled tasks at the right time. The objective is to bring consistency of treatment to all agricultural operations at all times through a programme which can take into account all the factors — agronomic and economic. Such a programme must cover each estate, each division, each field and indeed each plant and tree regularly, with specific operations which incorporate the best practice, whether it be of clearing, planting, weeding, fertilising or harvesting. Moreover, each individual operation is the subject of constant study to improve its efficiency — to do it better and in less time, while simultaneously preserving and striving to improve the quantity and quality of the crop.

This is the unique and distinguishing central feature of the plantation — that it tends every tree and every bush regularly and with the same treatment; this treatment attempts to incorporate the best known practice, which is constantly being developed and improved, and its application is regularly supervised to fit in with a central plan designed over the years to produce the best quality and the greatest quantity. Such detailed improvements have evolved over a long time; they are the essence of plantation progress, whether it be the improvement of efficiencies in the milling of cane in the late eighteenth century in the West Indies,[12] or the detailed work on the methods of tapping rubber in the twentieth century.[13]

There are two main parts — two different sides — to the expertise that goes into the running of a plantation. They are shown in Figure 1.1. The first, with the links shown in dotted lines, is that which acquires and systematises the knowledge, whether of agronomy, engineering or management structures, into a form that can be applied towards the better performance of a series of individual tasks. The knowledge is split down into practicable applications, each on a narrow front, so that those whose task is the carrying out of these applications become more skilled, in depth, and are therefore able to bring a higher technical level of performance to each task for each crop and each tree.

The second, with the links shown in unbroken lines, is that which sees that this knowledge is applied — regularly and systematically — and that all the resources of men and materials are there to apply it. It is also responsible for the practical 'feedback' from grass-roots level that is needed to sustain and guide research.

Each of the two parts is the province of a separate management chain; each has its own operative channel. The first has to select out from a background of general and international knowledge that part (and it differs for each crop and each area) which is relevant to the country, climate and the particular soil and other characteristics of the plantation in which it is operating, and then to break it down systematically into tasks which can be performed with exactitude and continual repetition to produce a well-defined result: there must be exact methods of planting, tree by tree; detailed schedules for weeding and fertilising; a careful and critically timed programme for harvesting; rigorous and exact standards for processing.

The second part of the management chain has to see that these detailed formulae and practices are applied properly and effectively. It must make due provision for sufficient numbers of work-force and supervisors; it must train them and specify and allot the tasks to each man or each time; it must lay out the working area and the nature of the responsibilities. It must set up and adapt to daily circumstances the organisational framework that provides for the setting and control of these tasks, linking them together so that each stage of the process proceeds in step with the rest; the factory must

Figure 1.1: The Management Hierarchy

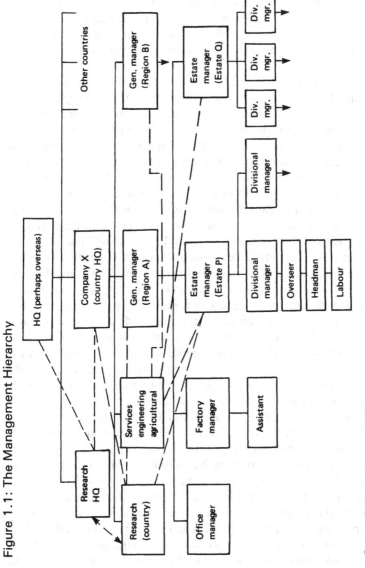

Source: Unilever, London 1983.

not stand idle for the lack of crops from the field, nor the field grow and harvest so much that the factory cannot process it. For this part, the management's province is the whole process and all that enters into it — from nursery seedlings to spare parts for generators; the whole is divided into separate areas on which the worker can specialise and become expert.

It will be seen that each part is a different sort of management, demanding different qualities. In business theory they are called 'advisory' and 'executive'. Day-to-day responsibility for achieving the planned result is put wholly into the hands of the executive channel. The limits of authority and the area of responsibility are defined at each level — horizontally as well as vertically. Each of the management and supervisory staffs answers for his own area to the one above him — who controls a larger number of units — so that the shape of the organisation becomes a pyramid. The higher you go in the pyramid, the wider is the span of authority; the lower you go, the greater is the degree of responsibility for detail in depth.

But success and efficiency depend also on the scientific expertise in the content of the tasks to be performed, and the way in which the job is devised and framed to be carried out by practical skills. To build in this content is the task of the advisory part of management. It is here that the expert in each particular field operates. He may be a mechanical engineer whose province is processing in the factory, an agronomist specialising in oil palms, or someone whose study has been insect life and who is called upon to provide for the effects of a tropical creature on a new plant introduced into a strange area. In each case the task is the same — to break down the sophisticated knowledge in a fashion which enables it, or the appropriate parts of it, to be embodied in a practical task. Each individual job then has in it the relevant part, distilled to the required degree of simplicity for practical application, from each area of knowledge; it should thus be possible to apply the best of practice in each task. The advisory channel has the responsibility for the quality and correctness of this technical content; the executive has to implement it, and thus has the immediate responsibility for success or failure in the final result.

The co-ordination of the two parts of management in carrying out their tasks and the ultimate responsibility for the venture lies with the general management at the top of the pyramid. Here above all it is critical that the area of power and answerability be accepted and agreed. Different organisations differ in the degrees to which authority is delegated. The amount of freedom of action allowed to individual units within an overall plan varies according to the philosophy and management style of the body concerned. Effective control at a distance is more difficult than the steering of operations immediately under the hand of the management. Operating practices therefore vary widely, over a whole gamut of management styles, between the greatest decentralisation and devolution of responsibility for operating decisions at the one extreme and, at the other, firm control of most decisions and close supervision of operations on a short time-scale by headquarters management. Whatever the system adopted, it calls for a network of information, regularly flowing up and down between top management and the man in the field, which produces in itself a range of specialised management and communications practice. It has made tremendous strides in the last 20 years with the advance of computers and the electronic communications industry generally.

The rewards for getting this part of the organisation right are more efficient and more economic use of top management and an ability to centralise research and development and then use their findings widely. Decentralisation tends to be greater in proportion to the distance that separates the levels of management. The difficulties of communication, and the advantages for decision-making of first-hand knowledge of the situation to be guided, favour this. But the most important requirement is that it must be clear where the final authority lies and what the nature of that authority is. Once that is established, the good top manager will exercise intelligent and inventive control within the framework that has been given to him, and do it better, because of his knowledge of the team who work with him and the familiarity he has with all the particular local factors, than could be done by detailed instruction from a distant headquarters which had not the same knowledge and the same familiarity. Any good institution is a living thing; in the best the lines of demarcation or specialisation are not so high that they cannot be crossed when desirable. It is the task of a good higher manager to create the spirit of a team and a practical working synergy across the divisions — in essence to make the system work by the occasional light adjusting touch at the right spot, while still keeping the unit's objective firmly in sight.

This system of management and supervision and the injection of specialist skills is the feature that most clearly identifies the modern plantation and gives it its specialised character, and the creation of such a system within a corporate institution has great advantages for the effective implementation of development plans.

A corporate body looks for direct and uncomplicated definition of responsibilities. Whether the ownership and shareholding of such a body is private or public — in the hands of citizens or the government of the country, international agencies or foreign investors — need make no difference to the way it functions, provided its task and the way it will operate are clearly defined and agreed in the instrument that creates it.

Of equal importance is the change that the plantation system brings to the tasks and indeed the everyday life of the work-force. Under ideal conditions, as found in growing oil palm, the labour force can become a regularly employed, formally organised group of workers along normal 'industrial production' lines, whose job all the year round is in the same place and within the same institution. Different crops vary, according largely to their harvesting pattern. Palm oil is the extreme example; the bunches of fruit ripen practically all the year round; thus palm oil can be harvested on practically any day in the year, with only two minor periods of reduced production in a cool or rainy season in most countries. The demand for labour is therefore steady, without the usual sowing and harvesting peak; there need be no hiring and firing for short periods. On the contrary, there is every incentive for worker and manager alike to undertake constant training to enhance skills and to build up work patterns on a regular and planned basis.

Similarly rubber can be regularly tapped, and coconuts harvested nearly all the year round. For other commodities there are varying degrees of difficulty over the deployment of the work-force in the same regular fashion, because the pattern of ripening for harvesting is not so regular. Tea occupies something of a middle position, for it has definite seasonal peaks of ripening; towards the other end of the scale lie cocoa and sugar, though experience varies between areas and countries. Both have a definite annual harvesting peak. Cane cutters on the sugar plantations of a hundred years ago were needed for only a few weeks at a time; crushing mills ran for only a slightly longer period; accordingly employment was highly seasonal, and could not produce the same type of work-force that became possible with the later plantation patterns for rubber and palm oil. It was therefore to be expected — in an effort to meet the characteristics postulated in our definition — that major efforts would be made in some way to lengthen the harvest period. Much progress has been made with the introduction of new types of cane for earlier or later ripening, with programmed planting and detailed irrigation time-tables, and with measures to delay and hasten ripening. The result has been a considerable extension of the harvesting period and consequent smoothing of the curve in the demand for labour.[14]

These conditions of continuity and regularity have other consequences. Plantation labour is often immigrant labour, usually because plantations are started on cleared ground where crops have not previously been grown and where there are therefore few if any indigenous residents. The provision of housing for the immigrants — particularly in remote areas — became the task of the landowner from the earliest times of the slave plantations; today it has come to mean the provision of estate housing and a whole municipal pattern of shops, services and communal facilities for recreation and culture. This has brought for managements a new dimension and a very difficult one, for the same authority sets the condition for the plantation worker at work and outside it. Moreover, regular hours of work on a regular pattern of tasks is strange to most recruits when they start plantation work. This strangeness is increased by the necessity to manage a weekly wage and live according to a set of rules that have no sanction in ancestral custom, in an entirely different environment. It is frequently a necessary part of the plantation system; but as a counterpart to its dangers and disadvantages, it can bring with it opportunities for desirable developments both in labour practice and social conditions; these will be examined later.[15]

This chapter has so far produced a general, if tentative, definition of a modern plantation, and a description of its organisation and the main principles behind it, with a first look at the working patterns of its labour force and the social problems that it can pose. The various definitions have brought out that it is an institution which cultivates large areas and uses a large management and labour force to do so. To focus the picture more clearly, it is useful to look at some actual examples of the size and cost of the sort of organisation that operates in the way shown in Figure 1.1.

Plantations are big institutions, as the definitions have specified. Size is essential to sustain the specialised and specialist organisation that has been described; even in a greatly curtailed form it would not be viable for estates that were of only a few hundred hectares in size. The distinction must be stressed, for many of the standard statistics in such basic authorities as Bauer and Barlow, dealing with the rubber industry, categorise 'estates' as being of areas of 40 hectares

(100 acres) upwards. Even at the smaller end — 40 hectares — such estates have, of course, to be run by more than one man; the work will be done by labour under supervision; but their size would not allow in full for the degree of detailed and specialist management that this chapter has described — and they would not therefore come into the estate definition or be governed by the same principles of management.

It is difficult to set parameters for size — and indeed there is no need to do so; the criterion is the management system used; it can vary in depth and complexity, and is very adaptable to the task that is required. The size of the estate and the complexity of the management system will interact, and each will play its part in determining the size and character of the other, with viability as the ultimate criterion. But for the full realisation of the advantages of the system, the venture needs to be on a certain scale. What then is of interest is to look at a range of units, whose size and management systems clearly identify them as plantation estates, and see how size, capital employed, numbers of management and the size of the labour force interact.

Some Examples of Modern Plantation Estates

The examples chosen represent a wide range of products (palm oil, copra and rubber) and a variety of countries and types of economy — Sabah, Western Malaysia, the Solomon Islands and Cameroon, giving a spread across South East Asia, Oceania and Africa as well. They are run by Unilever's Plantations Group (see Table 1.1, which shows the relationship between hectares planted, tonnage of crops produced and total world production).

Sabah, East Malaysia: Oil Palm (1981 Figures)

The total area under cultivation is 6,650 hectares; the management numbers 13 and the labour force, including supervisors, 2,180, although of these 500 are engaged on the special task of pollinating (see Chapter 4). The plantation is subdivided into three divisions — which here means the operational unit of control, usually about 2,000–3,000 hectares in size; the line of command follows that shown on Figure 1.1.

The estate was carved out from virgin forest, beginning in 1966; this means that large parts of it are only now coming into maximum

Table 1.1: Unilever Plantations Group: Area and Production, 1982

	Zaire	Malaysia	Cameroon	Ghana	Nigeria	Solomons	Unilever Total	World Total (1981)
Oil Palms								
Area (hectares planted)	31,228	13,400	9,165	41,092	—	—	57,885	
Production (tons)								
Palm oil	47,737	61,114	18,747	1,234	—	—	123,832	5,500,000
Palm kernels	13,733	19,653	5,485	264	—	—	39,135	1,600,000
Rubber								
Area (hectares planted)	7,145	—	1,886		5,348		14,379	
Production (tons)	4,799	—	1,739		5,823	—	12,361	3,800,000
Coconuts								
Area (hectares planted)	—	—				7,760	7,760	
Production (tons)	—	—				7,372	7,372	4,700,000
Cocoa								
Area (hectares planted)	3,780	—	—			710	4,490	
Production (tons)	882	—	—			299	1,181	1,700,000
Tea								
Area (hectares planted)	440	—	—			—	440	
Production (tons)	1,198	—	—			—	1,198	1,900,000

Source: Unilever, London.

production, since the oil palm does not begin to fruit until its fifth year and comes into full bearing around its tenth year onwards. Capital investment is nearing its peak: all roads are laid, the mill is approaching full capacity, handling, storage and office facilities are fully provided. Invested capital, on an indexed replacement basis (an 'indexed' replacement basis is one where fixed assets are written up in groups at considered intervals by a factor representing general inflation, without revaluing and recosting individual items), stands at £11.6 million, covering all fixed assets (machinery, housing, roads, planted trees, etc.); it will rise higher as the last extension to the estate is brought into full production over the next four to five years. Working capital is relatively modest at £1.5 million, in spite of the remoteness of the site; the difficulties of supply routes tend to make for higher stocks and longer transit times both in and out; bought-in supplies take longer to arrive and outgoing products, chiefly oil, are a long time in transit before customers pay. All labour is housed in estate housing, as is management; communication with the outside world is by air or water. This means that medical, welfare and shopping facilities have to be provided as part of the investment.

Johore, Western Malaysia: Oil Palm (1981 Figures)

The area is 4,700 hectares, with a management strength of six.and 1,550 supervisors and workers. Fixed assets, on the same estimated replacement cost basis, are worth £12.9 million and working capital — due to shorter lines of communication than in Sabah, and hence quicker transit to the point of sale for outgoing produce and shorter arrival times for bought-in inputs — is a low £0.6 million.

This is an old-established plantation, where the earliest planted palms are already being replaced under a replanting programme (according to varying prices of palm oil and yields, such replanting can now take place for palms from the age of 18 years upwards). It cannot expand, as there is no land available within reach of the mill — so that it can only invest afresh to make the best of the present limited area under cultivation. Production can only be increased by concentrating on efficiency and by the planting of new strains with high yields to increase tonnage per hectare of fruit, oil content and oil quality.

Located with it is the territorial headquarters — the 'country HQ' of Figure 1.1 — with a management strength of nine. It controls all the Unilever plantations within Malaysia — the older areas in the Malay Peninsula and the newer venture in Sabah.

Solomon Islands: Coconut Oil (1981 Figures)

Coconuts are less intensively cultivated and require less on-site processing: from the Solomon Islands, copra is dried in the sun and then exported in its dried state for the oil to be expressed in large mills overseas (when the crop is large, as in the Philippines, it is expressed in 'central' mills within the country itself, although still outside the plantations). As the factory is not included with the plantation, the fixed assets are less for a given area of cultivation than is the case with oil palm. The labour per hectare is lower because of the lower intensity of cultivation.

Thus, for an area of 7,500 hectares, fixed assets are £4.2 million — again on an indexed replacement basis. Managers number eleven, and supervisors/workers 1,385. Working capital, in spite of very long supply lines, is £0.2 million; buyers take the copra at the plantation, at the commencement of the sea voyage. As might be expected for a different commodity, the pattern is significantly different from that of palm oil.

Cameroon: Oil Palm and Rubber (1976 Figures)

The planted area is 7,900 hectares of oil palm and 1,780 hectares of rubber. The labour force/supervisors number 2,690, and the management 25. Fixed assets, on an indexed replacement basis, were nearly 4,000 million CFA francs (exchange rate in 1976 was approximately 400 CFA francs to £1) for oil palm and 580 million CFA francs for rubber.

In the year 1976 the company paid 515 million CFA francs in taxation and duties, including social insurance and pension contributions, and earned 484 million CFA francs in foreign exchange (only palm kernel oil is exported; palm oil is all consumed locally, either in food or soap production).

Palm oil production is split between two locations, connected only by water. One centre, as a result of its remoteness, runs medical, transport and radio services for the community in general, government departments included. Some of the land was originally planted in the 1930s; but the major development — and redevelopment of the old areas — has taken place since 1956.

The overall picture for Unilever's plantations, showing the relationship between hectares planted and tonnage of crops produced, is shown in Table 1.1. This question of size is not crucial to the definition of a modern plantation. Some forms of plantation — e.g. for the growing of sugar — can differ significantly from the examples given above, as can be seen from Chapter 9; they can be much bigger, but this is not a problem: the management pattern is easier to enlarge than to apply in all its specialisation to smaller units. What emerges as the common factor is the management organisation; capital intensity per hectare and number of workers vary with the crop, but the operating system is common throughout the range.

Conclusion

The principles and characteristics examined in this chapter give a general picture of the modern plantation; but the definitions have not yet been widely accepted even within the plantation industry itself. There is, therefore, no corpus of analysis or description of it as an institution or a management system, and comparisons with other forms of agricultural organisation (which suffer from the same lack of definition) are very difficult. There are economies of scale, and the complexity of the management system itself brings with it a cost that makes it not viable unless it is deployed in a large unit. As an example, 800 hectares is probably the smallest practical operating module for an oil palm plantation, and three to four of such modules will go to make up an estate; yet many government classifications only distinguish between units under and over 40 hectares (100 acres). There is as yet no basis for statistics, which would permit quantified comparison with other systems. Even such simple measures as tonnage per hectare are of little use unless other factors — e.g. size of units and management systems — can be seen to be comparable.

It is nevertheless now feasible to recognise the essential nature of the modern plantation estate, even if there has to be some latitude allowed for description or quantification of particular categories. To summarise, it is an agricultural production system where a single management controls all aspects of the operation as an integrated whole. But the operating management has to draw on a range of specialist agronomic knowledge which is in its turn essential to the system. The necessary and relevant part of each discipline is distilled into the formulation of the detailed tasks which the supervisory field management has to cause to be carried out. The separate parts of the system, when each part meshes together, produce the overall objective. Though everyone has a broad idea of what is in hand, only a few know each process in detail; it is the institutional system which produces the result.

Its task is to operate and improve productivity and quality standards from ground preparation, seed selection and planting through growing and harvesting to processing, grading and sale and distribution. Above and beyond this, it is the task of general management to optimise, short and long term, the mix of these factors.

Notes

1. M.R. Biswas, 'Agrarian reform and rural development', *Mazingira* (The world forum for environment and development), no. 12 (1979), p. 66.
2. World Bank, *World Development Report 1981* (published for the World Bank by Oxford University Press), Table 1.1, p. 3.
3. World Bank, *Accelerated Development in Sub-Saharan Africa* (Washington DC, 1981), p. 47.
4. B. Ward, *Progress for a Small Planet* (Penguin Books, Harmondsworth, 1979), p. 181.
5. P.P. Courtenay, *Plantation Agriculture*, 2nd edn (Bell and Hyman, London, 1980).
6. For example, G.E. Beckford, *Persistent Poverty: Under-development in Plantation Economies of the Third World* (Oxford University Press, 1972).
7. Cited in E.D. Genovese, *The Political Economy of Slavery: Studies in the Economy and Society of the Slave South* (Vintage, New York, 1967), p. 15.
8. Beckford, *Persistent Poverty*, p. 6.
9. R.E. Baldwin, 'Patterns of development in newly settled regions', *Manchester School of Economic and Social Studies*, vol. 24 (May 1956), pp. 161-79.
10. R.W. Fogel and S.L. Engerman, *Time on the Cross: the Economics of American Negro Slavery* (Little, Brown and Co., Boston, 1974), p. 38.
11. Ravindra K. Jain, *South Indians on the Plantation Frontier in Malaysia* (Yale University Press, New Haven, 1970), n. 5, preface p. xvii.
12. Until the end of the eighteenth century cane was crushed between two rollers (originally made of wood, later of stone and by the mid-seventeenth century of iron) set either vertically or horizontally. The juice extraction rate was of the order of 45%. Clearly a better system was needed to take advantage of the expanding area planted to cane — both to handle far greater quantities and to extract more juice. Technical progress came with the three-roller mill — invented by Collinge in 1794 — driven by wind power but soon to be driven by steam. Many subsequent refinements, which included setting 3 three-roller mills in tandem and treating the megass (crushed cane) with water between the mills, raised the juice extraction rate to 95.5%. Two interesting accounts of these developments are to be found in G. Martineau and F.C. Eastick, *Sugar*, 7th edn (Pitman and Sons, London, 1938), pp. 23-34, and Noel Deerr, *Cane Sugar: a Textbook on the Agriculture of the Sugar Cane, the Manufacture of Cane Sugar, and the Analysis of Sugar House Products* (Norman Rodger, London, 1911), pp. 170-81.
13. P.T. Bauer, *The Rubber Industry: a Study in Competition and Monopoly* (Longmans, Green and Co., for the London School of Economics and Political Science, London, 1948), pp. 254-6. Bauer describes the changes in rubber tapping that took place between 1930 and 1945, but this kind of work has continued, and at an increasing pace, up to the present.

14. See, for instance, the results that have been achieved in Guyana and Malaysia, as described by Courtenay, *Plantation Agriculture*, pp. 135–9; see also the general discussion of sugar research in Chapter 8 of this book.

15. See Chapter 7 for a discussion of the activities of the Federal Land Development Authority (FELDA), Malaysia, and Chapter 9 for an account of a sugar complex which came into production in 1980 at Simunye, Swaziland.

2 DEVELOPMENT ECONOMICS AND THE EVOLUTION OF PLANTATIONS

The previous chapter has identified the modern plantation as an institution with strong individual characteristics. The patterns vary between countries and with types of crop. Many of the features of the past have now changed. A plantation has become a tightly defined institution — not a broad agricultural concept.

This narrower identification is a much more particular use of the word 'plantation' than that which is usually employed in the writings of development economists. It is important to realise that in development theory the term has been used loosely; in this broader form plantations have received a good deal of attention — more indeed in the theoretical field than that which has been accorded to small-holdings and co-operative schemes which have occupied the greatest part of the literature on the practical side among geographers and allied academic disciplines.

Criticism of the part played in developing economies by plantations has been made under several heads and different economic theories — concepts of the 'enclave', 'dualism or the dual society' and 'linkages' — have all been raised as particular difficulties. In relation to general dependency theory,[1] the issues are questions such as expatriate ownership, commodity exports and vertical integration, and suspected seller disadvantages in commodity markets.

This chapter will define and examine these issues as they have been applied to plantations to discover how they have arisen and to relate them to the operation and organisation of plantations as they are today. Chapter 5 will examine some particular cases where up-to-date figures are available and quantification is possible.

The Enclave, Dualism, Linkages and Underdevelopment

The concept of an enclave in a dual economy is a mixture of history and development theory. It sees all plantations as enclaves — areas of agricultural activity closely circumscribed with a life and society of their own, alien and inward-looking and cut off from all links with the surrounding people and economy as well as usually with the political system outside. This has arisen, it is alleged, because plantations were set up to produce export crops for the metropolis by people and capital which came from the metropolis. Land was alienated and fenced off from the rest of the country, labour was hired (or in the early days bought as slaves), was given housing and incorporated into a new form of society, the pattern of which was dictated by the management of the plantation and designed solely to suit the needs of the plantation. All inputs to the plantation were and are imported, from seeds for planting, through fertilisers to the machinery and buildings for processing and storing. The managers too are said to be foreigners, equally imported; in so far as plantations have usually been established in forest areas or regions where the land was not being tilled and therefore there were few inhabitants, the labour force has been imported as well, either from different regions of the same country or as immigrant foreigners.

Similarly all the outputs are assumed to be exported. The produce itself is sent to overseas manufacturers or consumers and the salaries of the expatriates who are the managers are remitted back to their home country. The labour force lives in segregated dwellings and spends its money on goods which are imported by the management and sold to the workers through retail outlets on the estate. They have no links with the rest of the country even though they may well be nationals of it.

The result of all this is held to be a profit which accrues to the owners overseas and which is remitted to them, either straightforwardly in the form of dividends or by more dubious channels such as transfer pricing. The wealth which the operation produces is therefore rated as an addition to the wealth of the metropolitan country alone.

Much of this description is derived from history — largely Caribbean history; the difficulty is that it is used without reference to dates. It is clear that such an extreme definition cannot be applied today in all its particulars (what enclave, for instance, does not pay taxes to its host state?); but it has become a stereotype used by writers in discussions on plantations generally.

From this definition there arises the concept of linkages or 'externalities'. These are the contacts and relations between the plantation as an enclave and its surroundings. They can be economic, political or cultural, although under the extreme versions of the definition of an enclave they clearly will not exist at all.

There are social dimensions as well. If such constraints are real, the plantation, it is argued, must develop as a society in itself cut off from the outside world. It will find itself going in different directions from the rest of the country in which it is situated. Within it there will be from the start cultural and racial differences — the management as a minimum are taken to be expatriates — with perhaps a large element of imported supervisors and labourers who come from outside countries because they need work or because they have particular aptitudes for this type of agricultural task. With such a mixture the pattern of the internal society would develop differently in any case; but there is also the necessity to create a new physical environment, to build a new community, buildings and social patterns as a whole, before the venture can function, rather than to allow it to develop gradually and naturally over the years. It will, therefore, in many respects be different as a planned community from those which develop gradually. In any case, as its form will be determined by the management of the plantation, its design will tend to be set by the needs of the plantation: the layout will be so planned as to provide efficient working conditions over the plantation as a whole.

In other words, if the barriers against exchange with the outside world are indeed as assumed by the enclave theory, this will lead to a different form of society inside the enclave from that which continues to exist outside — which will be the traditional form of life of the country into which the plantation has been introduced. This becomes then the dualism or dual society of the development economist.

If the enclave has by definition no links with the surrounding countryside it has by the same definition strong links with its parent and founder in the metropolis. Its policy will be dictated from the metropolis and its operations will be run according to the ideas of its management in the metropolis. Ownership in the metropolis will mean an effort to maximise the benefits to the metropolis. Its technology and all its methods must be derived from the metropolis; their adaptation and application can be developed only within the enclave and cannot take account of experience outside. This reinforces the dualism.

The theory also considers the movement of the commodity from grower to user to be virtually integrated. If the metropolitan owner is a manufacturer and the plantation is a producer of his raw materials, the presumption is that the commodity will go straight from producer to manufacturer as a simple supply function. Prices and quantities can be dictated by the sole needs of the two parties concerned.

Similarly, if the relationship is that of a seller of a commodity to a monopoly user/buyer, the advantage will be presumed to lie with the metropolitan partner who will probably have other sources of supply and in any case is the owner and dominant operator in the venture.

The overall effect of such a pattern of relationships, if they are true, is clearly to keep the supplying unit, and therefore the country in which it is situated, in a position of dependency on the metropolitan owner.

At the same time the producing country outside the enclave will either remain in its traditional undeveloped state, because it has no links with the plantation which will bring it along the development road, or, alternatively, because the linkages with the enclave are haphazard and imperfect, it will develop in a haphazard fashion, changing only some random aspects of its economy and culture and allowing them to blend uneasily with a largely unchanged traditional pattern of life. The result is a society which enjoys neither a traditional pattern nor a satisfactory developing pattern. It is in a state which is now called underdevelopment.

This is a deliberately simplified description of the four concepts — enclaves, the dual society, linkages and dependency/underdevelopment. It has picked out from the general theories those aspects which have been applied particularly to plantations. An examination of the plantation estate is much more directly related to enclaves, linkages and the dual society — which are more particular concepts — than to the wide area of dependency theory. The rest of this chapter will therefore relate more to these first three; but the extent to which they are found to be valid must have significance for general dependency theory in itself. Later it will be asked whether the overall impression that these theories produce can be said to hold today; but first it is necessary to see whether in fact the historical development of plantations world-wide has been as described.

The Development of the Modern Plantation

For plantations the concepts of dualism and dependency have been carried to their most extreme manifestations by the West Indian School of Economists, in particular Beckford in his description and analysis of the Plantation Society.[2] He describes an institution and a society which is heavily overlaid with the associations and connotations of the early slave plantations of the Caribbean and makes of it a general model for world-wide application. It has acquired its own name — the PEM or Plantation Economy Model.[3]

But in fact even by the eighteenth century plantations in different regions were beginning to take a different pattern. Plantation development in North America — in a 'colony of settlement' — soon began to take another form from those in 'colonies of exploitation' such as the Caribbean and the Netherlands East Indies. When plantations began to be developed in Malaysia in the nineteenth century, they took a new direction again and were indeed the forerunners of the modern plantation as it has been described earlier.

Moreover, within the slave plantation pattern of the Americas itself, historians are now beginning to question some of the traditional assumptions on which the West Indian school has rested its case. An example is research that has been done on the degrees of skill that were attached to the labour force in slave plantations in the southern United States plantations in the *ante-bellum* period. It goes far to undermine premises on which a great deal of theory has been built. Baldwin's assumption[4] that there was and is little if any craft skill below the management level leads him to conclusions about wage levels, income distribution and consequent patterns of purchasing power which have been used to deny the suitability of the plantation as a factor in development. A mass of undifferentiated labour with undifferentiated wages has not, he believes, the dynamism for change that comes from a body of smallholders who can earn higher incomes because of their developing skills.

Yet, even at the time of the slave plantations, in the southern United States at least there was already a wide distribution of skills.[5] Today in the modern plantation the range of skills is wider and even more differentiated and specialised, and the scales of pay correspond to it.[6] Similarly for Beckford there is not only the straightforward form of the enclave described at the beginning of this chapter. He carries the case further and paints a picture of a unique form of society with complete separation between the races and a social structure which is heavily layered and stratified inwardly as well. It must be said that his description and the model that he constructs from it is an exaggerated position now recognised as unrepresentative of plantations world-wide. For instance Dennis Pantin concludes 'the generalisation is of little relevance to the case of most of Africa and Asia'.[7] Yet many of the assumptions on which it rests continue to be restated when development theory is argued in relation to plantations generally.

History too confirms that there is a major difference between the modern type of plantation which evolved towards the end of the nineteenth century and the New World plantations which have been most studied and have therefore tended to be regarded as the pattern. It stems from the crops themselves and more specifically from the pattern that the sowing and harvesting of each crop imposes.

Early plantations, largely in the New World, began by growing annual (cotton and tobacco) or nearly annual (sugar) crops. The labour force had to be big enough to handle all the planting and all the harvesting annually within a limited period; but outside these two peaks there was not enough work to be done directly on the crops to keep the large field labour force busy. Even if they were all slaves, such a large labour force meant high costs, for food, housing, clothing and tools and equipment. Though these might be at the lowest possible level, it was still inevitable that such part-time and inefficient deployment of the labour force would mean high costs for the product, which had to be sold outside the plantation economy and whose price was therefore fully determined by market forces.

In a slave society there could be no hiring and firing. The costs continued whether the slave was working or not. The answer, therefore, had to be to become as self-sufficient within that society as possible by using the surplus of labour when it was available. The plantation was led into growing its own food, making its own clothes, building its own buildings. It became almost a self-sufficient society within itself and its social and cultural pattern reflected this. Virginian plantations were good examples:

> The labour pattern was designed to achieve total self-sufficiency; the field workers raised corn and pork in addition to tobacco, and tended their gardens in off hours; slave spinners and weavers made cloth from local cotton and wool; slave shoemakers tanned and dressed local leather; the smiths and joiners made wagons, ploughs and hoes and shod horses, while the carpenters, masons and jobbers erected and repaired buildings. Work logs kept by the overseers show a definite seasonal rhythm, with a long slack period in the winter.[8]

This was Beckford's 'plantation society' where 'the master of the plantation was ruler of his principality'.[9] But such a pattern need only obtain with this annual type of crop. In commodities where there was a more steady all-the-year-round demand for labour, the number of workers were related directly to — indeed themselves were — the costs of production of the main crop alone. The price at which the crop was sold could then be a straight function of these direct costs; the proceeds could provide a margin of profit which would enable some or all of the food and equipment requirements to be bought in rather than produced within the plantation. It was much more possible for a sugar, and even more a coffee, plantation to develop in this way than those plantations where annuals were grown, and there were therefore already in the eighteenth century notable differences from the southern United States pattern in, for instance, the Brazilian coffee and Jamaican sugar plantations.[10]

The differences became much more pronounced in the nineteenth century, with increasing specialisation and growing demands for investment in new, industry-related, capital equipment, which in turn induced a changing ownership pattern. Moreover some West Indian islands not only switched from tobacco to sugar but also experimented at times with other crops, e.g. bananas, with a consequent change in the pattern of the labour force.

The greatest differences, however, arise in the patterns of Asian and African plantations. Here from the beginning there was little of the completely self-sufficient 'plantation society'. Early in the nineteenth century Chinese planters in Malaya were engaged in cultivating tapioca, gambia and pepper. Land was cleared from tropical forest, crops planted and processing capacity installed. Roads had to be built as well. These were all crops which quickly came to maturity: they gave an early return but they also, especially tapioca, exhausted the land. It was a system of shifting cultivation; as the land deteriorated so returns fell; yet it was continued until the last decade of the century, when the tide of official opinion finally turned against it. By the 1850s, however, another form of cultivation, which involved a longer-term and less harshly exploitative use of the land, was slowly gaining ground. Many of the European residents in the Settlements of Penang and Singapore had accumulated capital and sought local opportunities for investment which they could supervise; what better than to invest in *permanent* plantations, growing crops for export to the home market?

Longer-term cultivation, however, meant investments which could not pay in the early years and required large capital expenditure. It was difficult for the existing cultivators; to plant a crop which will not begin to bear for several years, but which needs a large capital investment in the form of a factory ready by the time it is bearing, is not attractive for any individual entrepreneur working on the time-scale of his own life span. Nevertheless, by the middle of the nineteenth century, the opportunity to create a new agriculture existed clearly in Malaya. Land and climate looked suitable and those who could envisage a longer-term venture began to arrive in the form of sugar planters from Mauritius, tea and coffee planters from Ceylon, to join those already in Malaya for other purposes. On land which was leased to them on condition that it was used on a long-term basis they began to experiment to find out what could be grown. Coffee and tea met with initial success. It began to appear that tree crops with a much less damaging effect on the soil could avoid the need for shifting cultivation.[11]

A great deal of the basic work was quickly done. By the 1890s, the problems and practice of the clearance of land, the patterns and density of planting, the use of manures and fertilisers and the organisation of transport and labour to achieve rapid and cost-efficient processing were being formulated, and steady development and study were devoted to them. There was already a government research effort and a Planters' Association before the end of the century. There were 50 years of experience in the growing of sugar and coffee in a pattern of European estates largely owned by private individuals. There was the even older tradition of mono-crop cultivation by the Chinese, much of which was very relevant to the questions that tropical agriculture was now posing to those who had begun by assuming that there were no differences except favourable ones from cultivation in temperate European lands.

But sugar in Malaya was under pressure from land and labour shortage and in growing disfavour with the government who wanted to increase the production of rice. At the same time the price of coffee was falling rapidly. It was the last straw for planters who had already struggled for too long with problems of disease. They looked urgently for a crop which could be grown on their already developed estates using the infrastructure which represented so much of their fixed invested capital. They found rubber, which government research in the face of much scepticism had already shown could be grown, and they found a rapidly growing world market.

This was the first stage in the birth of the modern 'industrial' plantation. It was here that, from the 1890s onwards, the prototype of the modern plantation estate industry developed rapidly under the stimulus of the fast growing demand for rubber. It was at first interplanted with the coffee which could give some cash flow while the new rubber trees came to bearing and the processing facilities were built. Experiments began with planting intensities, research went into tapping methods; the frequency of tapping, the depth of the cut, the pattern of the cut, the shape of the knife, were all intensively studied by central bodies such as the Planters' Association, with careful documentation of the results year by year. Progress was steady, scientific research led the way, technology had begun to arrive. Plantations now needed long-term finance and a quality and depth of management which could only be afforded by the bigger units. Ownership began to pass from the individual to the corporation. The final shape was set by the arrival of the limited liability company in the last quarter of the nineteenth century. It took over ownership increasingly, not only in South East Asia but in the Americas as well.

In such ventures there was no room for 'plantation society' — the 'principality'. The objective was not to provide a way of life for an owner class but to grow a commodity as competitively as possible for the market — and competition was severe for plantation crops, whether they were sugar or rubber, tea, coffee or later oil palm. Every effort had to be geared to a single end — the growing of the crop. There could be no scope for the creation of a privileged class.

In Africa it is equally clear that the plantation-society phase could not have existed. African historians of the period up to the First World War tend to use the word plantation as a description of 'gathering' activities — the concatenation of many small-scale peasant producers tied together by a collection system. This was the first method used to increase the supplies of palm oil from West Africa when European demand began to increase after the first half of the nineteenth century and when the existing trading machinery had to look for a replacement for the traffic in slaves. It is difficult to establish whether any of the supplies came from specially planted palms, but, if there was planting, there is no indication that there was any considerable method or technology behind it. Indeed the case is rather the reverse, for late in the nineteenth century there were several European-sponsored ventures which failed, apparently due to a lack of relevant technical knowledge as well as management failure.[12] Large-scale attempts to produce palm oil from Africa did not begin until the twentieth century. The best documented is Lever's pioneering co-operation with the Belgian government in the Congo from 1911 onwards. This too started as a 'gathering' activity, and Lever's initial undertaking was solely to establish oil mills in five specially reserved areas and to buy and mill the fruit gathered in those areas from the palms growing naturally there. Apart from a relatively small number of workers in the mills, there was no large labour force. The fruit was bought from individual gatherers who were under no sort of institutional obligation. In these circumstances, there was no chance of a 'plantation society' arising. By the 1920s the superiority of the fully integrated Malayan type of plantation began to make Africa too, and specifically the Belgian Congo (Zaire), move into planting in the orthodox fashion, but the pattern of development was by then along the lines of the twentieth century, not the seventeenth or eighteenth.[13]

These differing patterns of individual development clearly make it unsound to use one overall theory to create a general plantation model on the West Indian lines. A theory should be an interpretation of basic facts and an attempt to explain them or relate them to each other. If the basic facts are not there or have ceased to be true, the theory needs to be recast. It cannot stand as an explanation. Even on the broadest of bases, what has happened world-wide in plantations does not fall into one single pattern.

Nor does the idea of dependency generally stand up to historical analysis world-wide in the plantations context. The dependency of the periphery on the metropolis, and dualism of the society within the entities on that periphery, are said to have arisen from and still to exist as a result of the form of the ownership under which plantations were set up, the way in which their management was effected and the strategy that was imposed on their operations and progression by the metropolitan controlling power.

The roots of such ideas again lie in events in the Caribbean and Spanish America in the seventeenth and eighteenth centuries. Here the home government had a policy and a practice which gave firm directives for the activities of those of its citizens who were sent out from the Iberian peninsula to the Americas. They were a part of specific government ventures and their remit fell into well-defined channels for those commodities which the metropolis wanted and the colony could produce. The exploitation of silver and gold, for instance, was closely controlled and taxed by the state. Sugar, too, was encouraged and taxed early. It was the first plantation crop and was already paying duty at the Lisbon Custom House in 1526.[14]

Similarly, outside the Americas, in Java from the beginning of the seventeenth century, there was a considerable production of agricultural produce which was dictated by the Netherlands East

India Company and which, indeed, lasted in different guises until well beyond the middle of the nineteenth century, finishing with the Cultuurstelsel system. In these cases the crops, though new to the territory, did not add much to its wealth, for they were produced almost entirely for the benefit of the metropolitan power. Had there then been a theory of an enclave and a theory of dependency, the facts would have been seen to have fulfilled many of the conditions.

But the same could hardly be said of those settlers who set out to the eastern shores of North America to shake off and leave behind them all that they found displeasing in their lives in Europe. These were people who were setting out to provide for themselves a new economic and social pattern. What they grew was to feed themselves or to export for their own profit. The type of crop was for them alone to decide. They grew it and then set about finding a market for it back in the Europe that they had rejected. The structures of plantations and the policies adopted in North America differed widely from those found in the West Indian islands. Mercantilist ideas, with the control of shipping and the direction and origins of trade, came much nearer to modern complaints about metropolitan control in the hands of government and vertical integration within the capitalist structure.

Yet in fact in many cases, and in spite of such mercantilist legislation, the supply end, once commercial growing had started under the plantation format, was firmly at arm's length from the buyer and the crops were chosen by the producer. In Virginia, for instance, the first idea of the original planters was silk, but they soon found tobacco to be a much more attractive crop under the stimulus of strong market pressure from Europe.[15] The decision was taken in America, not Europe.

Similarly in the Far East, although the Cultuurstelsel system in Indonesia was for a time a clear instance of government control from the metropolis, it was finished by the 1870s; private investment then moved in and greatly diversified the range of crops on initiatives which, although they were taken by Europeans, were firmly rooted in local choice and interest and indeed possibilities. The story of Nienhuys in Deli in Sumatra and his introduction of tobacco in the 1860s is the most dramatic instance; but cinchona, tea and later rubber, sisal and oil palm were also introduced from the middle of the nineteenth century onwards in Java and Sumatra. Individual planters and corporation capital came in from Britain, Germany and

Switzerland in the 1880s.[16] This was hardly monolithic control from one metropolis. It was the periphery firmly inventing its own ideas and finding its own way.

Furthermore, for all his crops, the planter at the periphery had to develop his own local knowledge and nurture his own experience. He was not dependent on the metropolis, for in tropical agriculture the metropolis had no worthwhile knowledge to offer except what had been fed back from other periphery countries. Both in growing and in marketing his crop he had to start from scratch as far as local conditions were concerned. There was no precedent to guide him. He had to be the progenitor of a fresh set of knowledge and the creator of a new set of assets. By the very nature of the case, the growth of good agricultural practice and the development of crop technology had to come from the plantation itself. Even the technology that had been acquired in similar climates elsewhere was often found to be deficient when transferred to another country. Soil conditions were never the same in two locations. The way in which the land drained was vital and the traditional practices and skills of those who worked on the land varied widely, often for good reasons. These lessons have continued to be learned right up to today: it was not until the twentieth century, for instance, that planters began to realise that the degree of latitute alone was vital for some crops — the photosynthetic effect of the sun varies according to its declination and has a major effect on ripening. All these were lessons which could not be learned in Europe.

It is true that this growth of knowledge was often led by men of European descent and it is equally true that in the West Indies and in the Central American territories at least there was much stratification in the plantation societies. Nevertheless, recent work has shown that the skills and knowledge of plantation technology went from the top right down to the bottom even in the days of slavery. The slave foreman and slave manager were skilled and knew their trade, as did many of the black plantation workers who were working the soil with their own hands:

On the large plantations slaves actually predominated in the crafts and in the lower managerial ranks. To a surprising extent slaves held the top managerial posts. Within the agricultural sector about 7 per cent of the men held managerial posts and 11.9 per cent were skilled craftsmen, blacksmiths, carpenters, coopers etc. Another 7.4 per cent were engaged in semi-skilled and domestic jobs — teamsters, coachmen, gardeners, stewards and house servants.[17]

This was a very considerable accumulation of knowledge in the hands and minds of people who could by that time under no circumstances be thought of as alien to the economy of the country, however little they belonged to it politically and culturally.

Moreover, the owner/manager class identified strongly with the country in which they lived and worked, frequently opposing the government in colony and metropolis alike. Some in fact had no metropolis — like the Chinese in Malaysia. What they did — the building up of agricultural practice and the knowledge of their crops — is well documented.[18] The new enterprises were unique and could be identified only with the country where they came into being; they depended on nothing outside except for the initial capital — and even that only in some cases and to a small extent.

The planters of these crops — tobacco and cotton in North America, rubber and oil palm in Malaysia in the nineteenth century, sugar in both at various times — built up their own set of skills. But though they were not dependent on the metropolis for their knowledge, they soon became linked with it in a two-way trade, and the greater strength of the senior participant could and did sometimes impose one-sided conditions. Yet even so there was often an independent answer possible — to grow another crop for another market, as with the West Indian switch from tobacco to sugar in the seventeenth century. There was, of course, always considerable pressure from home governments and home traders. It was founded on the belief of central governments that the colony was there for the benefit of the metropolis, and that the periphery existed to serve the centre. But this was a belief of the centre, not shared by the periphery; there was resistance to such ideas from the beginning, as the independence wrung from the mother country by each former colony was to prove, beginning in the Americas.

For the study of plantations the important point is that such independence of regard and spirit meant that specialised knowledge and professionalism was built up in tropical countries rather than the 'home' countries from the earliest days. The sugar planter and the rubber grower may have returned at the end of their career to the land of their birth; but, while they were exercising their trade and building up their professionalism and their wealth, they were doing it in a land where most of the knowledge and its results were going to remain when they departed. Where it had been suitably developed, it would become a significant part of the wealth of the country concerned. When allied to a proper climate and soil, it would stand as a unique resource, ending up with a phenomenon like the present position of Malaysia in the growing of oil palm. She has international leadership in management and technology; it is within the country, in the minds of her people and the highly developed state of her plantations. She is in the best of positions to go on developing these resources of knowledge and production. So far from being dependent on a metropolis, the position is reversed, and many of the world skills in the growing of oil palm are closely linked to Malaysia and the programmes that can be carried out there. This is particularly the case, for instance, in the field of agronomy and plant botany. The majority of the work on the DxP strain of palm and the tissue culture of the palm at the nursery stage have been done there. Similarly the Rubber Research Institute in Malaysia has been a clear leader both on plant breeding and on tapping and cultivation techniques for rubber for many years.

Dependency has now in fact become interdependency, and for plantations most of it is interdependency between countries of the Third World. To use again the same examples, tissue culture started as a laboratory experiment in England but had to be developed on a field scale in Malaysia and Africa, and it is there that knowledge is now being built up. The DxP cross was started in Zaire and developed in South East Asia. The clue to successful pollination of the oil palm came out of work done in Cameroon and in Sabah (see Chapter 4). A technique for ground clearing using entirely indigenous resources and avoiding a necessity for imported machinery was invented in Ghana and transferred to Cameroon. The employment of draft oxen or the raising of cattle on the undergrowth under plantation trees have been the subject of experiment in both Africa and South East Asia — and each has fed his knowledge to the other.[19]

Plantation technology is today shared and diffused through a network of research institutions and plantation associations. The latest discoveries, the new strains of seeds or fresh ideas in methods of propagation pass from country to country, sometimes through the old metropolis which now screens documents and disseminates the latest advances; it has become a centre for the diffusion of knowledge and a convenient place — because of ease of communication — for the exercise of co-ordination between similar ventures in different types of country.

The modern plantation was clearly not an alien implant imposed on dependent and underdeveloped countries by Western capitalists. It was in most cases a local and autochthonous growth, a response to the peculiar needs and potentialities of each tropical country. It remains, however, to see whether these plantations constitute enclaves in their economies and what benefits they provide for host countries.

Notes

1. 'Dependency theory' is a vast subject in itself; there will be no attempt here to examine it generally. There are now several competing versions — and it has its detractors. See, for instance, Arghiri Emmanuel, *Appropriate or Underdeveloped Technology?* (John Wiley and Sons, Chichester, 1982), p. 103: 'Save in cases of direct political domination or violence, dependence cannot be the cause of economic backwardness; it is the consequence of it. One is as dependent as one is underdeveloped; one is not as underdeveloped as one is dependent.' See also Martin Godfrey (ed.), 'Is Dependency Dead?', *Institute of Development Studies Bulletin*, Sussex, vol. 12, no. 1, December 1980.

2. G.E. Beckford, *Persistent Poverty: Under-development in Plantation Economies of the Third World* (Oxford University Press, 1972).

3. D. Pantin, 'The Plantation Economy Model and the Caribbean', *Institute of Development Studies Bulletin*, Sussex, vol. 12, no. 1, December 1980.

4. R.E. Baldwin, 'Patterns of Development in Newly Settled Regions', *Manchester School of Economic and Social Studies*, May 1956, p. 166.

5. See pp. 44–5 of this chapter for quotation from R.W. Fogel and S.L. Engerman, *Time on the Cross: the Economics of American Negro Slavery* (Little, Brown and Co., Boston, 1974), p. 38.

6. A detailed account of the skills and corresponding scales of pay obtaining in the post-Second World War banana, oil palm and rubber plantations controlled by the Cameroons Development Corporation is to be found in E. Ardener, S. Ardener and W.A. Warmington, *Plantation and Village in the Cameroons* (Oxford University Press, 1960), pp. 13–22.

7. Pantin, 'Plantation Economy Model', p. 17.

8. R.S. Dunn, University of Pennsylvania, Oxford (England) seminar paper, September 1981.

9. Beckford, *Persistent Poverty*, p. 75.

10. See S.J. Steiner, *Vassouras, A Brazilian Coffee Country 1780–1900* (Harvard University Press, 1957); also M. Craton and J. Walvin, *A Jamaican Plantation* (W.H. Allen, London, 1970).

11. J.C. Jackson, *Planters and Speculators: Chinese and European Agricultural Enterprises in Malaya 1786–1921* (University of Malaya Press, Kuala Lumpur, 1968), pp. 76–81 and pp. 87–92; J.H. Drabble, *Rubber in Malaya 1876–1922: the Genesis of the Industry* (Oxford University Press, Kuala Lumpur, 1973), pp. 26–7.

12. A.G. Hopkins, *An Economic History of West Africa* (Longman, London, 1973), pp. 213–14. See also J. Forbes Munro, 'Monopolists and Speculators: British Investment in West African Rubber 1905–1914', *Journal of African History*, 22 (1981), pp. 263–78.

13. D.K. Fieldhouse, *Unilever Overseas: the Anatomy of a Multinational*

1895-1965 (Croom Helm, London, 1978), Chapter 9.

14. P.P. Courtenay, *Plantation Agriculture*, 2nd edn (Bell and Hyman, London, 1980), p. 25.

15. Ibid., p. 26.

16. J.S. Furnivall, *Netherlands India: a Study of Plural Economy* (Cambridge University Press, 1939, reprinted 1967), pp. 169–70, 204, and 309–12.

17. Fogel and Engerman, *Time on the Cross*, pp. 38–9.

18. See in particular Drabble, *Rubber in Malaya*, and Jackson, *Planters and Speculators*; Jackson, pp. 253 and 266, states there was a marked increase in Asian rubber holdings after 1910, and that by 1921 one-fifth of the estate area was held by Chinese.

19. Information arising out of discussion with L. Davidson of Unilever Plantations Group.

3 FOREIGN OWNERSHIP AND FOREIGN MANAGEMENT: COSTS AND BENEFITS

Two standard grounds on which plantations have often been criticised are, first that they are commonly owned by corporations whose headquarters and shareholders are overseas and, second, that senior management in the host Third World country is largely expatriate. Both characteristics are potentially objectionable, because they suggest an in-built conflict of interest which might adversely affect the benefits which — as argued above — the modern plantation estate may bring to a less developed country. This chapter examines both ownership and management patterns in the 1980s, laying particular emphasis on the changes that have taken place during the last three decades.

Foreign Ownership

Since 1945 the ownership patterns of plantations have moved fast towards indigenisation. Given the feelings that have always been raised by the issues of land rights, this is not surprising. Once it was in their power to do so, newly independent ex-colonial states have rapidly introduced legislation insisting on major or majority indigenous shareholding, as in the case of Nigeria and Zaire, nationalised the whole, as in Guyana or Tanzania, or introduced a phased programme for local ownership, as in Malaysia. Over and above government decisions have been the changes caused by the policies of such international institutions as the World Bank or the Commonwealth Development Corporation (CDC), so that major participation by indigenous capital, either government or private, is the first requirement as a matter of principle in setting up any project for foreign aid, and so that provision is always made for the proportion of that capital to increase by indigenous interests buying out the foreign shareholder.[1]

The result is that today expatriate ownership has either been greatly modified or disappeared. As is argued in Chapter 5 on linkages, the available figures already show considerable movement but still fail to reflect the full effect of the change, since the process of indigenisation continues and accelerates, whereas the latest statistics are several years old. This is particularly significant for expatriate ownership, for change has been very rapid indeed since the middle 1970s. Thus, in Indonesia by 1976, 66 per cent of plantations in the main growing area — North Sumatra — were owned by the Indonesian state, having been originally almost 100 per cent Dutch, and the share of overseas capital had shrunk to 33 per cent.[2] In Malaysia many of the biggest formerly expatriate plantation companies transferred their ownership and domicile to the country during the 1970s and such landmarks in the plantation world as Sime Darby were fully owned and controlled locally before the beginning of the 1980s. Guthries and Barlows both became locally owned as to the majority of their shareholdings in 1981. This, indeed, was an example of the wheel coming more than full circle, for in some cases (e.g. Guthries) the change brought with it ownership or part-ownership by Malaysians of businesses that were situated in the UK. The majority of the shares in Harrisons and Crosfield's Malaysian business passed into Malaysian ownership in 1982.

In South America palm oil, which had been comparatively unknown, became a much more interesting crop for various countries from the 1960s onwards; but, although in many cases expatriate capital took part in the creation of oil palm plantations, it was restricted to around 50 per cent of the equity as a maximum by the provisions of the Andean Pact. Thus Unilever in their first entry into the plantation business in South America made an agreement in Colombia which gave them a minority (49 per cent) of the total shareholding, although they were responsible for the technical and commercial management.

The same story was repeated in Africa. By the end of the 1970s majority holdings in all plantations in Nigeria and Ghana were indigenised by government decree. Kenya saw a very successful partnership between the government and the CDC to grow tea and sugar with majority indigenous shareholdings. On the other side of the continent the Cameroons Development Corporation, based entirely today on indigenous funds, has become the sole owner of large plantations producing palm oil, cocoa and rubber.[3] In three of these countries, Ghana, Kenya and Cameroon, the World Bank and the CDC played a major part in forming the pattern of indigenous ownership in line with their overall policy. The result is the existence of businesses which are committed to a steady decrease in overseas ownership and a corresponding increase in indigenous ownership which is in any case already in the majority.

Quite apart from 'dependency', the ownership and management of plantations is important politically (in the country concerned), whether it lies with overseas proprietors or particular indigenous groups or classes. In the last 30 years the least controversial formula has been held to be government ownership. This has its own disadvantages and recognition of them is changing sentiment in some quarters.[4] Government control in its usual form is distant and bureaucratic. Decisions are slow and sometimes related to factors far removed from the requirements for producing a good crop. Management changes particularly at the top are often dictated by party or political considerations rather than the needs of the operation.[5] There may well be a tendency to produce short-term solutions and short-term results under the pressure of vote-commanding necessities in an industry which, even in its shortest time spans, involves a ten-year programme.

An equity-based management corporation can overcome these objections. Ideological and political aims can be met by the government or a public body owning all or part of the equity. But the essence of the success of its operations is that it should be allowed to operate as a management corporation and manage according to the principles that are emerging in these chapters. No matter who the owners are — government, parastatal bodies, private individuals or overseas investors — the policies required for high productivity and maximum production will be the same in the long term. Indeed the options for plantation owners are much more limited than is sometimes imagined. There can be few businesses so deeply attached to a country and its fortunes as a plantation. Once the initial establishing and planting have taken place, the money is irrevocably invested and the assets must either be worked or deteriorate within one or two short years. Successful working means a period of at least 20 years for crops such as the oil palm and 30 years for rubber — this is the time that it takes for trees to mature and pass through their most productive phase before beginning to decline and need replanting.

The owner of a plantation, whether he comes from overseas or is indigenous, is therefore effectively 'locked in' to a far greater extent than in almost any other economic activity; few of his assets are moveable nor can they be used for any other purpose. Management policies must therefore be geared to operating over the same period of 20 or 30 years and their direction will be determined by the weather and the movement of commodity prices much more than changes of policy by the owners. Even in the most extreme case, an overseas owner with 100 per cent of the equity and large multi-national interests in other countries can expect today only to steer for a few degrees to left or right; the basic course can only be set within the main current of a country's policy. He can only invest or refrain from investing in accordance with the overall direction of the country's development. Practical wisdom usually indicates a continuance, with perhaps variations of pace, of the course already begun. The assets of a plantation will sink or swim with the country in which it is situated. If it belongs to overseas interests it is nevertheless as much a part of the country as any local business, for it is unalterably rooted in it. The only real sanction in the hands of the overseas owner is to withdraw, which is likely to lead to the loss of all his assets. Indeed the decision may well not be his, for, if he departs too far from a course laid down by the government of the country in which he is operating, he is more likely than most businesses to be taken over by the state; such is the strength of feeling about the use of land and he must remember it.

The division of the profits made is the one issue which must be directly affected by the pattern of ownership. Dividends can only be paid to those who own the shares. There is no need to enter here into the balance of advantage when ownership lies overseas — whether more wealth is created within the country concerned than is remitted to the owners of the equity outside the country. Much has been written on this subject, but controversy continues.[6] Plantations are not among the highest earners on capital employed and the pattern of overseas remittances will vary with the crop and with the seasons, climate and commodity prices. The important thing to recognise is that dividends are paid to the owners of shares and that, therefore, as the percentage in the equity rises in the hands of local shareholders, so the amount of the dividends paid to them will rise equally. If, as has been instanced, the majority of the equity is owned within the country, the majority of the dividends will stay there.

This changing pattern of ownership also has conclusive consequences for the possibilities of 'transfer pricing'. Unless the ownership of the metropolitan user and the periphery producer are the same — and 100 per cent the same — there will be a clash of interests which will arise immediately any attempt is made to transfer production from a plantation on any other than an arm's length basis. A price too favourable for one must be to the direct disadvantage of the other — a state of affairs which is unlikely to continue for long if the ownership of both buyer and seller is not the same.

In any case such pricing mechanisms are today in most cases impossible, given the existence of marketing boards and terminal commodity markets in most of the countries involved.

The Nationality of Managements

There is a further and most important change which has greatly affected many of the patterns previously attributed to overseas direction and ownership. It lies in the management area where expatriates have now been largely replaced by indigenous managers from the country concerned. As with other areas of rapid change, it is difficult to give precise figures; but the stances taken by Third World governments have become increasingly firm on the subject, and quotas for the employment of expatriates are a very widespread phenomenon in developing countries at all levels. The figures for Unilever are indicative of what has happened (see Tables 3.1 and 3.2). The pattern of change has perhaps been carried further here than for other international businesses, since the policy of the company has been to encourage indigenous management since before the Second World War.[7] The details show that, out of a total of 3,676 in 1982, only 220 of Unilever's managers employed in their overseas businesses were expatriates — and 'expatriates' means literally what it says: it includes Third World management posted to another developing country as well as people from the centre sent out for specialist jobs or the training of indigenous management. Moreover this total had hardly changed in 15 years, while indigenous management had increased from 1,366 to 3,456 over the same period. The full story appears in Table 3.1; an important incidental point is the disappearance of 'expatriate only management', i.e. businesses where, in the earlier years, there were no indigenous managers. Table 3.2 shows the figures for the plantation industry alone.

This is a change of pattern which is fast overcoming the cultural gap that has caused so many difficulties between different countries at different stages of development. It can also give a different aspect to the questions that have been seen as a clash of interest between the planation and its original founders from overseas — if they still exist as such. Top managers in developing countries are important

Table 3.1: Summary of Management in Unilever Companies Overseas, 1968–82

	30 Sept. 68		30 Sept. 69		1 Jan. 71		1 Jan. 72		1 Jan. 73		1 Jan. 74		1 Jan. 75		1 Jan. 76		1 Jan. 77		1 Jan. 78		1 Jan. 79		1 Jan. 80		1 Jan. 81		1 Jan. 82	
	NATS	EXPATS	NATS	EXPATS	NATS	EXPATS	NATS	EXPATS	NATS	EXPATS	NATS	EXPATS	NATS	EXPATS	NATS	EXPATS	NATS	EXPATS	NATS	EXPATS	NATS	EXPATS	NATS	EXPATS	NATS	EXPATS	NATS	EXPATS
CENTRAL AND S. AMERICA																												
Mexico	20	10	21	11	37	9	8	3	4	—	—	2	9	2	3	2	7	1	8	1	—	—	—	—	—	—	—	2
Argentina	18	11	32	7	46	9	44	12	61	11	52	8	54	5	64	4	93	4	97	5	97	6	98	9	92	9	91	8
Brazil	100	7[a]	121	7	118	10	138	14	162	18	205	20	234	33	298	33	339	38	382	33	470	27	508	34	509	27	514	24
Chile	—	—	—	8[a]	—	8[a]	43	3	40	3	32	3	41	4	50	6	56	6	55	5	63	3	64	7	58	6	57	5
Colombia	—	5[a]	—	5[a]	8	6	7	5	13	5	14	4	22	4	26	6	28	6	29	6	38	6	45	7	44	7	40	8
El Salvador	—	4[a]	—	—	9	6	12	6	17	5	19	5	23	6	22	5	24	4	28	4	40	4	43	3	42	3	42	3
Peru	13	7	17	7	17	3	—	2[a]	—	2[a]	6	2	13	2	17	2	—	—	—	—	—	—	—	—	—	—	—	—
Trinidad	15	5	14	2	12	2	11	3	16	3	20	1	18	1	21	2	21	3	19	3	19	4	21	4	25	5	25	3
Venezuela	7	5	8	5	8	6	13	6	15	4	18	4	18	4	17	4	16	4	19	4	21	3	23	3	19	5	20	7
AFRICA																												
East Africa	10	13	11	13	17	16	19	16	32	9	40	8	44	10	45	11	59	9	61	13	65	13	82	12	78	12	88	7
Ghana	12	8	14	8	17	8	20	6	3	6	27	4	24	3	22	3	28	2	28	8	23	2	24	1	21	1	21	1
Malawi	1	10	1	9	1	11	2	11	3	10	3	10	3	8	6	6	6	7	8	8	10	8	11	8	12	6	14	5
Nigeria	18	17	11	11	39	13	32	15	41	16	42	12	51	11	52	16	70	19	93	22	102	23	127	26	143	24	175	29
South Africa	220	8	261	8	307	8	323	7	322	10	348	14	381	8	382	8	463	12	488	16	488	16	525	18	556	17	544	14
Tunisia	—	—	—	—	—	—	—	—	—	3[a]	—	3[a]	2	3	2	3	—	3	2	2	3	2	3	1	3	1	5	1
Zaire	9	8	10	8	12	12	16	12	19	11	23	11	26	9	—	8[a]	—	5[a]	39	3	38	4	40	5	41	6	30	6
Zambia	—	15[a]	3	15[a]	3	21	4	19	4	13[a]	—	10[a]	—	—	—	—	—	—	—	—	—	—	—	—	—	—	—	—
Zimbabwe	—	—	—	—	—	—	—	—	—	—	40	1	43	2	45	2	47	1	45	1	43	2	45	3	50	3	48	8
REST OF WORLD																												
Bangladesh	—	—	—	—	—	—	—	—	4	1	5	1	8	1	8	1	8	1	9	2	9	2	10	2	9	1	9	1
India	208	10	223	13	238	8	243	10	248	9	264	8	278	5	288	3	296	6	318	5	336	1	446	2	456	4	482	6
Indonesia	60	7	59	10	65	9	65	10	67	9	80	10	83	12	88	12	106	18	110	19	133	22	169	25	180	24	207	24
Japan	31	7	33	5	33	5	25	5	22	4	30	5	28	8	31	8	36	8	79	10	83	12	89	13	92	14	96	12
Malaysia/ Singapore	28	10	30	6	35	5	38	6	38	5	40	4	57	3	64	4	54	4	62	3	68	3	72	7	67	8	68	6
Pakistan	43	5	44	5	46	3	46	3	43	6	41	2	40	2	41	2	39	2	38	2	40	2	44	2	42	2	77	6
Philippines	43	8	49	8	62	2	70	6	70	6	72	7	76	6	80	7	89	5	96	7	102	9	101	6	100	7	87	4
Sri Lanka	25	3	24	2	26	7	25	1	26	1	25	1	24	7	25	1	24	1	25	8	26	7	26	1	27	1	30	2
Thailand	26	5	34	7	31	7	31	7	31	7	38	6	32	7	40	6	43	7	45	3	50	7	52	6	55	4	59	5
Turkey	41	6	37	6	56	6	58	9	57	5	61	4	68	5	74	4	85	5	84	3	83	12	82	7	79	3	74	4
Australia	333	4	337	9	359	10	372	9	390	8	391	8	409	11	406	12	409	15	431	16	464	12	479	7	502	15	468	16
New Zealand	85	8	93	6	93	5	95	4	87	4	82	5	87	6	89	6	79	3	85	2	80	1	84	2	85	2	82	3
Total	1,366	211	1,487	207	1,695	215	1,760	207	1,852	190	2,018	183	2,196	182	2,306	186	2,526	199	2,783	206	2,994	199	3,313	214	3,387	217	3,456	220

Note: a. Expatriates only.
Source: Unilever, London.

Table 3.2: Manpower Statistics for Unilever Plantations Group, 1972–82

	1 Jan. 1972			1 Jan. 1977			1 Jan. 1982		
	Nats	Expats	Total	Nats	Expats	Total	Nats	Expats	Total
Belgium	5	1	6	8	2	10	7	3	10
Colombia[a]	–	–	–	–	–	–	1	1	2
Cameroon	6	10	16	15	7	22	16	6	22
Gabon	–	1	1	–	–	–	–	–	–
Ghana[b]	–	–	–	4	4	8	6	3	9
Nigeria	6	2	8	7	2	9	8	1	9
Zaire	24	68	92	50	36	86	49	32	81
Malaysia	14	5	19	16	5	21	21	4	25
Solomon Is.	–	6	6	4	3	7	3	7	10
Total	55	93	148	104	59	163	111	57	168

Notes: a. 1 Jan. 1982 included the newly formed company, Plantaciones Unipalma de Los Llanos SA.
b. 1 Jan. 1977 included the new development of Benso Oil Palm Plantation.

Source: Unilever, London.

members of the community with their own ideas about its true interests. If they work within an organisation that they respect (and there is no need for them to continue to do so unless they do respect it for the outside opportunities in such circumstances are great), they can exert a major influence on policies and on the pattern of management and operations — and indeed do so.[8]

With this change the complete technology — operational management techniques, technical and research progress, agronomic discovery — all lie in the hands and minds of citizens of the country concerned. It is an asset which is often considered more important than all others in the discussion of the differences between the developed and the developing world. Today the developing world cannot be deprived of it by its export and is not dependent for it on any metropolis.

Costs and Benefits

The commercial return on investment in plantations is now usually modest. Profit is not a prime consideration in government or parastatal ownership; the more important objective for most projects is the production of the crop. Where private capital is concerned, the investment is seen as a long-term venture, often allied to other activities, and sometimes subsidised by tax and other incentives from a government which wants to promote agriculture. In other words, whatever the ownership, the return on the capital invested is not always the only criterion.

It is in fact more important to try to assess what are the social costs and benefits to the country concerned — if only as a guide to, or justification for, agricultural policy. It is a question that arises throughout development economics; a major attempt was made to answer it by the OECD Development Centre, Paris, in 1968 and 1969.[9] Little and Scott[10] then took up the original methodology, which was designed for the appraisal and evaluation of investment projects in manufacturing industry, and from 1968 began to apply them in other fields, especially agriculture. One such study was carried out for an oil palm plantation in Malaysia — a CDC company, the Kulai Oil Palm Estate.[11] The technique is a complicated one, involving a mixture of actual costs and estimations on the basis of stated hypotheses ('shadow pricing'); but various versions of it have been widely adopted for independent assessments of projected schemes, notably by international organisations such as the World Bank, in deciding which projects to finance. It has been used less frequently on organisations which are actually in operation; but in that it represents a dispassionate and independent view of the 'social' value of a plantation, it is obviously of importance for the present examination.

The whole case study is worth careful reading. It gives a description of the history of the venture and describes in some detail the agricultural operations. It then goes on to an analysis of costs and benefits for both CDC and Malaysia as the host country. The conclusions are clear (p. 54):

> The most noticeable feature of the results shown . . . is the size of the difference between the commercial and social profitability. By 1969, ignoring any terminal value the private return was only 1.2 per cent compared with the central estimate of 16.4 per cent social return. For the owners, the investments at Kulai are only now beginning to pay off, and the estimate of final profitability is very sensitive to the assumptions concerning future costs and reserves. From the social point of view, the future does not make nearly so much difference to the final result. In terms of 1950 present values, most of the social net benefits had accrued by 1969.

A further breakdown, Table 3.3, splits the benefits between Malaysia and CDC.

Table 3.3:   Malaysia: Value of Benefits from the Kulai Oil Palm Estate, from 1950 (M$ 000, 1967 prices)

	1950–69	1970–	1950–
Discounting at 7%			
Benefits to: Malaysia	9,030	7,115	16,145
CDC	– 3,430	5,930	2,500
Total	5,600	13,045	18,645
Discounting at 12%			
Benefits to: Malaysia	5,655	1,735	7,390
CDC	– 4,065	1,445	– 2,620
Total	1,590	3,180	4,770

Source: I.M.D. Little and D.G. Tipping, *A Social Cost Benefit Analysis of the Kulai Oil Palm Estate, West Malaysia* (OECD Development Centre, Paris, 1972), p. 56.

Finally, there is a comparison (p. 87) with a similar exercise by a different team (Bevan and Goering) in 1967 on a different oil palm estate and a rubber estate in Malaysia which produces higher figures — but the social rate of return is again greatly in excess of the commercial rate.

Conclusions

The limited empirical evidence contained in this chapter can prove nothing in general. It does, however, suggest three broad conclusions that are important for the argument of this book.

First, the old bogy of foreign ownership has been effectively laid in the last three decades. There is nothing intrinsic to the plantation that requires it to be a tool of international capitalism; and a large number of Third World states have used their sovereignty to acquire all or a majority of the equity in plantations previously owned by foreign corporations. At the same time the case for a continuing element of foreign involvement remains, in that some large international firms possess a stock of knowledge and the research facilities that are critical for the most efficient use of resources. In principle, knowledge and technology can be bought, along with foreign experts, without involving investment or ownership by foreign corporations. In practice the most efficient and economical way of acquiring these things may well be for a Third World government to enter into partnership (with or without participation in the equity) with a large international enterprise, thus maintaining the pattern of management set out in Figure 1.1. Certainly a number of less developed countries (LDCs), after experimenting with complete local ownership and management, have decided that partnerships are more effective. Some of the reasons for this are set out in Chapter 5 below.

Second, whatever the pattern of control and ownership, management of the plantations on the ground is now predominately in the hands of nationals of host LDCs. This process has, of course, gone hand in hand with the transfer of management in industrial and other enterprises that were originally owned and run by expatriates. The main condition for continued efficiency involved in this transfer is that the host society should be able to provide managers with the necessary administrative and technical skills. Thirty years ago, with the very small number of people with tertiary, or even secondary, education in many African and Pacific countries, this problem was significant. By the 1980s it has virtually ceased to exist. The only remaining case for retaining a limited number of expatriate (which is not to say necessarily European) managers is to ensure the transmission of new ideas and to prevent insularity and complacence.

Finally, there is the question of costs and benefits. The potential costs of the plantation, as defined by hostile writers such as Beckford, have been summarised above. Some of these costs remain and may be intrinsic to intensive methods of agricultural production in the tropics. In particular, the plantation uses land which might be used for other purposes; it requires a large labour force, and much of the work is repetitive and rigorous; by some standards wages are likely to be relatively low, given the constraints of the commodity market on selling prices; and the plantation may (though it need not) form a partially insulated segment of the economy. But equally many of the old charges are now invalid. If the equity is wholly or largely owned within the host country, the drain of profits overseas will be minimal. Moreover, the charge that plantations are natural enclaves within the host economy can no longer stand up. If the host government insists, most of the inputs will be bought locally, which will ensure backward linkages. These are discussed in Chapter 5. Increasingly the product of the plantation is consumed locally or used as an input by local industries. Even if the product is sold abroad, it uses transport, warehousing and other local facilities and ultimately earns foreign exchange which can be used to finance imports of capital and other goods essential to economic development in other sectors. Perhaps most important, the cash-benefit analysis adopted by Little and Tipping suggests that the social gain from a well-run plantation is far greater than its obvious commercial value. The basis of their calculation was shadow wages. Given the validity of their assumption — that in a LDC such as Malaysia the marginal value of labour in the subsistence sector was very low — the plantation constitutes a most efficient means of employing factor endowment and significantly increases the real wealth of the community.

The general proposition, then, is that the modern plantation estate is potentially an asset to a developing country and that it no longer represents the intrusion of foreign capital. This proposition will be developed and tested in later chapters.

Notes

1. The Overseas Resources Development Act (ORDA) of 1948, which established the Colonial (later Commonwealth) Development Corporation (CDC), was drawn up in very wide and general terms. While there was general agreement that economic development was being held back in the underdeveloped territories owing to the existence of a gap between the development activities of governments on the one hand and commercial operations on the other, and that this gap required to be filled, there was no consensus on what was the precise nature of the gap nor experience on how it should be filled. There was no blueprint. CDC's rationale for operating had to be worked out through trial and error: 'Like so much in CDC there was a gradual process by which the policy was extended and refined as experience from actual operations accumulated.' (Sir William Rendell, *The History of the Commonwealth Development Corporation 1948-1972* (Heinemann Educational Books, London, 1976), p. 195.) Rendell's authoritative account, so alive to the political issues of the day, describes how the CDC seeks to maintain a careful balance between meeting the needs of some of the least well-endowed territories and at the same time keeping its overall account in the black. CDC has tended over the years to evaluate projects from the point of view of the government and people of the territory concerned, and to make their co-operation a major prerequisite for CDC involvement. This did not always imply an indigenous or local injection of capital for agricultural projects. However, CDC's ultimate aim in all its agricultural development work has been to encourage and promote self-sufficiency, and to this end the eventual 'disposal (of land) to local citizens was firm CDC policy by the end of the 1950s'. (Ibid., p. 277.)

2. P.P. Courtenay, *Plantation Agriculture*, 2nd edn (Bell and Hyman, London, 1980), p. 116.

3. See Rendell, *Commonwealth Development Corporation*, pp. 75, 119-21 and 130-3.

4. See World Bank, *Accelerated Development in Sub-Saharan Africa* (Washington DC, 1981), pp. 37-40, 49-51 and 61-9; see also R.H. Bates, *Markets and States in Tropical Agriculture: the Political Basis of Agricultural Policies* (University of California Press, Berkeley, 1981), pp. 46-9 and 114-18.

5. See, for example, Bates's discussion of the uses to which funds of the marketing boards in West Africa have been put following independence. Ibid., pp. 12-19.

6. See D.K. Fieldhouse, *Unilever Overseas: the Anatomy of a Multinational 1895-1965* (Croom Helm, London, 1978), pp. 577-98, for an excellent analysis of a very large case study in India.

7. Ibid., p. 191.

8. For a general history of this indigenisation process see A.M. Knox, *Coming Clean* (Heinemann, London, 1976), pp. 162-5.

9. This method of project appraisal was originally put forward by I.M.D. Little and J.A. Mirrlees, anonymously, in the *Manual*, vol. 1, 1968, and subsequently rewritten by them in 1974: *Manual of Industrial Project Analysis in Developing Countries,* vol. 1: *Methodology and Case Studies* (OECD Development Centre, Paris, 1968); vol. 2: I.M.D. Little and J.A. Mirrlees, *Social Cost Benefit Analysis* (OECD Development Centre, Paris, 1969); I.M.D. Little and J.A. Mirrlees, *Project Appraisal and Planning for Developing Countries* (Heinemann, London, 1974).

10. I.M.D. Little has specialised since 1958 in the economics of developing countries, and was Professor of that subject at Nuffield College, Oxford. He has been Vice-President of the OECD Development Centre, and is a member of the UN Committee for Development Planning.

M.FG. Scott has worked as an economist for international organisations, and is a former Fellow of the OECD Development Centre. He collaborated with J.D. MacArthur and D.M.G. Newbery in writing *Project Appraisal in Practice: the*

Little-Mirrlees Method applied in Kenya (Heinemann, London, 1976). He has helped evaluate projects in India, Mauritius and Pakistan. He is a Fellow of Nuffield College, Oxford. See I.M.D. Little and M.FG. Scott, *Using Shadow Pricing* (Heinemann, London, 1976), p. vi and Introduction.

11. I.M.D. Little and D.G. Tipping, *A Social Cost Benefit Analysis of the Kulai Oil Palm Estate, West Malaysia* (OECD Development Centre, Paris, 1972).

4 THE ROLE OF MANAGEMENT

Chapter 1 described the organisation of a plantation and how it is set up to produce its results, the nature of its labour force and the untraditional features that it introduces. Examples suggested the numbers of managers and men and the size of the capital commitment involved. In describing these features it was stressed that the unique nature of these arrangements lies in the specialised management content that is involved and in the systems and methods that are adopted to apply it. Subsequent chapters referred frequently to it.

What is this management content? What do managers do? What are the problems to which they apply their skills?

The business of management is to make things happen according to a plan. The aim is always to produce a greater quantity and better quality with a given set of resources — by using them better, by studying the detail of where significant adaptations can be made to make the greatest impact on the process as a whole. There are theories and principles behind it, but the achievement of the objective is essentially a pragmatic process; some specific examples should make clearer the nature of what is involved.

Planning and Design

Much of the pattern of costs and productivity is set unalterably in the first design of the plantation. In the factory, for instance, the major features are fixed when the building is built and the machinery installed. Similarly the layout of the crops and the estate housing, and the roads which will evacuate the produce, are set from the beginning. So is the endemic fertility of the stock that is planted: much has been done to introduce higher yielding varieties for many crops, but once planted they will normally be there for the term of their natural lives, no matter what superior strain arrives on the market in the next season.

In all the decisions that have led to these designs, whether of factory or estate layout, management knowledge has played the major part. The pattern of the factory process has to be provided for in detail in the building; the installation of the machinery in the most efficient layout and the design and choice of the machinery must be thought out against a background of past experience and development of the plantation. As experience is gained, and experiments are successful, the results are fed back to become part of management knowledge, or to suggest adaptations and change in machines and techniques. Mill machinery today, for example, whether for oil or sugar, bears little resemblance to its ancestors of even 50 years ago. Similar skilled planning, using the latest experience, must go into the layout of the estate, the pattern of the roads, or the choice of other means of transport, water or rail; the location of the factory, of the water reservoirs, of housing and amenities. Bad management at this stage brings penalties for many years.

Repetitive Field Tasks

But there is a second area where improvement and change are constantly possible — this lies in the maintenance and day-to-day running of the estate. It is here that much of the skill and ingenuity of the field management — those who work directly on the crops — is deployed. Of these direct costs, under the immediate control of the estate management, the largest is that of cutting and evacuating the crop. It is twice the cost of the maintenance of the estate on average; and, although some of the pattern is already set by the layout of the estate, distance between roads, and access to outside transport, there are variable factors which can often be very favourably affected by good management.

Let us take as examples the 'ripeness standard' and the 'optimum harvesting round'. Both apply to the harvesting of bunches of fruit from the oil palm.

Ripeness Standard

The product of the oil palm is called a 'fruit' in the shape of a very large nut, golden yellow in colour, embedded in the 'bunch' in which it grows and ripens. There is usually only one bunch ripe on the tree at one time — though it may be up to 20 kg in weight. But one part of the bunch is more exposed to the ripening effects of sun and rain than the rest, and on this part the fruit ripens more quickly. It is usually the top, and the ripe fruits fall out while on the underside the fruits are still unripe. The puzzle is then that of deciding which is the best time to harvest; sooner, and the higher proportion of the lower fruit will be unripe; later, and a greater amount of the top fruit will be over-ripe and will have fallen.

In Malaysia a bunch is usually considered ripe when ten loose fruit have fallen out, and this standard obtains throughout the year. In West Africa the figures vary according to the season from 15 at the top to as low as one. The further variant is the speed at which the fruit matures — an alternation of sun and rain will make it ripen very quickly. So there will obviously be variations and compromise in deciding the optimum ripeness standard. Its importance is the commercial effect that it has on oil production and costs. This appears in the next section.

Optimum Harvesting Round

There is one day for each bunch when it reaches its maximum oil content. In the case of each fruit this is the day when it is just correctly ripe and should be harvested. But, in the case of the bunch, not all the fruits are ripe, and the unripe fruits will have less than the maximum oil content. Yet, if the bunch is left, the ripe fruit starts to fall out and can be lost in the undergrowth or eaten by vermin; in any case the quality of the oil starts to deteriorate — the fruit should be processed within twelve hours of picking.

If the maximum amount of oil were the only objective, all ripe bunches would be cut every day. This would call for a very large harvesting force — it could only be justified if labour costs were very low and oil prices very high. But in practice it is always necessary to sacrifice some oil to achieve a reasonable harvesting cost.

There are, in fact, always market price factors which must be considered when deciding on the optimum harvesting round and setting the ripeness standard. The points at which they are fixed will vary with the weather, the price of oil, the cost of processing and the cost of harvesting operatives. The experienced manager will be able to work largely on a rule of thumb; but it will be a rule which is really the result of a series of judgements of variables, and will depend on the existence of a system around him — an institution of which he is a part and can draw on the other parts — which will identify these factors and quantify them as they vary. He will permute the use of his workers and the allocation of the tasks, the length of the round and the number of men he uses, accordingly.

So the content of the management's task is to consider all these specialised details and variable factors and to dispose resources so as to obtain the most cost-effective results. It is a task which demands a series of decisions taken out of a background of specialised knowledge, reinforced and constantly updated by institutional support, and applied flexibly in continually changing circumstances. It is a process which is possible only within a closely knit organisation designed for the purpose, and therein lies its strength; it is this which should produce results superior to those open to the unsupported single worker on the land.

Plant Research

Such management skills are as it were the tactical end of the battle to grow the crops; though there are general principles behind them, they need to be applied individually, and need adaptation for each use. But there are also wider areas for the application of more fundamental disciplines, for instance in the natural sciences, where what is studied and invented can have world-wide application.

New Strains

A particularly important example can be found in the oil palm industry. Today, and from the 1960s onwards, almost the entire area under oil palm throughout the world is planted with one variety — the DxP, produced by research workers in the Belgian Congo (now Zaire), by crossing the shell-less Pisifera variety with the fruit type then planted throughout the Far East, the thick shelled Deli-Dura variety. This in itself had seen its yields greatly improved throughout the 1950s by commercial seed producers in work associated with the big plantation companies in Malaysia and Africa. The rise has been dramatic. In one plantation in Johore (Malaysia) for instance, the yields have risen from 1.8 tons of palm oil and 0.5 tons of palm kernels per hectare in 1951 to an average of 4.6 tons of palm oil and 0.9 tons of palm kernels per hectare in 1980 — with the best of the areas yielding over 5 tons.[1]

This has been the result of steady work over 30 years. But more recently fundamental research has made a leap which promises to bring the industry into a new phase altogether. The story is a fascinating one, not least for the way in which it demonstrates plantation management at work and the range of sciences and disciplines which it brings together in its service.

Vegetative propagation is a very old and well-known technique. If you take a cutting or a bud graft from a tree and succeed in getting it to grow, you produce a 'clone' — and, unlike sexual reproduction, clonal propagation produces a plant which is genetically identical to its parent. So it is simple and quick to multiply the best plants by clonal propagation, and indeed rubber plantations throughout the world are planted mainly with clones.

Grafting is unfortunately impossible with the oil palm — it will not reproduce from cuttings. Improvements to the oil palm stock have always had to be by sexual reproduction from high yielding varieties aimed at producing high yield progenies. It is necessary to test the progenies before selecting the parent palms for the programme, and there are individual differences between palms in the same progeny; in any hectare of palms of the same progeny there are both high yielders and low yielders, and several years are needed to identify the high yielders.

What was needed was a clonal palm — and it was this that the research scientists set out to produce. They worked on 'tissue culture'. Within the tissues of each plant are cells which are capable of growth into a complete plant, identical to the tree from which the tissue came; and each plant should therefore be identical with others from the same tissue. They needed a medium to make them grow — a 'culture'. After several years of experiment with different culture techniques, 'test-tube' plants were produced from root tissues. The experimental techniques moved into commercial production, and by 1980 there were units in both England and Malaysia multiplying up clonal material. First tests in the field suggest an increase of 30 per cent and more in the volume of palm oil.

Pollination

Cloned oil palms should be of world-wide application. But there are also problems which demand an equally broad spectrum of scientific effort to be deployed for the benefit of particular areas. Such is the case with the variations in successful pollination that occur in different parts of the world. Although the problem is not great in Africa and South America, in the Far East, and particularly in East Malaysia and New Guinea, natural pollination was so deficient that it was necessary to pollinate artificially throughout the life of the palm. The pollination process itself required the invention of new techniques, both for the collection of the pollen and the method of dusting the female flower. Every palm had to be inspected; any receptive flower had to be dusted with pollen every three days. The result was a considerable increase in fruit, but the expense was high (approximately US$250 per hectare per year). Obviously it would be extremely valuable if the natural pollination rate could be increased.

The story of what happened when the problem was well enough defined is very illuminative of the accidents and benefits of a management institution — as well as the unexpected discoveries that can emerge when a problem is looked at over a wide front, rather than the setting of one country or one region. Most of the studies of pollination had been done in South East Asia — for the simple reason that there was no problem in Africa, where palms were pollinated satisfactorily by natural means and there was therefore no cause for investigation. Moreover it was traditionally believed — and never questioned — that the oil palm was wind-pollinated, that the pollen was carried from male to female flower by the wind rather than insects — the other possibility. And indeed, in the Malaysian context, for such pollination as takes place naturally this is probably nearly always right.

It should be noted here, in parenthesis, that pollination in this fashion is relatively inefficient; the ratio of the fruit to the bunch, which determines the amount of oil, is about 54 per cent in Malaysia, as opposed to approximately 65 per cent in Africa. The difference is masked by the fact that the productivity of the oil palm is much greater in South East Asia than in Africa, but if the fruit:bunch ratio in Malaysia were as high as in Africa the yield would become significantly greater. Yet the reason for the difference in the fruit:bunch ratio was never examined; it was never related to the efficiency of pollination.

Unilever operates plantations both in Africa (Zaire, Cameroon and Ghana) and in East and West Malaysia. Some of its planters who had worked in both areas were convinced, in defiance of the text-books, that in Africa at least — its original home — the oil palm was insect-pollinated. They cited as an example Cameroon, where, in spite of the fact that it rains every day in August, the flowers pollinated naturally when wind could obviously not be a factor, and produced excellent bunches five to six months later.

In 1977 Unilever approached the Commonwealth Institute of Biological Control (CIBC) with the problem and some of their theories about it. As a result a CIBC entomologist visited Cameroon to examine natural pollination. He established, in a much admired series of experiments, that the oil palm in its natural surroundings is insect-pollinated. He found that about a dozen species of insects are associated with the male inflorescence and he identified two weevils as the main pollination agents. He calculated that more than 20,000 individuals might visit a female flower while receptive and that these could carry more than half a million pollen grains into the inflorescence. (Artificial pollination blows a cloud of pollen at the surface of the inflorescence, and clearly cannot hope to compete thus with the natural pollination — hence the much better natural pollination in Africa.)

It was clear in retrospect that the early pioneers who had brought oil palm seeds from Africa to the Far East had left behind not only pests and diseases which afflicted it (they are much rarer than in Africa) but also beneficial insects which had established a symbiotic relationship with the oil palm. If these insects could be introduced to the Far East, in carefully controlled conditions, it would complete the palm's ecosphere and refill the artificially created vacuum. The Malaysian government was approached and co-operated with the CIBC in a series of experiments, over a period of three years, to establish that no harm would come from the introduction of the insects. All fears were assuaged; the weevils were introduced early in 1981, and the result is estimated to be an additional 400,000 tonnes of palm oil per annum in Malaysia as a whole.

It is also interesting that the discovery has been particularly valuable for smallholders in Malaysia and elsewhere. On large estates pollination could be done efficiently; but for smallholders it was difficult to organise pollen collection, oven drying and application; as a result artificial pollination was much less effective. But insects do not differentiate — they pollinate the smallholders' flowers just as efficiently as they treat those of the estate. It has been equally advantageous to spread the technique geographically, and the weevils have accordingly been released in Papua New Guinea, the Solomon Islands and Thailand — though Unilever has plantation interests only in the Solomons.

Conclusion

Any one of the examples quoted could be regarded as the exercise of a particular craft or profession: of measurement and accounting for the ripeness standard and the optimum harvesting round; of botany and chemistry for the tissue culture discoveries; of entomology and botany for the discoveries in pollination. What makes them relevant to plantation technology is the conspectus that the institution — the co-ordinated plantation management — brings with it. It is because it sees the operation as a whole, and then seeks to isolate in detail the parts whose improvement would make tangible progress with the whole crop, that it can focus research on areas which are the most likely to produce valuable results. Unless there is some part of the organisation whose task it is to relate scientifically what is done to what is produced and what is earned, there is no criterion for identifying those activities where successful investigation and change would bring improvement in the way of greater quantities or better quality. Nor is there the mechanism outside of an institution, once the areas for change of practice are identified, of introducing that change — of changing the length of the harvesting round, of introducing artificial pollination and then in its turn superseding it when something fundamentally better can be substituted. The institution has no limit to its life span; the organisation is naturally working always to perpetuate its existence; provided that its efforts at perpetuation are always related to the original purpose, and not merely to securing its own existence, it will constantly seek improvements. In this it will be more single-minded than the individual, and will also gain from the synergistic effects of the efforts of many individuals, each with their own specialised capacities, in a way that could never be possible for a single cultivator working on his own, and with only his own resources. Individual growers there are and must always be; and they must be enabled to partake of the fruits of the technical advances, no matter from where they come. This too will be a matter of organisation and institutionalisation — the co-operative or the extension services. But for most advances the lead and the initiatives, as well as their development and advance to a practical stage, depend on a more centralised form of institution and management; one which can take the clues in whatever part of the problem they are found and then follow them through, solving the puzzles, bringing specialised expertise to bear, and then working out the usefulness and methods of application of the new discoveries.

The task of management, in short, is to ensure that it can command, identify or reach a very wide range of resources and then expertly apply them to problems that it is another part of its task to identify.

Note

1. I am much indebted for a great deal of the material in this chapter to Leslie Davidson of Unilever, and a paper he gave in Bombay on 13 December 1980 to the Oil Technologists' Association of India.

5 THE PLANTATION AND THE HOST ECONOMY: STUDIES IN LINKAGES AND COMPARATIVE ADVANTAGE

This chapter will seek to compare up-to-date facts and statistics on the question of linkages with some of the difficulties raised by the theories outlined in Chapter 2. Part of the evidence will have to come from general observation and the known and changed situations of recent years in many Third World countries which have plantations today. To this picture it is possible to add some detailed and quantified work which has been done in particular countries.

There is, however, a general difficulty which applies to a great deal of the presentation of up-to-date facts in this book. It has been argued that the modern plantation is a much changed institution from that phenomenon to which the word was applied even in times as recent as the years immediately following the Second World War, and that development of the plantation as an institution has been at its most rapid in the last 20 years. As progress has been so rapid, it is vital to such an argument that those facts and statistics which are quoted should belong to the present or the very recent past.

But the laborious nature of the task of gathering together evidence, for instance of linkages, which by their nature must depend both on particular industry or case unit studies and also on more general national statistics, and which themselves tend to be both incomplete and much in arrears, will always mean that quantification will trail a long way behind the rapid changes that are taking place. Where concrete evidence is available then, and provided that the trends continue in the same direction, it is always likely to underestimate the real effects of change. This is particularly true of a phenomenon like linkages, where development is cumulative; one successfully created trade tends to make the case for others. One example below shows the difficulty clearly and is particularly apposite in that it is taken from an excellent and most exhaustive study of the whole subject of linkages as seen in the plantation industry. It comes in Thoburn's very detailed study of Malaysia.[1] This is a book published in 1977, based on a household budget survey of 1957–8, which is used to give a pattern of domestic consumption for tin and rubber industry workers and rubber smallholders for

1968. The section deals with final demand linkages — where the proportion of the consumption expenditure of the plantation workers that is satisfied by local production from within the country is measured. But between 1957 — the date of the household budget survey — and 1977 — the date of the book — there was a lot of change in a rapidly developing country such as Malaysia. Thoburn himself recognises the difficulty over dates and the obsolescence of the statistics in note 1 on page 184. Here, too, he acknowledges the impossibility of applying the statistics to the oil palm industry; what makes the comparison even more difficult is that in the intervening years there has been a massive switch in relative importance away from rubber and in favour of palm oil; so that, as a picture of the pattern of locally produced supplies at the date of the book, it must be a significant underestimate.

This is one particular case; more generally, the same is true of the Malaysian economy as a whole. There have been major changes in Malaysia since 1957 and they are changes which have significance not only for such matters as final demand linkages; they show clearly that its development is now inconsistent with the rigid application of the theory not only of the enclave but also of any suggestion of a pattern of underdevelopment for the country as a whole.

For those who knew Malaysia as far back as 1957 and still know it today, there will be little difficulty in acknowledging the major changes that have taken place in consumption patterns, and in many of the indicators which are used to define the standard and the quality of life. Independence came in 1957 but the Emergency continued. In contrast, by the start of the 1980s the country had become one of the richest of the developing world economies. By 1980 the GNP had expanded at more than 6 per cent per annum for the previous 15 years. Its people had by then a life expectancy of 68 years, an average daily calorie intake 15 per cent above FAO's minimum requirements and access to safe water for 62 per cent of the population. The overall mortality rate fell by 22 per cent between 1970 and 1978, and the number of villages supplied with electricity increased by 186 per cent between 1970 and 1978 — from 1,223 to 3,498. Agriculture still represented 62 per cent of GNP but manufacturing had risen to 18 per cent and GNP was growing at the end of the period at the rate of 8 per cent per annum and the balance of payments was very favourable.[2]

The growth of manufacturing and services has been at the forefront of government policy throughout, with specific arrangements to ensure increased and continued participation by indigenous Malay capital: the manufacturing product more than doubled in seven years, from M$1,858 million in 1971 to M$2,768 million in 1974 and M$3,735 million in 1977 at constant prices. Plantations by the beginning of the 1980s were suffering from a shortage of labour, while their wage rates, under continuous and effective union pressure, were comparable and in some cases superior to those of factory workers in nearby towns. In Johore in West Malaysia, for instance, palm oil harvesters on piece-rates and using draught animals were earning over US$12 per day plus free accommodation, services and medicine in 1980. This was considerably more than workers were earning in factories in the town less than 10 kilometres away.[3]

Malaysia is perhaps the best and indeed most extreme example of a plantation economy, though its growth, especially on the export side, has been helped over the whole of the period by the tin and timber industries and in the last few years by mineral oil (14.1 per cent of export value in 1977–9). Its recent performance does not suggest either underdevelopment or the existence of enclaves. It points to an open market economy functioning freely and effectively. There is an increasingly complex and interlocking system of economic activities, and plantations are an integrated part of this system.

This is an impressionistic view over the whole of the economy, but it has as much validity as detailed case studies based as they must be on imprecise and outdated figures. The truth is most likely to come from marrying the two together — having a look at an overall view of the economy and then at such particular case studies as have been validly researched.

Malaysia — A Case Study in Linkages

Such a quantified examination of the direct effects of plantations on surrounding economies is found in the work of Thoburn on Malaysia to which reference has already been made. Though his book is recent (1977) it does not fully represent the extent of the integration of the rubber and palm oil industries into the Malaysian economy today. Nevertheless, the picture that emerges already bears no relation to the concept of the enclave; linkages are abundant and very important, to both the plantation and the economy as a whole.

Thoburn's analysis is a full and convincing recital. It depends on assumptions which in places, from their very nature, must be guesswork; but they are informed guesswork and constitute a framework which will stand scrutiny. Most importantly the conclusions are so arithmetically and overwhelmingly convincing that there is room for considerable error without the danger of invalidation.

Chapters 6 and 7 of Thoburn should be read for the methodology and the detailed arguments, but four of his calculations by themselves identify conclusively the close economic associations which tie the plantations into the life of the country. These are the extent to which local resources are used in the original establishment of a plantation: its capital costs; the backward and forward linkages between the plantations' inputs and outputs and the local economy; the final demand linkages which reflect the volume and pattern of the impact of the spending of the wages of those employed in the plantation; and engineering linkages.

Capital Costs

Rubber Estates.   There are two main cost components called by Thoburn 'field establishment costs' and 'factory capital costs'. The figures seem to be an underestimate of the full establishment costs in that he does not take account of the costs of providing the infrastructure — the original clearing of the land with the building of estate roads, workers' housing, communal buildings, etc. Nearly all such costs are money spent on local labour or local materials so that the 'local content' figure would be higher. His figures are therefore more conservative than a complete calculation would produce. Nevertheless they are most convincing; they show a major part of the setting up of the so-called 'enclave' as an input from the Malaysian economy.

Of field establishment costs, i.e. the costs of preparing and planting the whole area with rubber, Thoburn produces references to suggest that on private estates at least 50 per cent of the expenditure is on labour, with a further 20 per cent spent on fertilisers and weeding chemicals. If a further 10 per cent is estimated for materials used by the labourers, at least two-thirds of the direct field costs will be for labour; and, since much of the fertiliser and other agricultural chemicals is manufactured locally, he calculates that the total local content of field expenditure could well be over 75 per cent. On factory capital costs he gives the itemised figures for a rubber factory producing Standard Malaysian Rubber (SMR), and he describes it as having a lower local content than some others for which figures were obtained. The table is reproduced as Table 5.1 — the detail is interesting as an indication of which parts of an exercise of this sort can be supplied without imported content. The proportion would certainly be higher today in the early 1980s, more than ten years later.

Table 5.1: Malaysia: Itemised Capital Costs of a SMR Factory, 1970 (capacity 8 tons per day)

	Cost (M$ 000)	% Local Content	
1. Site preparation	11.1	100.0	
2. Main drains	8.6	100.0	
3. Factory compound and approach roads	16.4	100.0	
4. Factory buildings, office, workshops, etc.	199.1	100.0	
5. Machinery and equipment	268.7	28.9	
6. Water supply	54.2	n.a.	
7. Electrical installation	34.8	n.a.	
8. Weighbridge and house	26.0	10.0	
9. Firefighting appliances	1.2	—	
10. Equipment for office, store and workshop	2.6	100.0	
Total	622.7	51.4	Minimum
		65.4	Maximum

Thoburn's sources and notes:
(1) Information from interview in Malaysia, October 1970.
(2) Factory not designed for further expansion.
(3) Local content of item 8 is estimated. The weighbridge is imported, and the house is local.
(4) Imported structural steel in item 4 will account for 50–75% of cost of buildings. This reduces local content by between 21.6% and 32.4%.
Source: J.T. Thoburn, *Primary Commodity Exports and Economic Development: Theory, Evidence and a Study of Malaysia* (John Wiley and Sons, London, 1977), Table 6.22, p. 157.

Putting together the field establishment costs containing 75 per cent local expenditure and factory capital costs as above (up to 65 per cent) and counting day-to-day material costs at 10 per cent of the total, the overall local content works out at not less than 70 per cent. Here is strong material evidence of substantial linkages and refutation of the sort of separation that an enclave would entail.

Oil Palm Estates. Field establishment costs are very similar to those for rubber so that the local content will once again be in the region of 75 per cent or higher.

A palm oil mill is a more expensive and more complicated asset than the processing capacity required for rubber. Table 5.2, taken from Thoburn, shows the cost as ten times higher, though the capacity is much larger (54 tons per hour). Again the detailed breakdown is interesting. There is a high imported content only in the oil press and the boiler and power plant. Even in 1970 this could be improved; Thoburn cites a factory where only one-third of the cost was due to imported items as against 55 per cent in this table.

Table 5.2:   Malaysia: Itemised Capital Costs of a Palm Oil Mill, 1970 (capacity 54 tons of fruit per hour)

	Cost (M$ 000)	% Local Content
1. Reception	400	90.0
2. Sterilisation	400	50.0
3. Threshing	450	55.6
4. Pressing	700	14.3
5. Clarification	350	28.6
6. Depericarping	200	62.5
7. Kernel recovery	500	46.0
8. Oil storage	700	99.6
9. Steam plant	1,200	31.3
10. Power plant	250	2.4
11. Piping valves, etc.	300	16.7
12. Water supply	200	50.0
13. Electrical installation	300	40.0
14. Buildings	350	85.7
15. Civil works	400	100.0
16. Fees	250	50.0
Total	6,950	45.3

Thoburn's Sources and Notes:
(1)   Only for item 14 is cost of imported structural steel known to have been deducted (estimated by manufacturer at 100 tons, at say M$500 per ton). If structural steel for complete mill is estimated at, say, 600 tons (less 100 already included = 500 tons) at M$500 a ton, total local content is reduced to 41.8%.
(2)   Information from manufacturer in Malaysia, October 1970.
Source: Thoburn, *Primary Commodity Exports*, Table 6.25, p. 167.

Backward and Forward Linkages

Thoburn deals with these in detail both for rubber and for palm oil (pages 158–67).

Rubber.   Backward linkages are unimportant; chemical products for coagulation, fertilisers, weed-killers, etc. take less than 1 per cent of output value. With forward linkages, however, it is a different story. There are three main heads: the off-estate processing sector, the manufacture of rubber goods and the processing of rubber wood.

In off-estate processing 11,000 persons were employed full-time in 1971, while in the manufacture of rubber goods 9,000 people were employed in 50 establishments and the total value added was M$46.6 million. Moreover within this total were five large public companies — a new type of industry, capital intensive with tariff protection and pioneer status. Among them was Dunlop making tyres. It is more difficult to be specific about the manufacture of products made from rubber wood, but that it was not insignificant is shown by the quantity, 6 million tons in 1974/5. Half of this may have been used as fuel, but the rest would produce chipboard and similar wood products.

Palm Oil.   Information is not as full as that for rubber, which has for long been extremely well documented in Malaysia. Among backward linkages the importance of fertiliser is greater than for rubber — usage is much higher for the oil palm. Indeed it was calculated in 1972 that palm estates were the purchasers of 55 per cent of the output of fertilisers within the country. There are also factory linkages into the engineering industry to which Thoburn devotes a special chapter which will be discussed later. Among forward linkages, transport was more important than for rubber — palm oil needs tanker lorries and rail tankers and specialised oil bulking installations. But when Thoburn wrote, forward manufacturing linkages consisted only of some soapmaking, the processing of palm kernels and some modest processing in the way of refining part of the palm oil exports. This side of the industry has seen major development in the intervening ten years. During the 1970s it became the policy of the Malaysian government — as with some other governments in South East Asia, e.g. the Philippines — to encourage the further processing of edible oils by the introduction of differential export duties. There was a heavier tax on unrefined oil and major government encouragement for the building of bleaching and refining capacity. Technical exactitude is difficult as to the degree of refining and processing, but the result was a very large increase in the proportion of oil that was treated in some way before export. For example, volume increased by 34 per cent between 1978 and 1979.[4] There have also been important developments depending on sophisticated technology into the field of edible oil products and the processing of fatty acids.[5]

Final Demand Linkages

Thoburn has a very interesting and ingenious chapter on final demand linkages and the development of the local market for consumer goods. It is of limited specific value for application to the plantation industry by itself, since the figures aggregate the demand from the rubber estate and smallholders' sectors and the tin-mining industries in one set of totals and do not include the palm oil effects. But he comes to the conclusion that from these two industries the consumption expenditure of the workers is satisfied up to a proportion of 70 per cent by local production. From the assumptions that he makes in arriving at these figures, it is clear that, although the inclusion of the palm oil sector would increase the totals, it would not significantly alter the pattern. Indeed his conclusions tie in well with the official Malaysian statistics for 1980 which show that by that year local production was responsible for 69 per cent of final sales of all goods and services.[6]

Engineering Linkages

Thoburn firmly concludes that 'primary product exports have given rise in Malaysia to a substantial light engineering industry'.[7] His estimate of the local content of rubber investment and maintenance expenditure is 60 per cent and of palm oil, which developed later, 45 per cent in 1972.[8] He believes that 'the development of firms producing SMR machinery is due predominantly to sales to the export sector and is thus an example of linkage investment'. In the case of palm oil the linkage investment is not so direct since the seven firms working on palm oil machinery were not originally founded to manufacture for this sector. Nevertheless, palm oil work is now over half their turnover.[9]

Case Study Conclusions on Malaysian Rubber and Palm Oil

Natural linkages — economic and social — do then exist and function between the modern Malaysian plantation and its surrounding economy. The theory of the plantation as an enclave with links only outside the country in which it is situated and with all its wealth fed out to an outside owner cannot be squared with the facts. The importance of palm oil and rubber production in the total economy and the broadly impressionistic conspectus of the rapid advance of Malaysian society in the last 20 years seen at the beginning of this chapter confirm, at the level of the whole country, what has been seen in the facts of the detailed linkages. The wealth of Malaysia has advanced with the growth of the plantations step by step. It is only in recent years that it has received help from the development of the petroleum industry. There are differences between town and country and between standards of living in different parts of the country. But these are differences that are found in all developed countries, and are not the specific result of plantations.

It is an elementary error to lump all developing countries together or indeed all plantation economies. Malaysia is in many ways better than an average case, especially in its stability and wealth, and particularly very recently because of petroleum. But there are other countries where the growth and importance of plantations have brought with them similar major advances in related industries and patterns of consumption. In South East Asia, both the Philippines and Indonesia are clear instances. In South America, Brazil has built a large part of her economy on coffee and sugar. In Africa, Cameroon owes a very large part of its recent development to oil palm and rubber plantations. In Malaysia the plantation industry and its links have been documented in detail. In many other plantation economies the linkages can be seen equally well even though they have not been so clearly quantified.

Comparative Advantage in Third World Countries: Exports and Home Consumption

Exports

Definitions of the plantation have usually described its product as 'export crops', in line with the concept of the enclave and the concept of dependency. This has been another reason for their condemnation.

Even if it were universally true that all plantation crops are exported, condemnation should properly await the result of an examination of how comparative advantage applies: at its simplest, whether the amount of foreign exchange which the country acquires in payment for its exports enables it to bring in a larger quantity and a better variety of imported goods for the use of the inhabitants of the country than would the devotion of the whole of the efforts to growing their own crops from their own resources.

There are two points to be made. First, to take the example of food, that a better and more nutritious variety is possible for any country through a mixture of growing certain crops and importing those which cannot be grown at all or cannot be grown efficiently. Cereals are a good example: they can usually be better grown in countries outside rather than inside the tropics and are so important as an element of diet that they have tended to become almost synonymous with food generally in the discussions of world trade in food commodities. It is impracticable to pretend that each country could grow all its cereals. It seems logical to suggest that countries should grow that which they can produce very efficiently and export it to pay for the cereals and other goods that their diet needs.

Calculations of comparative advantage are difficult to do within a single country for one commodity against another — e.g. palm oil against cereals. In even the simplest of economies there are manifold links with too many other factors. But the questions begin to be answered at market prices on a world level where the world export price for cereals (which is often a subsidised one) has a long-term, though fluctuating, relationship with the world market price for palm oil. Any country can then calculate the attractiveness of producing by comparing its own production costs with the costs of importing. This is the standard approach to the evaluation of any new project for growing a crop for export; those who then go ahead with the project to grow such export crops do so because they are convinced that it will bring a comparative advantage to them. A variation can be that such an evaluation of the growing of a particular commodity may show that it would be possible to produce it for home consumption, which would free foreign exhange from paying for imports of it, and so, as with exports, enable more other goods to be imported. In this case again it is common sense to go ahead; this indeed has been done, e.g. in the case of Ghana for palm oil.

The second argument in considering 'tied' export as an alleged basic characteristic of plantations is once again that the facts have now changed. For a period in the early twentieth century there was indeed 'vertical integration' of the type described by Beckford.[10] It developed mainly out of earlier buyer and seller relationships, when larger and better established corporate customers took over from individual planters, who had run into financial difficulties at times of depressed prices. This was a process which began in the last quarter of the nineteenth century. A manufacturing company in Europe would thus find itself to be the owner of a plantation growing some of the raw materials that it used in its processes. In other cases, a manufacturer might set up a procurement agency in a tropical country to buy his raw materials from a series of small producers, collating his requirements through a series of collecting points. Such arrangements certainly added to the power of the buyer and were therefore unpopular with the sellers. The pattern existed, for instance, in Nigeria and Ghana in the 1920s and 1930s. Margarine and soap manufacturers had their buying arrangements for edible oils and seeds. Cocoa manufacturers purchased their supplies direct from farmers. Some small quantities were grown by direct subsidiaries.

But this direct contact disappeared when the chain was broken, first by the interpositioning of marketing boards by the colonial governments in the early 1940s, and then by the successor controls established by the newly independent governments when they came to power. These statutory marketing boards soon became a favoured device of many governments for commodities as different as the cocoa and oil seeds of West Africa and the meat of Argentina. The new boards took complete charge of the crop, constituting themselves often as the sole final buyer and fixing a producer price for universal application throughout the country. If the price was always set well below the world export market price, they could build up large funds. Indeed the surplus which arose from the wide difference between buying and selling prices became the largest element in the government revenues in many cases. The history and theory of marketing boards is a separate and fascinating study in itself.[11]

With such arrangements, vertical integration was split wide asunder. There could no longer be any idea that the periphery's low priced commodities were subsidising costs in the metropolis. Domestic prices and quantities for export were fixed by the marketing board, and export prices had to be in line with world prices. Even when a transnational owned a plantation which grew its raw material, it could no longer control either the amounts or the costs for delivery to its factories. The production of its subsidiaries was as much at the mercy of world forces — government controls and international commodity markets — as any material which came from a completely arm's length grower. Where marketing boards and terminal markets existed, it was indeed itself at arm's length.

It was not only price and quantity that were now controlled at the periphery. Primary producer countries began to look at the possibilities of processing their commodities before export so as to add value and to carry out some of the operations that had previously been carried out in the developed world where the final consumer bought the finished product. Differential duties were introduced favouring those products which had undergone local processing, as with palm and coconut oils in the case of Malaysia and the Philippines and groundnuts in the case of Nigeria. In addition to the financial sanctions, quotas were sometimes introduced as well.

It is worth quoting a striking set of figures which were the result of the Malaysian government's decision to encourage the processing of palm oil before export. It was a decision which prima facie was not the easiest or most acceptable from a technical point of view. There are large processing facilities in all user countries and a strong body of technical opinion which maintains that palm oil is of better quality when refined as near to the final manufacturing stage as possible. Nevertheless, the view of the producer government prevailed as the following quotation demonstrates:

> Exports of processed palm oil comprising refined palm oil, palm kernel oil, palm stearine and palm oil acid continue to show an impressive growth in export volumes due to the expansion in the domestic palm oil refining and fractionation industry. For the whole of 1979 total exports of crude palm oil are estimated to have declined by 6% over 1978 to about 539,000 tons compared to a decline of 18% in 1978. This is due mainly to increase in the domestic consumption of crude palm oil in 1979. Exports of processed palm oil in 1979, on the other hand, are estimated to have increased by 34% over 1978 to 1.25 million tons. The share of Malaysian palm oil (crude and processed) in the total world exports of palm oil is expected to have increased to 70% in 1979 from 68% in 1978.[12]

Similarly, the Philippines had entirely ceased to export copra (the unprocessed form of the coconut) by the beginning of the 1980s and was the supplier of 85 per cent of world coconut oil exports. A levy on the price of copra has been used over a period of eight years to build up a large vertically integrated group of institutions which bought up existing oil mills and refiners and some exporting firms. The operation was financed by a levy through the United Coconut

Planters Bank, which was itself purchased as to 70 per cent of its shares by the proceeds of the levy in 1975 and has consolidated under interlocking managements the processing and exporting trade. The parallel institution to the Bank — United Coconut Mills, which carries out the milling and trading — now controls 93 per cent of milling capacity and is responsible for 80 per cent of oil exports.[13]

This is a picture of events which have moved a long way from the vertical integration which Beckford describes. The same effective division between buyer and seller has been achieved in most other plantation economies, though the arrangements vary from country to country. Good examples are the controls for the marketing and export of tea in India, Ceylon and Kenya.[14]

Home Consumption

The growth of internal wealth and a money economy, together with rising populations, have also greatly modified producers' dependence on external markets.

There are many well-documented examples: for example, increased local consumption turned Nigeria from a major exporter of edible oils in the 1950s to a net importer in the 1970s. Up to 1965 she was the world's leading exporter of palm oil. Recently her exports have vanished. The reason is that since 1948 consumption has been rising: for the period 1948-67 it rose by 3 per cent per annum.[15] But on average the annual growth in production of palm oil for the period 1962-75 was only 1.9 per cent.[16] Similarly, the share of all agricultural products in total exports declined from 77 per cent in 1960 to 30 per cent in 1968, and has now almost

Table 5.3: Nigeria: Contribution of Major Export Crops to Total Exports, 1960–78 (as percentage of total)

	1960	1968	1972	1975	1978
Cocoa	22.2	10.0	3.0	2.7	3.3
Palm kernels	15.7	6.1	1.0	0.7	0.5
Palm oil	8.4	2.3	0.5	0.1	—
Groundnut oil	3.2	1.5	0.4	0.2	—
Groundnuts	13.8	6.4	0.8	0.1	—
Cotton	3.7	1.1	n.a.	n.a.	—
Rubber	8.6	2.5	0.9	0.6	—
Beniseed	1.1	1.0	0.3	0.1	—

Source: International Labour Organisation, *First Things First — Meeting the Basic Needs of the People of Nigeria* (ILO, 1981), Table 18, p. 86.

disappeared, as Table 5.3 indicates. Marketing board purchases also dropped over a similar period: for the years 1960-4 palm oil purchases averaged 161,878 tonnes and palm kernels 413,754 tonnes; a decade later, for the years 1970-4, they averaged 23,899 tonnes and 282,291 tonnes respectively. The very large drop in palm oil purchases reflects greater local consumption, with fruits going direct to small local processors rather than to the supposedly monopsonist board.

In Zaire, production of palm oil fell heavily over a period of nearly 20 years due to the civil wars and disturbed conditions. However, though the total has diminished, and is only just beginning to recover, Table 5.4 shows that the swing from export to home consumption has been steady throughout the period. These are Unilever figures, which are lower than those given in a World Bank Report of 29 March 1978. (The World Bank gives higher production figures, which therefore allow for higher exports.)

Table 5.4:   Zaire: Palm Oil Production and Export, 1970/1 to 1980/1 (000 tonnes)

	Total	Export	Consumption
1970/1	210	117	93
1971/2	193	98	95
1972/3	166	69	97
1973/4	167	68	99
1974/5	155	54	101
1975/6	149	46	103
1976/7	132	26	106
1977/8	119	9	110
1978/9	115	1	114
1979/80	124	7	117
1980/1	128[a]	7	121

Note: a. An estimate. However this figure indicates that additional expenditure five years earlier (using loan from World Bank to rejuvenate oil palm plantations) is beginning to show results.
Source: Unilever, London, 1983.

A South American country, Colombia, shows the other side of the coin; no exports of edible fats and oils, increasing consumption within the country, increasing production within the country and imports continuing since home production cannot keep up with the increased pace of demand.[17] In this particular case, Colombia's encouragement to foreign technology, touched on in Chapter 3, is an attempt to increase production for home consumption — not for export.

The foregoing sample is taken from a range of countries from South East Asia, Africa and South America. In no instance do the facts suggest that plantations are geared exclusively to the production of a commodity which is then totally exported in an unprocessed state. On the contrary, they suggest that plantations produce crops which are then often processed and consumed in the country of their origin, with a diminishing balance in some cases going overseas and earning foreign currency.

Indeed, the realities of plantations as they are today suggest a very different picture of the modern plantation from that outlined in Chapter 2. Almost none of what Beckford describes as 'the major development obstacles' have been found to exist nowadays. It is clear that there are no true enclaves today; that expatriate ownership and vertical integration have in most places ceased to exist and in others been greatly modified; that the metropolis and the periphery belong now only to history.[18]

The institution of the plantation has perhaps now arrived at a stage where it need not fear the strictures of those who have criticised it on the strength of out-of-date facts and outmoded concepts. In many countries it offers a set of skills and constantly renewable assets which today constitute a major part of the wealth of those countries. The modern plantation estate has been seen as an institution which has adapted itself to an efficient role in the agricultural and economic life of the Third World. It has already changed and fitted itself to meet criticism and the progressive needs of the countries in which it operates. The process of adaptation is continuous and has by no means ended. Further change and further uses for it as an institution are the subject of the later parts of this book. But, as a management system and an agricultural institution, it has already shown its effectiveness to those who have now taken up its use.

Notes

1. J.T. Thoburn, *Primary Commodity Exports and Economic Development: Theory, Evidence and a Study of Malaysia* (J. Wiley, London, 1977), p. 173.

·2. World Bank, *World Development Report 1981* (published for The World Bank by Oxford University Press, 1981), Annex of World Development Indicators; and *UN*

National Account Statistics 1979.

3. Unilever Plantation Group say that over the ten-month period June 1980 to March 1981 harvesters earned an average M$459.16 for a 26-day month, compared with factory workers in Kluang who earned M$208 for the same period. Using the exchange rate of US$1 = M$2.297, harvesters therefore earned an average US$7.68 per day. Top men earned much more on piece-rates. See also C. Barlow, *The Natural Rubber Industry: its Development, Technology and Economy in Malaysia* (Oxford University Press, Kuala Lumpur, 1978), Table 7.24, p. 282.

4. Ministry of Finance, Malaysia, *Economic Report, 1979/80* (Director General of Printing, Kuala Lumpur, 1979), p. 94. For the full quotation, see p. 82 of this chapter. The report also notes, p. 58, 'that export duty on palm oil would have been higher but for the revenue foregone due to the shift from the export of crude palm oil to processed palm oil, which is eligible for exemption on the total duty payable ranging from 65% to 70% depending on the degree of processing'. In 1978 processed oil amounted to 62% of the total palm oil exported, and exemptions on duty amounted to M$150 million; in 1979 the comparable figures were expected to be 70% and M$390 million.

5. Unilever Report and Accounts 1981, London.

6. Ministry of Finance, Malaysia, *Economic Report, 1979/80*.

7. Thoburn, *Primary Commodity Exports*, p. 203, point 4.

8. Ibid., Table 8.1, p. 188.

9. Ibid., p. 193.

10. G.E. Beckford, *Persistent Poverty: Underdevelopment in Plantation Economies of the Third World* (Oxford University Press, 1972), Chapter 5.

11. See, for instance, G.K. Helleiner, 'The fiscal role of the marketing boards in Nigerian economic development 1947–1961', *The Economic Journal*, vol. 74, no. 295, September 1964, pp. 582–610.

12. Ministry of Finance, Malaysia, *Economic Report, 1979/80*, p. 94.

13. G. Sacerdoti, 'Cracks in the coconut shell', *Far Eastern Economic Review*, 8–14 January 1982, pp. 42–8.

14. For India, see, for example, R.C. Awasthi, *Economics of Tea Industry in India* (United Publishers, Gauhati (Assam), 1975), pp. 144–8; National Council of Applied Economic Research (NCAER), *Techno-economic Survey of Darjeeling Tea Industry* (NCAER, New Delhi, 1977); for Sri Lanka, see a series of essays on the tea trade edited by Godfrey Gunatilleke, Marga Institute, Columbo, in a special issue of *Marga*, vol. 3, no. 4, 1976; for Kenya, see D.M. Etherington, *An Econometric Analysis of Smallholder Tea Production in Kenya* (East African Literature Bureau, Nairobi, 1973), Chapter 1, pp. 1–16; D.K. Leonard, *Reaching the Peasant Farmer: Organisation, Theory and Practice in Kenya* (University of Chicago Press, Chicago and London, 1977), Chapter 12; and J.R. Moris, 'Managerial Structures and Plan Implementation in Colonial and Modern Agricultural Extension: a Comparison of Cotton and Tea Programmes in Central Kenya' in D.K. Leonard (ed.), *Rural Administration in Kenya* (East African Literature Bureau, Nairobi, 1973), pp. 97–131 (esp. 120–4).

15. S. Olayide and D. Olatunbosun, *Trends and Prospects of Nigeria's Agricultural Exports* (Nigerian Institute of Social and Economic Research, Ibadan, 1972), pp. 17–29.

16. International Labour Organisation, *First Things First — Meeting the Basic Needs of the People of Nigeria* (ILO, 1981), Table 17, p. 85.

17. The following information on Colombia is taken from Alfred E. Persi, 'Colombia expands palm oil output', *Foreign Agriculture* (published monthly by United States Department of Agriculture), 9 January 1978:

(1) *Human consumption of fats and oils for the year Oct. 1979–Sept 1980*
275,000 tonnes, i.e. 10.2 kg *per capita.* This was made up from 10,000 tonnes butter, 14,000 tonnes lard and 251,000 tonnes soya and palm oil.

(2) *Industrial consumption, 1979/80*
96,000 tonnes, of which 41,000 tonnes were vegetable oils and 55,000 tonnes tallow for soap. (Of the total 96,000 tonnes, 88,000 tonnes go to soap.)

(3) *Human and industrial consumption, 1979/80*
Total of edible oils and soapmaking fats (excluding castor and linseed oil which are not used in any great quantity) was 371,000 tonnes.

(4) *Local production in relation to total consumption, 1979/80*
Out of 371,000 tonnes consumed, 196,000 tonnes were produced internally. The breakdown was as follows: 8,000 butter, 14,000 lard, 12,000 lauric oil for soaps (coconut and palm kernel), 60,000 liquid oil (sunflower, cotton, groundnut, soya), 67,000 palm oil and 35,000 tallow.

(5) *Future prospects*
In 1979/80 Colombia imported 127,000 tonnes edible oils. Even the planned doubling of palm oil production (67,000 tonnes at present) over the next two decades will not make Colombia self-sufficient. Moreover, consumption *per capita* per annum of edible fats and oils is rising: in 1970/1 7 kg; in 1979/80 10.2 kg — a rise of almost 50%.

18. For a convincing argument that enclave theories, whether applied to plantations or other productive systems, are now irrelevant, see the paper by David E. Hojman, 'From Mexican plantations to Chilean mines: theoretical and empirical relevance of enclave theories in contemporary Latin-America', presented to a meeting of the Development Studies Association in Liverpool in March 1983. The standard article on linkages is A.O. Hirschman, 'A Generalised Linkage Approach to Development, with Special Reference to Staples', *Economic Development and Cultural Change,* 25 (1977), Supplement.

PART TWO: APPLYING THE PLANTATION PRINCIPLE

6 DIFFERING INSTITUTIONS AND ALTERNATIVE STRATEGIES

It has been suggested in previous chapters that the plantation as an industrial institution makes a more efficient use than the individual farmer can of scarce inputs — whether they be land and fertiliser or labour and management expertise — because of its greater specialisation and more effective adaptation of the new technologies that are the fruit of world-wide research efforts. Later chapters provide case studies of some individual institutionalised systems such as the Federal Land Development Authority (FELDA) in Malaysia and Mumias in Kenya, which show the principles of the plantation technique working in different organisational settings. But first we need to consider what objectives any innovator in the agricultural field should have before him.

The Organisation and its Task

Organisations are created to achieve a particular purpose. There are often other considerations of politics and personal power and prestige, but the basic requirement is that the nature of the institution and the specific form that it takes should be shaped by the task that it has to perform. Moreover, a specific task and aim will be more likely to be carried out efficiently if it is narrowly defined and has few extraneous issues included in its field and its brief. In other words, the narrower the span of its tasks and hence of the issues it has to face and the problems it has to solve, the more it will be able to devote an undistracted attention to the prime purpose that has been put in front of it.

Here the management corporation type of institution which has descended from the birth of the limited liability company in the nineteenth century has a natural advantage in that it is specifically constituted with one task in mind. It has its 'Articles of Association' which in their strictest legal form can completely debar it from venturing on other activities which are not related to its defined task and hold it responsible to its owners — its shareholders — for keeping to the area they have originally defined. It has moreover a very clear criterion for most of what it does in a profit and loss account, though the balance between short- and long-term profit on the one hand, and the considerations which social desiderata and its duties as a 'good citizen' impose on the other, complicate decision-making. The government department, in contrast, usually has political or welfare objectives as well as the aim of running an agricultural project as efficiently as possible; matters which for the independent management corporation are only related issues can be for the government institution a major part of its task. It may well be that it is accepted that this should be so; but it ends in a trade-off of these benefits against the more efficient production which will be forthcoming from an institution whose brief is more single-minded. There is also the tendency in government operation of such enterprises for management and instructions to be filtered through different levels and chains of authority, gaining in obscurity and losing in impact on the way.[1]

The parastatal corporation is frequently the solution adopted in an effort to resolve these difficulties. It is framed in the image of the commercial management corporation and has its task defined in terms of commercial aims — it is told to grow a crop and make a profit on it with the nature of the profit sometimes well defined. It will be owned in whole or in part by the state, which for many schools of thought resolves the doubts about profit-making in such projects. Its other objectives, social and welfare, can be allowed for in the appraisal of its primary objective of agricultural production.

Nevertheless the parastatal organisation has frequently become notorious for its inept performance, achieving neither its crop production nor its social aims.[2] The reason has usually been found in its management and more particularly in the organisation or pattern of its management. Within this the trouble has often lain in the span of responsibility that this same management, often in the initial and inexperienced stages, has had to cover.

If management skill in an individual consists in an ability to get a given task or plan carried out, largely through co-ordinating and directing the efforts of others, it is clear that it is likely to be most effectively exercised when the numbers of helpers are low and contact with them is direct. Guidance, training and instruction can be given face to face, questions can be put and answered, misunderstanding and errors cleared away immediately. Supervision of the next level down in the operating hierarchy is simple and direct. Equally important, there is direct feedback from the working level providing for adaptation and adjustment. With no intervening barriers in the communications, understanding and synergy can be immediate. This state of affairs constitutes the strength of the small unit with a well-defined objective. But, when many managers or operators are reporting up to a superior who has a very extended area of supervision and responsibility, the situation changes quickly. He has not the same knowledge of the background to all the areas which his subordinates manage; he will need a preliminary briefing on each of them before he can pronounce on achievements or problems; he may well require regular reports and standardised figures before he can understand exactly what has been going on in one area and perhaps relate it to another. Management thus becomes a very different task.

Usually management training begins at the simpler level; the art of operating through others is more easily learned on a small scale and with direct communications between manager and managed. The opportunity to learn the sciences of control in the bigger unit can naturally only come when bigger units are functioning efficiently. The ability and the techniques to control a large organisation are therefore more rare and indeed more crucial, for, if they fail, the disaster is a large one. It is also the case that the opportunities for learning in the Third World have been much more restricted than in the industrialised countries where the institutions concerned have been growing in size and complexity over a long period of time and the ability to manage has had to grow with them. Good management is short in all countries; managers who can use the complicated techniques that are now necessary to direct large concerns with a wide range of responsibilities, and frequently an extended geographical spread, are particularly scarce; and, because such institutions have only in the last 20 years begun to make their appearance in the developing world, the scarcity is at its most acute there. So, from the point of view of the suitability of the organisation itself in terms of its concentration of purpose and in consideration of the availability of those who can bring to it proper management, there is a strong case, whatever the actual type of organisation which is being created to carry out a project, to keep it small and within well-defined limits and to refrain from marrying it to a project in a different area perhaps with different peripheral aims. It needs to be limited in its aims and reasonably autonomous in achieving them. The object should be to avoid giving responsibility for a wide and heterogeneous range of tasks to top managements; instead they should be organised into providing single-minded attention to the desired well-defined aims in smaller units.

The need is particularly clear in agriculture, where weather and climate alone require a flexibility in tactical planning which is not demanded in the more standardised operations of industry. It would seem sensible to limit consciously the size and the span of control of agricultural institutions designed to deal with specific crops. Development thinking is now moving this way, impelled by the acknowledged need to find new approaches; a general examination and a series of case studies in Africa published by the World Bank makes a well-argued and supported case for a fresh approach.[3]

With this case for more flexible forms of institution goes an argument for the association with developing world governments of overseas private enterprises who already manage and are constantly developing this sort of institution and the technology and systems that go with it. Moreover, because of their spread through more than one country, international companies can bring with them international standards of management to maintain quality and productivity at an international level — something which is certainly required if there is any question of exporting and which is desirable in any case in the close links that obtain between all countries involved in international trade today.

The Need to Monitor Performance

Chapter 1 described the arrangements for the systematic and regular application of a series of well-defined operations in plantation agriculture and singled out the proper performance of these individual tasks according to an overall plan as the identifying feature of plantation cultivation. If it is a proper plan scientifically based and the individual parts are carried out to the correct standards, the optimum quality and quantity of the crop under cultivation should be assured and the land itself should be so treated that it remains in good heart for future years. But, if individual error is allowed to creep in and individual tasks can occasionally go by default, the results will not be so rewarding. Thus, the minimum requirement in any form of agricultural organisation is a mechanism which will monitor performance; if monitoring is not carried out or is not acceptable and performance of the individual task is allowed to slip, output and quality will suffer. On this issue compromise is not possible — or if accepted it must be paid for in worse results; there is a direct trade-off.

There are two sides to such a trade-off; while for the individual cultivator there may be a perfectly legitimate choice between more leisure and more income, where he is producing agricultural output from the land the community as a whole will usually have a very direct interest in the optimisation of the crop. If the output is food, more leisure for the farmer means less food for his family or community; if a cash crop, more leisure for the producer means less cash in the community and therefore less choice and a lower standard of living. It is thus highly desirable that the nature of this monitoring be well planned, effective, understood and accepted. Without it there cannot be an 'industrial' approach to cultivation.

There are three basic ways in which such supervision and monitoring can be carried out: by its operation through a management hierarchy; by self-supervision and control among members of a group, perhaps by the delegation of control responsibility to specifically elected individuals; or by the direct planning and allocation of tasks among a very small number of individuals who are always in direct touch with each other and the job in hand. The nucleus plantation or estate is a variant of the first of these.

The Management Hierarchy

The management hierarchy has been described in Chapter 1 (see Figure 1.1). What is perhaps more important than its format is the motivation and ethos that makes it work. The superior gives an order to his junior; it may be in harsh or polite terms or may even seem to be an agreed course of action between them; but the essence of it is that a specific operation is required to be carried out. What makes this happen?

It is in the determination of this triggering action that adaptation to different cultures and customs is possible. Though the task must be performed and performed in the way agreed and required, the incentives and the stimuli to perform it can be suited to the local situation and will change with changing ideas of what is suitable and acceptable. Thus in the West one sees constantly changing patterns of piece-work, hourly rates, incentive bonuses, participation in profits and differential gradings of jobs, while in the socialistic states of Eastern Europe quotas and norms have traditionally played a larger part than direct money incentives. All these variations and other particular ones, such as work and payment by family units, are both known and used in Third World countries. By a skilful mixture and adaptation of them, patterns can be found which will engage the willing exchange of labour on closely defined terms for rewards which are acceptable and appropriate in the country concerned. In plantations, for instance, employment may be extended to a whole family unit and pay may include housing, food and social services such as medical attention. Such complications are usually not popular with employers but have to be provided because they cannot be made available on the spot by any other agency and are necessary to do the job — as is the tied farm cottage in the United Kingdom; they bring problems of the same kind.

The hierarchical approach is the most straightforward of the mechanisms to permit the essential monitoring and ensure performance. But it must be recognised that it encourages, and indeed sometimes introduces to a society, a new pattern of living that must go with a daily wage and fixed hours of work. As such it can initially be suspect to those who are planning a project and thereby deciding the type of society in which the workers will live; yet, in spite of abuses in the past, it is now becoming clear that a regular wage and well-defined conditions of work are as acceptable to a large part of the population of the developing world as they are in the West.[4] Equally and essentially in all countries such a system entails an active supervision being exercised by someone in authority. Good practice will constantly look for ways of making it totally acceptable — of identifying the efforts required from labour with the aims that management plans set out to achieve. Anything that can unify the efforts of workers, supervisors and management plans so that the interests of each — wages, quantity and quality of production and profit — are maximised, must be the constant concern of all.

Again, as with improvements in technique and agronomy (Chapter 4), a good corporate organisation is well fitted to study and develop such efforts towards better performance in everyone's interest and will do so as a part, and a very important part, of its management task. Likewise, a system of wages and incentives such as that described will normally be found only in a large and formally organised concern. Its constant adaptation and improvement to match changing circumstances require a real professionalism and have to be matched with systematic recruitment and training.

Self-supervising Systems

For any working group, as has been said, the requirement remains the same — a systematic monitoring of the proper routines of cult-ivation with a central direction to make and apportion out the parts of the plan. The management hierarchy was invented for this purpose, but for some schools of thought hierarchies are not popular. They are not liked by those who do not cheerfully listen to orders from others. Indeed some societies and tribal customs do not provide for leadership in the usual way of life. Other groups, for political, idealistic or even religious reasons, may seek to equalise exactly the profits and benefits from a communal agricultural effort. For these and other reasons 'co-operatives' are formed. The essence of such an organisation is that a group of farmers or peasants pool their resources — whether capital, collective enterprise, labour or sales outlets — for the purpose of agricultural crop production. It is a 'tying together' of individual effort. In these conditions the per-formance of the routine must be assured by some type of self-supervision and there must also be provision for the feeding-in of the proper technical content — which comes from the advisory side under a management organisation (see Figure 1.1) It is in these two areas of supervision and technical content that co-operative systems find their greatest difficulties and where external help is most needed.[5]

There is a wide range of such co-operatively managed organisa-tions. The best, with the highest operating standards, are usually those where there is a management structure created within the co-operative with a salaried staff who perform in much the same way as the staff of a commercial corporation, interpreting and imple-menting policy on behalf of the whole organisation and acting throughout with its overall will behind them.

The crunch comes when this will is not effective: the issue always has to be faced of the participant who does not do his job properly or indeed at all. What can be done to improve his performance?

Many of the best-known schemes have long struggled against accepting the logical, and indeed, the only answer: in the end such an individual has to cease to be part of a scheme. This is the supreme sanction; in a case where a venture has been set up in such a way that each member closely interlocks with all the others — for instance, with contiguous plots of land which are meshed into a common set of extension services providing fertilising, growing, harvesting, collec-tion and perhaps processing patterns in common — this will mean that he has to leave not only the scheme but also his land as well. It is to strike at the roots of many of the original ideals, but it is a measure

which in the end was found necessary even for such admired proto-
types as FELDA in Malaysia. In the 1960s this parastatal organisation had to be given the power by law to turn a settler off his plot as a
last resort.[6] It is a sanction which will be found in the constitution of
most co-operative organisations today, just as it had to be included
as early as 1936 in the arrangements for such pioneering institutions
as the Gezira scheme.[7]

There is, however, a greater and wider danger than the threat to an
individual holding in this difficult area of self-supervision. It is the
obstacles that stand in the way of the maintenance of truly high standards of performance. To raise and maintain operating levels is the
aim of any agricultural institution and the central task of its management. If there is a single clear criterion, such as a profit and loss
account, the level of performance can be properly evaluated; but for
a co-operative type of institution the amount and quality of the work
put into the tasks depend on a common standard agreed or accepted
among all the workers. The danger is that it can become something
nearer to a lowest common denominator rather than a higher
common factor. In such a framework the raising of standards is difficult. The danger is that performance and productivity will be lower
under this form of incentive and motivation because compromise is
acceptable — that less effort will be regarded as a legitimate trade-
off in terms of human satisfaction against greater production.
Again, this may be acceptable for the organisation that is setting the
standards, but it falls short of the demands of those who look at the
gap that will then arise for the community as a whole.

In many countries various types of co-operative or communal
organisations have been adopted for social reasons; but it must be
recognised that there is sometimes a price to pay in terms of less production than would be possible with a fully-fledged corporate management corporation such as a plantation.

Direct Planning Systems

The systems so far described are designed to motivate large numbers
of workers on the land in tackling formalised tasks and ways of
working. With such crops as palm oil, cocoa, coconuts and coffee
the employment of a large labour force will always be necessary
within the foreseeable future, for they all require operations, particularly in harvesting, which cannot easily be mechanised. Where
machines rather than the number of workers can provide the means
of handling the necessary scale of operations, the organisation of a

functional unit for agriculture can begin to take a form which is much nearer to the farms of temperate climates. The owner himself can directly arrange the work and supervise the standards of the small numbers of workers who are needed to man large capacity machines. He will also have to be a man who can ensure that he himself keeps up to date with the latest developments in technology and markets, in fact becoming himself his own professional manager. Of all the producers of tropical crops, only the cane planter is near to this in some places; for example, the Queensland sugar farmers referred to briefly in Chapter 9, n. 81. Here the motivation of the producer is the same as that of any other commercial venture — the satisfaction of running his own business for his own benefit. It is not the same problem — of motivating large numbers of men and organising their work — that arises in developing countries where the nature of the crops to be grown and the need for employment for large numbers of rural workers will continue to impose a different pattern.

To sum up, the political and social and cultural problems that arise from the ownership of the land have obscured the problems of how it can most effectively be worked. Agricultural development and research have produced new discoveries and techniques which can usually best and most efficiently be deployed at a level where they can bring economies of scale. The modern plantation estate has become an institution specifically designed to do so. It is now clear that smallholdings are moving along the same road. To achieve results which will produce the necessary quantities of agricultural produce and provide a proper standard of living for the smallholder himself, unifying systems are needed which will enable the same technology to be used on the 10-hectare plot as on the 15,000-hectare plantation. Such systems will need to provide the framework and the techniques and motivate the owners of the smallholdings to adopt them and continue to practise them, so as to satisfy the quality and quantity standards of an external market outside their own organisation.

The Nucleus Estate

A variation which attempts to combine the virtues of the plantation system of management and consistent standards and practice with the social attractions of the smallholders' schemes is the recent development of the 'nucleus estate' or 'nucleus plantation' which promises well in several countries and indeed has already proved itself in ventures such as the Mumias Sugar Company in Kenya, which is described in detail in Chapter 7.

The nucleus plantation is centred on a core plantation run to the highest standards and the latest technology for the crop that is being grown, in accordance with the methods described earlier in this book. This central working unit sets the standards and teaches the methods not only for the workers of its own estate but also for a number of smallholder growers of the crop on its periphery who are formally linked with it. It will probably also provide seeds, fertiliser and perhaps processing for the smallholders within the scheme. Certainly it will buy and market their produce, insisting on its own quality standards, and the smallholders may become shareholders of the central organisation. But it is the essence of an arrangement such as this that there should be an independent core of professional management, often with an international component, which will form and maintain standards and keep up to date with research and development on a world-wide scale.[8]

For a well-run organisation of this type results can be very good. Productivity can be high while at the same time the social and the cash benefits to the smallholder participant are clear. It is also a deliberate part of the process that good agricultural practices and their rewards are spread out in ever wider circles. Moreover, this idea of the nucleus centre of knowledge is obviously capable of extensive adaptation and indeed is now beginning to be widely used.[9] The combined incentive of good examples and personal profit clearly related to a tangible series of measures and results can be seen to motivate the smallholder very powerfully.

The general point, then, is that the principles of efficient management in agricultural production, which — it has been argued — are most clearly evident in a conventional modern plantation, can be extended and applied to other methods of production. Indeed, given the special characteristics of seasonal food crop production and contrasting social and political conditions in Third World countries, such adaptation is essential. The case studies in Chapters 7, 8 and 9 indicate the range of such possibilities. They also, however, suggest that, in making adaptations, there is the danger that dilution of the basic principles of efficient management may reduce the efficiency of the operation in both commercial and social terms. It is a matter of policy how such a trade-off should be arranged.

The following chapters differ intentionally in style and content from what has gone before. Earlier chapters defined the concept of the modern plantation estate and set out the case for its wider application to the production of certain tropical crops in the Third World. The arguments in favour of this industrial approach to agriculture were examined in some detail, and the strengths of the system so described were used to refute misconceptions that still prevail when the word 'plantation' is used today. Chapters 7, 8 and 9 provide evidence that the system and its variants work well in certain situations. They aim to show how its principles can bear fruit when correctly applied.

Chapter 7 illustrates what has been discussed in this chapter by describing two successful variants of the plantation estate: the system devised by FELDA in Malaysia for the large-scale cultivation of rubber and oil palm, and the nucleus estate at Mumias in Kenya, where thousands of outgrowers have been introduced to sugar cane cultivation. Since many of the references in earlier chapters were to rubber and oil palm, Chapters 8 and 9 then concentrate on cane sugar, a commodity that is of great value to, and is very largely produced by, developing countries. Chapter 8 outlines those factors governing the world market for sugar that are of particular relevance to Third World producers, before moving on to a brief analysis of the production processes in field and mill, and the related issues of efficiency, costs and yields. Chapter 9 emphasises the importance of a political environment conducive to the exercise of modern management principles before presenting three case studies of national industries which are analysed with reference to those principles. Their structures, their adherence to those principles, and their achievements vary considerably. In the Dominican Republic political considerations appear to override economic in the state plantation sector, which performs significantly less well than the private plantation sector. In other countries whose governments have enthusiastically espoused the modern plantation estate — the second case study looks at selected examples in central and southern Africa — the beneficial results are clear. These two studies also describe the important contribution small farmers are making alongside larger units. In Thailand, the subject of the third case study, independent farmers supply all the cane. Though the plantation is unknown here, it is argued that the application of the principles of modern management to Thailand's existing structure would do much to consolidate the country's position as a leading sugar exporter. Chapter 9 concludes that size is not of the essence; what matters most is that the production unit — whether a plantation estate or a smallholding — should enjoy proper management and have effective access to up-to-date technology. In the world of cane sugar there is room for both the modern plantation and the independent farmer.

Notes

1. See Chapter 9 for an analysis of why, in the Dominican Republic, the state sugar plantations perform less well than those in the private sector.
2. See World Bank, *Accelerated Development in Sub-Saharan Africa* (Washington DC, 1981), pp. 35–40.
3. The joint need for good management and smaller organisational formats is stressed by the World Bank, ibid., Chapter 5, 'Policies and Priorities in Agriculture'. Throughout, this report emphasises the desirability of promoting smallholder agriculture and describes several successful ventures. For example, Box A, p. 51, discusses the rapid expansion among Kenyan smallholders of hybrid maize production, and of tea under the aegis of the Kenya Tea Development Authority (KTDA). Box B, p. 53, describes three pioneer development projects in Northern Nigeria which were created to assist small farmers raise their output of sorghum, millet and maize. 'The projects contained few novel elements. Success was due in large part to the reasonable autonomy granted in day-to-day operational matters and to the government's willingness to compensate local manpower deficiencies through liberal recourse to expatriate managerial and technical skills.' Box C, p. 54, discusses the contribution private enterprise can make in the context of mixed public–private companies with reference to two cotton-based projects, the Mali-Sud project and the West Volta project in Upper Volta. The two areas are contiguous, located in a zone where annual rainfall equals or exceeds 900 mm.

> Both projects are based on populations known for their industriousness and community spirit; this facilitates collective action. [Another] feature of key importance is the well-established structure of cotton projects, which is based on a proven system of extension organisation and a confirmed technical message . . . Finally, the minority partner, the Compagnie Française pour le Développement des Fibres Textiles (CFDT), can claim credit for a good portion of the success. The company provides technical know-how and management (about half a dozen expatriates hold technical or managerial positions); the international structure of the company permits it to keep abreast of market developments and research results in other countries and to take advantage of CFDT's expertise in bulk buying of certain inputs.

4. See the reference to the manpower problem of 'securing unskilled and semi-skilled labour to meet the needs of new farms, factories and mines' in E.J. Berg, 'The development of a labour force in Sub-Saharan Africa' in Z.A. and J.M. Konczacki (eds.), *An Economic History of Tropical Africa* (Frank Cass, London, 1977), vol. 2, pp. 157–75. Berg writes:

> Though in much current discussion the 'labour recruitment problem' tends to be seen as a problem of securing an industrial labour force, it has no necessary connection with 'industrialisation' narrowly defined. Its essence is the transfer of labour resources out of subsistence agriculture into paid employment. This is the truly revolutionary change in early economic development everywhere: inducing

men to work for others in return for payment rather than remaining in their traditional, subsistence production-oriented villages . . . The recruitment problem has
largely disappeared in contemporary Africa, completed before industrialisation
has made large strides forward . . . A labour force has come into existence, eager
to take up industrial employment as it becomes available. It is not a skilled labour
force. Nor is it, by and large, a labour force fully committed to paid employment;
to an important degree it remains 'migratory', shuttling periodically back and
forth from village to town or mine. But it is a labour force — mobile physically and
in an economic sense sensitive to job opportunities, and disposed in growing
measure to undertake final commitment to paid employment when it is possible
and worthwhile for it to do so.

5. See, for example, the description of two cotton-based projects — one in Mali,
the other in Upper Volta — in n. 3 above. They are also referred to in Chap. 7, n. 39.
    6. See Chapter 7, n. 17.
    7. Article 13 of the Standard Conditions of Tenancy (1936) states that

if the Tenant neglects or is careless in the cultivation of his crops or neglects to
carry out the reasonable orders of the Syndicate's officials . . . the Syndicate shall
have the right to terminate the tenancy forthwith without any compensation to the
Tenant (except as hereinafter provided) and to hand over the land and cultivation
to a new tenant who shall take over the land and cultivation subject to the debts to
the Syndicate secured thereon but free from any claim by the old tenant (except as
hereinafter provided). (Arthur Gaitskell, *Gezira: a Story of Development in the
Sudan* (Faber and Faber, London, 1959), Appendix I, p. 342.)

8. The Commonwealth Development Corporation (CDC) claims with a measure
of pride and justification that it was largely responsible for initiating and promoting
nucleus estates, beginning in the late 1950s. The CDC report for 1957, p. 10, states
that 'producer co-operatives and smallholder schemes attached to estate projects and
central processing plants are being established'. Sir William Rendell writes:

A nucleus estate in CDC jargon was a plantation/estate run on commercial lines,
next to which would be a smallholder scheme. The estate management by practical
demonstration and technical advice would typically help the smallholders to plant
and establish their crops, train indigenous managers under local circumstances to
supervise and administer the scheme, process the smallholders' crops in the estate
factory and, if required, help market the product if it was exported. As a continuing function the estate management could keep the smallholders abreast of
developments in cultivation techniques and market requirements. In CDC experience, nucleus estates performed a most useful function, and the Corporation
liked to think that the concept represented a distinctive CDC contribution to
development techniques. (Sir William Rendell, *The History of the Commonwealth Development Corporation 1948-1972* (Heinemann Educational Books,
London, 1976), pp. 277-8.)

See also D.J. Morgan, *The Official History of Colonial Development*, vol. 2, *Developing British Colonial Resources 1945-1951* (Macmillan, London, 1980), Chapter 6.
    9. The model of the nucleus estate with attached smallholders is being adapted to
a variety of tropical crops, as this brief list of some schemes with which CDC is associated indicates:

(1) *Tea*
    The Malawi Tea Factory Company handles tea grown by more than 4,500

smallholders in the Mulanje and Thyolo districts of southern Malawi. The prices obtained by the Malawi Smallholder Tea Authority are the best achieved by any Malawian producer.

(2) *Cocoa*

BAL Estates in Sabah have 2,300 hectares planted to cocoa, and are now extending assistance to smallholders.

PT Coklat Ransiki, Irian Jaya, Indonesia, is developing a 1,000-hectare cocoa estate with associated smallholdings.

(3) *Oil palm*

Twifo Oil Palm Plantations in Ghana are developing a 4,800-hectare nucleus estate, a factory capable of processing 30 tonnes of FFB per hour, and 1,200 hectares of smallholder oil palm farms.

Mostyn Estates in Sabah run an estate of 3,300 hectares, and a pilot small-holders' co-operative of 100 hectares.

The Higaturu venture in Papua New Guinea comprises a nucleus estate of 4,300 hectares, a mill processing 60 tonnes FFB per hour, and a large smallholder scheme with 4,200 hectares planted with seedlings provided by the nucleus estate.

(4) *Sugar*

For various schemes in Africa, see Chapter 9.

7 TWO VARIANTS OF THE MODERN PLANTATION: FELDA AND MUMIAS

Ingrid Floering

The previous chapter outlined the ways in which the principles of corporate management may be applied to more loosely structured organisations than the modern plantation, to similar productive effect; it stated that sometimes there was a price to pay in terms of lower output than could be achieved under a fully-fledged corporate management, and conceded that this could not be avoided in those situations where social or political constraints made the choice of a different type of organisation more appropriate. Such considerations invariably carry weight in the planning of any resettlement scheme, and in all those projects which have as their goal the adoption of a new cash crop and new ways of doing things by established subsistence farmers. What is not in doubt, however, is the farmer's response to any such new economic opportunities; provided he is given the means to take advantage of them, the enthusiasm of his response will determine in large part the degree of the project's success.[1]

Two examples of the successful adaptation of the modern plantation system to the needs of the small farmer will be examined here, the rubber and oil palm settlement schemes established by the Federal Land Development Authority (FELDA) in Malaysia and the Mumias sugar venture in Kenya. FELDA's aim is to open up new land and resettle poor rural families, creating 'a stable and prosperous landowning peasantry enjoying through co-operative institutions the advantage of large-scale estate agriculture'.[2] Mumias, on the other hand, is a nucleus estate (see definition in previous chapter) with an unusually large number of outgrowers.

FELDA

FELDA can best be described as a multi-functional agency, and the biggest, of the Malaysian government. It was created in 1956 as a supervisory body charged with financing but not implementing land development projects, which at that time were the responsibility of various state authorities, in order to help the government of the day combat the twin problems of rural landlessness and rural poverty. From its inception it received strong backing from the politicians, and after the Alliance victory of 1959 it was transformed into the executive instrument for the direct Federal implementation of government development policies; FELDA's powers and functions have grown over the years, and it is now regarded as a major tool of government in modernising the rural Malaysian.

FELDA has devised an integrated approach to the problems that accompany large-scale development and resettlement projects, and by giving equal weight to economic and social objectives has not only opened up large tracts of land to profitable crops but also created a widespread scatter of 'urban villages'[3] where the settlers and their families lead lives that differ markedly from the traditional ways of the village — the *kampung*. By March 1980 FELDA had cleared 497,885 hectares for settlements and crops, developed 286 schemes and settled 58,803 families.[4] It had created jobs for at least 80,000 people on its land schemes, in its rubber processing factories and oil mills, and for private contractors. By 1980 the area of FELDA's land planted to rubber amounted to more than 10 per cent of peninsula Malaysia's total; meanwhile the area planted to oil palm had risen to a third of the country's total, with FELDA already producing a quarter of Malaysia's palm oil, though much of its planted area was still immature.[5]

The settlers are the nucleus of FELDA's programme, being both the reason for and the means of development; they are selected with regard to two sets of criteria, one being concerned with family size and family needs for land and work, and the other with skill and age factors. Because it is now understood that resettlement demands a major adjustment from the settler — in breaking with past attitudes, having to make a fresh start in unfamiliar surroundings, learning new skills, accepting for the first time the need for a daily routine — FELDA aims to give the settler the maximum of support during the early years by taking responsibility for the planning and initial development of the scheme and providing him with the framework within which he will work, together with the necessary supervision and training.

Until the early 1970s the average size of a scheme was approximately 1,820 hectares (4,500 acres), designed to support about 400 settlers and their families (i.e. a settlement of about 2,000). FELDA has consistently regarded this as the viable minimum: it justifies the capital outlay for the infrastructure of access roads, village roads and piped water, comes within the government's qualifying limit for the provision of certain essential services such as a midwife's clinic, primary school, police post, etc., and permits the application of modern management techniques to a plantation crop. However, in keeping with the government's urbanisation policy, which seeks to direct future urban growth towards a few large cities rather than towards several small provincial towns, FELDA now envisages centres with upwards of 1,000 settlers wherever conditions are suitable. Besides the economies of scale that will result if processing units can be established within these larger schemes, larger urban centres will offer more amenities and job opportunities to the children of today's settlers.[6]

In all schemes, the settlers and their families arrive on site at the end of the development stage, after contractors have cleared the jungle and planted the main crop, after the infrastructure and basic amenities have been established, and when their houses are ready. Before the main crop reaches maturity — about six years for rubber and three years for oil palm — the settlers are kept busy learning to tend their main crop (which, if it is oil palm, will be one with which they are unfamiliar) and cultivating short-term cash crops such as bananas, vegetables, maize and rice under the guidance of FELDA staff, who may also give advice on livestock production and freshwater fish culture. During this maintenance stage the settlers receive a subsistence allowance of M$4.00 (in 1975 the equivalent of US$1.60) for each day worked in the scheme, and can also supplement their income by working as contract labour in a subsequent phase of their own, or on a nearby, FELDA scheme. As the main crop matures, the settlers can look forward to a new phase during which they are able to earn a good income, repay their loans and accept responsibility for the organisation and execution of their agricultural tasks. FELDA provides processing and marketing facilities and other inputs on a charge basis. Once their loans have been paid off, the settlers acquire title to their land (to an individual holding in the case of rubber, to a uniform share in the profits of a co-operatively owned and managed block of about 80 hectares (200 acres) in the case of oil palm). FELDA's social development strategy envisages the settlers becoming 'self-reliant, progressive and responsible rural people, capable of making their own decisions and taking care of their own welfare . . . so that each land scheme becomes a viable, cohesive and progressive rural community';[7] its ultimate objective is therefore the settlers' full participation in the administration and management of their schemes and communities, with FELDA continuing to provide the extension, processing and marketing services. This fourth stage has yet to be reached; for the time being FELDA must continue in its role of initiator and mentor, maintaining the organisational, administrative and supervisory framework essential to success.

The income a settler receives from his mature crop will depend upon several factors, among them the size of his holding, the quality of his husbandry, the prevailing market price for his produce and the amount of loan[8] to be repaid to FELDA. Over the years the size of individual holdings has tended to rise as commodity prices have declined, though in the interests of sharing the land among greater numbers it may be reduced again. To begin with, a 2.4-hectare (6-acre) rubber holding was considered the right size for a settler and his family to manage and from which to draw an adequate income; in the early 1950s this was raised to 3.2 hectares (8 acres) and in 1973 to 4.9 hectares (12 acres); holdings in oil palm (a tree that reached parity in area with rubber only in 1972, before surging ahead) have always been slightly larger, and in 1973 the maximum of 5.7 hectares (14 acres) was established. Upon entering the scheme the settler joins a group of 15–20 settlers who, operating as a socio-economic unit, are allocated a block of about 80 hectares (200 acres) which they regard as their own. They are trained in a variety of skills while acquiring a sense of personal commitment to each other, to the tasks in hand and to the scheme as a whole. In rubber schemes this group method gives way to the subdivision of the block into individual holdings in the fourth year after planting, when the settler is judged able to tend his own trees though continuing to have access to FELDA staff and training schemes should he need help in tapping them. In oil palm schemes — this is a crop which requires methodical team-work at harvest and which, before FELDA entered the field, had been developed only by the estate sector — the group approach is maintained throughout the life of the scheme; the block continues to be worked collectively, and the settler is rewarded in relation to the amount of effort contributed. For both crops the rewards are such as to provide an income and standard of living well above what the settler and his family had previously known.[9]

The government has never attached a specific figure to the concept of poverty to which it has addressed its attention since the 1970s, merely stating that the 'poverty line income' provided only for minimum subsistence needs, taking into account the basic nutritional requirements plus the clothing, housing, household management and transport requirements of each household to 'sustain a decent standard of living'.[10] However, more detailed analysis of the 1970 Population Census suggests that the poverty line may be defined as an income per person in cash and kind of M$25 (in 1970 the equivalent of US$8.00) or less per month;[11] assuming an average household numbered seven people, this could indicate a monthly family income of around M$175. With such figures receiving media attention, a consensus has emerged that a family income of M$300 to M$350 is reasonable, and this is FELDA's goal for its settlers.[12] Inevitably, some schemes have done much better than this, while others — particularly some of the first rubber schemes that still suffer from poor planting programmes — find it difficult to reach this level; but in general the settlers' average monthly net income (i.e. after deduction of loan payments, land rents and inputs) reached M$300 during the 1970s, as Table 7.1 shows.

Table 7.1: Malaysia: FELDA Settlers' Average Monthly Net Income, 1972–6 (M$)

	Oil Palm	Rubber
1972 (June–Dec.)	250	124
1973 (12 months)	247	251
1974 ''	819	250
1975 ''	442	209
1976 ''	361	338

Source: Tunku Shamsul Bahrin and P.D.A. Perera, *FELDA: 21 Years of Land Development* (FELDA, Kuala Lumpur, 1977), p. 78.

Some settlers can do even better. At Ulu Jempol, an oil palm scheme with 3,800 inhabitants situated on the eastern edge of the Jengka Triangle,[13] settlers' monthly earnings in 1975 (taken over three months during the low season January to July) averaged M$545. Moreover, 62 per cent of the settlers showed considerable initiative by taking advantage of the opportunities for earning additional income, whether by running their own small businesses such as tailoring and furniture-making or a taxi service, setting up their own transport for carrying fresh fruiting bunches (FFB) to the mill instead of relying on outside contractors, working as labourers or drivers, growing and selling vegetables, owning their own shops or from many other activities which would improve the quality of life in their new and isolated settlement; they were able to supplement their FELDA income with an average monthly M$177 (range M$50–750). As a result, more than half the settlers said they were saving regularly, while the majority also spent money in improving their houses and valued their household possessions at more than M$4,000. The detailed pattern of ownership that has emerged is high by Malaysian standards: 76 per cent of settlers own motor cycles, 64 per cent radios, 58 per cent television sets and 13 per cent cars.[14] Within a decade, the Ulu Jempol settler has moved from an impoverished rural situation into a middle-class environment, living in his own house on his own plot of land.[15]

Ulu Jempol is no exception, being typical of a well-established oil palm scheme, and the achievements it illustrates stem from the interaction of certain hard-headed policy decisions by FELDA. For example, FELDA made no bones about giving 'opportunities to those who have initiative, rather than charity to those who haven't', and insisted that 'the best land [be found] for the best people'.[16] Having selected its settlers, FELDA spared no effort (or expense) in getting them off to a good start, for its field personnel had learnt from experience the overriding importance of getting the early stages of any agricultural enterprise right. But it also reserved the right to evict any settler, and swiftly recognised that the block method made

> eviction of any settler, if this becomes necessary, easier . . . should a settler slacken in his work, the common opinion of the rest of the members of that block would weigh against him and would induce him to work hard, as representations are normally made to the management by the remaining members of the block if the settler concerned does not change his ways.[17]

FELDA's management structure has changed gradually over the years in line with its tasks, becoming more decentralised as its activities increased. Today, policy is decided by the Board, and implemented by the Director-General and a highly-qualified team with well-defined roles, as Figure 7.1 shows. Each of the ten regions has its own Area Controller, who is responsible to one of three Operations Directors. Each scheme is run by a manager with overall responsibility for its agricultural and social development, and he is helped by an assistant manager, a number of field supervisors and assistants, besides social development officers and office staff. As a

Figure 7.1:   Malaysia: FELDA Organisation Chart

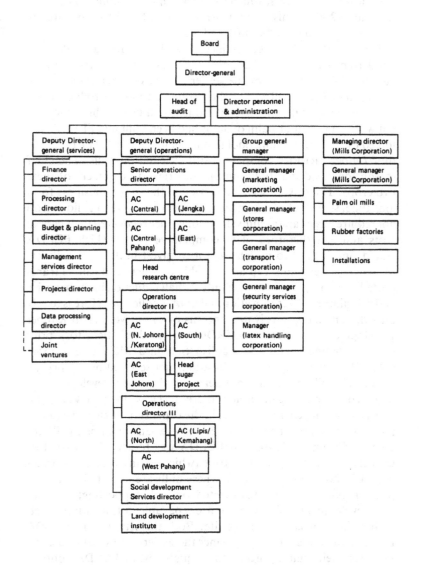

Note: AC: Area Controller.
Source: .Tunku Shamsul Bahrin and P.D.A. Perera, *FELDA: 21 Years of Land Development* (FELDA, Kuala Lumpur, 1977), Figure 5.2.

means of decentralising its commercially-orientated activities, FELDA has also established six corporations each covering a specific line of business, which together employ a minimum of 1,200 staff and 2,400 daily paid workers. In total, FELDA directly employs more than 9,000 staff and workers.

Though FELDA, since its inception, had planned to develop 'modern processing and marketing facilities to ensure efficient production and fair prices for the settler',[18] it has concentrated on the processing of palm oil rather than rubber. Rubber production by 1966 was sufficient to justify investment in a large rubber factory, but within a year four palm oil mills had been built and FELDA had joined the palm oil selling pool to market its oil. Today FELDA has four rubber factories compared with 29 palm oil mills. The chief reason for this disparity lies in the historical development of these two crops. The private sector has been in the rubber business for a long time, so its factories (which are relatively simple to build and do not require large capital sums) have long since recovered their capital costs and can therefore offer competitive prices which FELDA would find it hard to match were it to invest in its own facilities. Moreover, latex and scrap are valuable products and can be transported over long distances with only a small reduction in the net price and a minimum of deterioration. FELDA's policy therefore is to rely on selling its latex to private concerns or to the Malaysian Rubber Development Corporation (MRDC) provided a satisfactory price can be obtained, and to establish Standard Malaysian Rubber (SMR) factories only in those locations not serviced by the private sector. The oil palm, on the other hand, has been developed on a large commercial scale much more recently in Malaysia, and FELDA has played a major role in the expansion of this new industry. In fact, so great has been Malaysia's expansion of palm oil production during the 1970s that FELDA was forced to construct its own mills to process its own fruit (which in any case deteriorates within 24 hours of harvesting). These mills are operated on a nonprofit-making basis but are expected to be self-supporting; loans for mill development and operation are repayable in full with interest, within the project's operative life. Both the settlers and FELDA benefit from this arrangement, since the settlers receive a fair market price for their fruit according to its quality while FELDA controls the quality and the marketing of its oil.

FELDA has been judged commercially and socially successful. It has added to the wealth of the country and has helped to create a group of progressive farmers whom some would regard as a new rural elite. But in certain quarters there has been criticism of the high degree of subsidy involved.[19] FELDA's increasing operational complexity is reflected in the rapid growth in the inflow of funds: in the early 1960s these funds averaged M$30 million a year, topping M$100 million in 1971 and rising above M$250 million in 1975. By the end of 1978, total drawings amounted to almost M$2,000 million, the bulk of it coming from Federal sources and the remaining 11 per cent from external sources.[20] Of the total, about 25 per cent has been granted outright by the Federal government to cover infrastructural costs and all the costs of administration which, since FELDA has had to train its staff and management, have of necessity been high. The administrative expenditure per plantable hectare (i.e. not including settlement area) was estimated in the mid-1970s to be in the region of M$210.[21]

Table 7.2: Malaysia: The Cost of Settling a FELDA Family, 1976 (M$)

	Oil Palm	Rubber
Infrastructural development	5,200	5,200
Management and administration	3,700	4,200
Agricultural holding (4 hectares) development	15,500	14,800
Settler's house and houselot	2,200	2,200
Total	26,600	26,400

Source: Shamsul Bahrin and Perera, *21 Years*, p. 79.

It costs FELDA at least M$26,000 to settle one family on a scheme of approximately 1,800 hectares (4,500 acres). This is not excessive in view of what the settler is provided with at the outset, as Table 7.2 shows. Broadly speaking, the settler is expected to pay back about two-thirds of this sum over 15 years, to cover the cost of the preparation of his land, the planting and maintenance of his crop until maturity, his subsistence allowance received during that time, his house and an overall interest of 6¾ per cent.[22] Loan recovery from oil-palm settlers has been almost total, while the harder-pressed rubber settlers have managed 85 per cent, but FELDA itself has repaid only a tiny proportion of its loan principal so far. Some authorities regard this as a dangerously growing commitment, while others more properly see it as indicating the real cost of a development of such a comprehensive nature. After all, the FELDA scheme is widely recognised as an integrated model for rural development; recent studies acknowledge that, while costs are high, the economic returns more than compensate the investment[23] and the social benefits that accrue from having promoted achievement-orientated settlers who are able to grow crops as efficiently as the private estate sector are considerable.[24] Having established productive rural schemes that will yield more as those areas planted to oil palm and rubber during the late 1970s reach maturity, FELDA is now turning its attention to creating industrial employment so that second and third generation families will be encouraged to stay.[25] If during the next decade it can successfully promote new agro-based enterprises and local service industries in its centres, it will have provided further support for the World Bank's thesis that sound agricultural development and the alleviation of rural poverty provide one of the surest foundations for subsequent economic advance.

Mumias

FELDA's concepts have taken root on a national scale in a country amply provided with fertile undeveloped land. The nucleus estate of the Commonwealth Development Corporation (CDC), on the other hand, provides a model that may be applied on a much smaller scale and in densely populated rural areas where the indigenous people are likely to be subsistence farmers with few if any other employment opportunities. One successful and well-known nucleus plantation is Mumias, the sugar project in Kenya which was initiated by Bruce MacKenzie, then Minister of Agriculture, and subsequently put into effect with the full agreement and participation of the Kenya government and the support of CDC; it is managed by Booker Agriculture International (BAI), agribusiness managers and consultants.[26] Three features appear to provide the key to Mumias's success: the adaptability and enthusiasm of the local farmers, the tight controls exercised by BAI who have insisted on commercial guidelines throughout, and the nature of the agreement between BAI and the Kenya government which gave BAI the financial incentives to maximise production while retaining for the government the major stake in the enterprise. These features are discussed in detail below.

A traditional plantation was out of the question in the poor and over-populated Nzoia valley of Kenya's Western Province, where subsistence farmers grew maize on their own land. The government was anxious to reduce its dependence upon imported sugar, and hoped in time to produce sufficient to meet the demands of an expanding home market. It was also aware of the need to improve the living standards of the rural population. But a scheme had to be devised that would encourage the farmers to participate while leaving their family-based land rights untouched. As the climate at Mumias's altitude of 1,100 metres is uniform, with an annual mean temperature of 23°C and rain each month of the year, sugar cane could be grown without irrigation. Therefore the adaptation required of local farmers if they were to cultivate this new crop would not be too great, and well within their capacity if given material assistance and advice. And so sugar cane was chosen. This in turn would necessitate investing in a factory, which would require a steady supply of cane if it were to operate economically. These considerations prompted the eventual adoption of Mumias's two-tiered structure, with the Mumias Sugar Company (MSC) being responsible for the factory and a small nucleus estate of 3,400 hectares which supplies about one-tenth of the factory's cane requirements, and the Mumias Outgrowers' Company (MOC) representing the interests of 23,000 outgrowers who supply the rest of the factory's requirements from their own farms — in total some 29,000 hectares. In time MOC may take over the organisation and supervision of outgrower cane; for the present this important task remains the responsibility of MSC, while MOC is the source of finance for outgrowers' credit besides acting as the outgrowers' forum, with four of the nine members of its board of directors being outgrowers' elected representatives.

The most striking characteristic of the Mumias project is the extent to which the criteria of efficiency have outweighed all others. BAI was free to establish the commercial principles which it judged essential to the success of the scheme in this particular physical and social environment, and to select those outgrowers who would be permitted to grow cane in accordance with those principles. To be eligible, a farmer had to own land within a 21-kilometre radius of the factory, with at least 1.2 hectares suitable for cane plus sufficient on which to grow his subsistence crops should he wish to do so; moreover, his plot had to be adjacent to other suitable plots, so that farmers might operate in 6-hectare units to facilitate mechanical cultivation and a straightforward harvesting routine. Once he had been contracted to grow cane, the farmer had to follow MSC's procedures. He had to clear his land before the company, using its own equipment and labour, ploughed, harrowed and ridged his ground in preparation for planting, which was the farmer's responsibility, using seed cane supplied at cost by MSC and later applying fertiliser in the correct amounts as distributed by MSC. He was then responsible for the maintenance and weeding of his land until the cane was ready for harvesting some 18 months later, when MSC took over again, organising the cutting gangs (which included farmers and male members of their families) and providing the transport of cane to the factory. This interdependence of MSC and the farmer is at present vital for the success of the scheme as a whole. With MSC taking care of two important stages, the farmer is also responsible for two, and the weeding he must attend to is crucial to the crop's growth; in fact, MSC operates a sanction of a kind during this stage, with the right to enter a farmer's land if his weeding is not up to standard and do the work with its own labour force, charging the farmer for it later. The ultimate sanction — annulling or refusing to renew a contract — has rarely been invoked because of the need to maintain viable 6-hectare units.

While outgrowers have yet to match the cane yields achieved on the nucleus estate, they have on occasion come close to it;[27] more important, their enthusiasm for this new cash crop has permitted a more rapid expansion of the scheme than was originally envisaged, with sugar production rising from 21,000 tonnes in 1973 to 110,000 tonnes in 1979 and over 200,000 tonnes in 1982.[28] Mumias's performance compares well with that of four longer-established sugar schemes which continue to rely on government-sponsored, co-operative systems of cane production; it is not surprising, therefore, that the nucleus estate/outgrower format with expatriate management has recently been adopted for two new sugar schemes, which were scheduled to begin production in 1983.[29] Mumias presently contributes more than 40 per cent of Kenya's sugar output — an achievement which has been instrumental in turning the country from a sugar importer into a small sugar exporter.[30]

This record may be directly attributed to the rigorous studies and financial and supervisory controls that BAI has insisted upon from the outset. It spent longer than many other management consultants would have considered necessary on its feasibility study and pilot project, building up some 35 demonstration plots throughout the area between 1967 and 1970 so that farmers might judge for themselves the benefits of mechanical cultivation, chemical fertiliser and intensive weed control. In effect, BAI was determined that both it and the farmers should be convinced that sugar cane was a feasible crop before entering into a development contract with the government, and the Mumias Sugar Company was formed only in June 1971, with the government the major shareholder (see Table 7.3).

Table 7.3: Kenya: Mumias Sugar Company Shareholders, 1974 and 1978

	Dec. 1974	Dec. 1978
Total equity (K£ millions)	2.9	8.5
Total capital employed	5.7	16.4
Shares of equity (percentage)		
Government of Kenya	69	71
CDC	12	17
Kenya Commercial Finance Company	9	5
Booker McConnell	5	4
East African Development Bank	5	3

Sources: W.D. Ware-Austin, 'Report on a Visit to the Mumias Sugar and Mumias Outgrowers' Companies, 1978', CDC mimeograph, July 1978, p. 1; George R. Allen, 'Mumias Sugar Company', a paper presented to the Mohonk Conference in April 1980 and circulated by the Fund for Multinational Management Education, New York, p. 7.

In leasing the land from the government for its factory and nucleus estate, MSC immediately became responsible for employing and training a work-force which, in the ten years since the factory came into production, has grown to around 8,500: 4,000 are employed as cane cutters, almost 1,000 in the factory, and 2,000 in the agricultural services department which looks after the workshops, land preparation and cane transport, with the remainder working on the nucleus estate. In addition, BAI has had to train a small but highly skilled management team (see Figure 7.2) to supervise and deal with the problems of the 23,000 outgrowers. MSC is providing work for more than 31,000 people, who, together with their families, probably represent about 8 per cent of the 2 million people of the impoverished Western Province.

Who has benefited most from MSC's success? Since it is generally agreed that the company has been operating efficiently as Table 7.4 indicates, it is reasonable to conclude that all parties have benefited — government, employees and outgrowers, and BAI. This has been the case, but it should be remembered that the government retains the power to decide cane and sugar prices, and should its policy, in the interests of a low consumer price, become too restrictive, then

Figure 7.2: Kenya: Mumias Outgrowers' Development Service Organisation, 1983

MSC Outgrowers' Development Section
Assistant Agricultural Manager

Area manager (H.K. Khalumi)			Area manager (S.O. Otieno)		
Supt (K. Kimeli)	Supt (N. Atakos)	Supt (Vacant)	Supt (D. Kalangi)	Supt (R. Kulo)	Supt (G. Sagalla)
Supvr (4)	Supvr (4)	Supvr (4)	Supvr (6)	Supvr (3)	Supvr (2)
Headmen (15) South Wanga	Headmen (16) North Wanga	Headmen (16) North Wanga	Headmen (24) East Wanga	Headmen (13) Marama	Headmen (12) Seed Cane Administration

Source: Booker Agriculture International, London, 1983.

everyone involved in production suffers. And if any such restrictive policy coincides, as it recently did, with a severe drought,[31] then some outgrowers may be discouraged and MSC's profits will decline further.

Table 7.4: Kenya: Financial Summary of the Mumias Sugar Company Limited, 1974-9 (K£ 000)

	1974	1975	1976	1977	1978	1979
Gross turnover	4,635	6,676	9,792	15,674	16,954	21,499
Excise on sugar	1,241	1,309	2,470	4,176	4,396	5,521
Net turnover	3,394	5,367	7,321	11,497	12,558	15,978
Payments to cane farmers	710	1,345	1,979	3,238	4,131	5,285
Profit before taxation	751	1,291	1,702	3,020	2,278	145
Taxation	—	111	605	1,330	707	(246)
Profit after taxation	751	1,180	1,097	1,690	1,571	391
Equity 31 December	3,317	3,917	4,724	9,235	9,582	9,123
Profit after tax (as percentage of equity)	22.6%	30.1%	23.2%	18.3%	16.4%	4.2%
Dividends	348	580	290	1,279	1,274	850
Dividends (as percentage of equity)	10.5%	14.8%	6.1%	13.8%	13.3%	9.3%
Direct revenue to Government by way of excise on sugar and income tax	1,241	1,420	3,075	5,506	5,103	5,521

Source: Mumias Sugar Company Annual Reports and Accounts as presented by Allen, 'Mumias Sugar Company', Table VI.

During the late 1970s, as Table 7.5 shows, the Kenya government was the chief beneficiary, averaging more than K£6 million (the equivalent of £8 million sterling) a year between 1977 and 1979. It is not so easy to be precise about the individual sums the outgrowers received during those years, since their plots range from 1.2 to 1.8

Table 7.5:   Kenya: Payments by Mumias Sugar Company, 1976–9 (K£ 000)

Recipients	1976	1977	1978	1979
Government of Kenya				
Dividends	200	908	904	680
Taxes (excise and income tax)	3,075	5,506	5,103	5,521
	3,275	6,414	6,007	6,201
Outgrowers	1,979	3,238	4,131	5,285
MSC Kenyan employees	1,165	1,599	1,921	2,585

Source: Allen, 'Mumias Sugar Company', p. 22.

hectares, and they are paid after their cane has been harvested, which may be at any time between 19 and 26 months from planting; there is no doubt that farmers' incomes had increased by many times their expectations of ten years earlier, since the returns from cane were then ten times that of maize; one reliable authority estimated that the average ex-factory returns per outgrower ranged between K£500 and K£700 (equivalent range £670–£930 sterling), and commented that the farmers had invested

> their new-found wealth in additional cane land, improving their houses, ensuring their children's schooling, engaging in some form of public transport enterprise or in a shop. The fact that the money was usually not ploughed back into other enterprises on their farms is not altogether surprising as the general level of soil fertility did not appear to be particularly high.[32]

Then came the severe drought which began in 1980, by which year, according to MSC accountants, the growers' margin per tonne of cane after all costs had been deducted had shrunk to less than KShs5.84.[33] A grudging price increase of 10 per cent helped a little, but as the drought continued into 1981 it was reported that more than 60 per cent of the growers were in difficulties, with some of them wondering whether to replant. With yields picking up again as the drought ended,[34] and the promise in 1983 of a more rewarding cane price,[35] the more efficient farmers should regain their confidence, though it is unlikely their profits will reach those of the heady days in the late 1970s, when the disparity in rural incomes between the more fortunate Mumias outgrowers and those subsistence farmers living just outside the 21-kilometre radius threatened to provoke economic and political unrest.[36]

As for BAI, its reward is to be found as much in the acknowledged success of the Mumias project, which augurs well for BAI's future prospects in other Third World countries, as it does in the sums it has received for work done. The contract negotiated between BAI and the Kenya government demonstrates a realistic approach on both sides, containing four component parts which have been adjusted from time to time as the project progressed beyond the planning stage. Initially, the Kenya government wanted Booker McConnell, the parent company which is generally referred to simply as Bookers, to take at least 10 per cent of the equity; this Bookers were reluctant to do, and finally persuaded the government to agree to a 5 per cent share of the equity (reduced during the expansion programme of the late 1970s to 4 per cent) on the understanding that BAI would also take over the management of the ailing Chemelil Project in neighbouring Nyanza Province. During Mumias's development stage, while the mill was being constructed, the estate developed and the outgrowers organised, BAI required a large fee which was reduced once the project was firmly established and in part replaced by an agreed percentage of the profits. This allowed the other three components of the fee, which were in operation between 1 January 1976 and 30 June 1978, to be defined; they were a fixed fee to cover the general manager's salary and Bookers' relevant overheads, linked to the UK retail price index, together with an agreement that other staff were to be seconded at cost; a production commission on net MSC revenues (i.e. the value of sales to the Kenya National Trading Corporation less government excise duty; this was arranged on a sliding scale to encourage BAI to maximise output); and a commission of 2.5 per cent of the pre-tax operating profits of BSC, which was regarded as an incentive to BAI to manage the project as efficiently as possible. Since 1978, payment arrangements have been adjusted downwards in view of output which has been so much larger than expected, but it is understood that the incentives to maximise production remain.[37] MSC's accounts, which published BAI's management fees until 1977, are sufficiently detailed to indicate that in that year Booker McConnell and BAI together earned K£598,000, or 3.8 per cent of gross turnover.[38] Since then MSC's profits have been substantially lower (and therefore BAI's also); but BAI's reputation is established, and, since the company may move from a management agreement to a technical services agreement in the mid-1980s, it is probably satisfied with its present remuneration. In conclusion, few would dispute that, whatever MSC's present financial difficulties, the organisational structure that has been evolved for this nucleus estate/outgrower complex demonstrates one sound approach to the problems of development by giving due consideration to the needs and aspirations of the local inhabitants while adding to the wealth of the country as a whole.

Conclusion

Here, then, are two different agricultural schemes, for different commodities, flourishing in widely different settings. Both are forms of co-operation with ambitious social development aims, especially so in the case of FELDA. Yet they are able to combine these aims with efficient production of three different commodities — rubber, palm oil and sugar — and where many other schemes fail. There are, of course, a number of other schemes operating on similar principles of central control and looser association among farmers, such as the well-established Gezira cotton scheme in Sudan, the ambitious Niger Project in Mali and the expansion of smallholder tea production in Kenya under the Kenya Tea Development Authority (KTDA), besides the more recent cotton-based projects in Mali and Upper Volta which got under way in the mid-1970s.[39] They are all successful, though to varying degrees, because they have produced an operating organisation and a management system which is capable of applying and supervising the best of international technology, suitably adapted to local circumstances. The principles are consciously those of the modern plantation.

These projects raise important issues concerning the relative efficiency of small individual farmers producing tropical commercial crops within a guided framework. The subject will be further discussed below in Chapter 9 in the context of cane sugar production in Thailand, and a general comment is therefore postponed until that evidence also can be taken into account.

Notes

1. World Bank, *World Development Report 1982* (Oxford University Press, 1982), Foreword p. iii, pp. 4–6, 43–56 and especially 90–3.
2. Tunku Shamsul Bahrin and P.D.A. Perera, *FELDA: 21 Years of Land Development* (FELDA, Kuala Lumpur, 1977), p. 25.

3. Colin MacAndrews, *Mobility and Modernisation: the Federal Land Development Authority and its Role in Modernising the Rural Malay* (Gadjah Mada University Press, Yogyakarta, 1977), pp. 200-2. MacAndrews values FELDA's subsidiary role as an urbanising agent, seeing it as a vital link in the evolution of a more balanced urban growth over the next 15-20 years. The 1970 Malaysian Census defined as urban any centre with more than 10,000 people.

4. Sue Jones, 'The Political Implications of Resettlement Policy in Malaysia', unpublished MA thesis, School of Oriental and African Studies, London University, 1980.

5. The following facts may help to set FELDA's contribution to Malaysia's production of rubber and palm oil in perspective:

(1) *Area planted with rubber*

At the end of 1980 the area planted to rubber was estimated at 1,998 million hectares (4.9 million acres), of which 85% was in peninsula Malaysia. Of the total, FELDA had developed 167,200 hectares (413,150 acres). Taken from Bank Negara Malaysia Annual Report 1980, quoted in *Natural Rubber News*, May 1981.

(2) *Area planted with oil palm*

By the end of 1979, the area planted with oil palms was estimated at 854,990 hectares, of which 758,190 hectares (89%) were in peninsula Malaysia where some 607,680 hectares already supported mature trees. By the end of 1979 FELDA had planted 283,180 hectares. *Economic Report 1979-80* (Ministry of Finance, Kuala Lumpur), pp. 107-9.

(3) *Rubber production*

In 1981 Malaysia produced 1,590,000 tonnes, which amounted to 42% of world production (3,807,000 tonnes). *FAO Production Yearbook 1981*, vol. 35.

(4) *Palm oil production*

In 1979 the production of crude palm oil was expected to increase by 17% over 1978 to reach 2.09 million tonnes. Production by FELDA, Malaysia's largest single producer, was estimated at 501,120 tonnes, or 24% of Malaysia's total output in 1979. *Economic Report 1979-80*, pp. 107-9.

In 1981, Malaysia produced 2,821,700 tonnes of palm oil, which amounted to 52% of world production (5,383,960 tonnes). *FAO Production Yearbook 1981*.

(5) *Value of trade by commodities 1977-79 for Malaysia, in M$ bn.*

	1977	1978	1979	1979 (% of total value)
Rubber	3.38	3.54	4.56	19
Tin	1.70	1.92	2.30	10
Logs and timber	2.31	2.31	4.22	18
Palm oil	1.80	1.74	2.45	10
Petroleum	2.01	2.52	4.13	17
Others	3.78	4.72	6.36	26

Source: *Quarterly Economic Review of Malaysia, Singapore and Brunei, Annual Supplement 1980* (Economist Intelligence Unit, London).

6. The Jengka Triangle, in Pahang, was the first of the major regional schemes to be launched during the 1960s; by 1975 it encompassed 23 settlements with between 325 and 535 settler families per village. In contrast, in the Keratong Project in Pahang, which was initiated during the 1970s, 3,500 settler families will be concentrated in 2 towns servicing 9 agricultural schemes, i.e. Keratong Town with 2,500 families and Town 21 with a little under 1,000. By 1990, the total population for Keratong Town is

expected to reach 36,000, and for Town 21 7,000. Shamsul Bahrin and Perera, *21 Years*, pp. 70–1.

7. Ibid., p. 86, quoting the definition and concept of settler development as laid down by FELDA.

8. The question of how much the settlers should repay, in view of fluctuating and frequently low world prices, has presented FELDA with both financial and operational problems over the years. In 1960 FELDA accepted that 'expenditure connected with scheme management and the provision of basic facilities should not be charged to the settlers' account, and that they would only be responsible for the repayment of loans, in the form of subsistence allowance, cost of their houses, and the direct cost for developing their individual holdings, and the accrued interest therein'. However, as it has always been FELDA's intention to give the settler a certain minimum standard of living (set at M$100 in 1971, and raised to M$150 in 1976), a new scheme was initiated in January 1975 to help those rubber settlers with 3.2 hectares (8 acres) or less, and also those oil palm settlers who faced a severe drop in income during the low-crop months of January–July. In effect, a sliding scale was adopted for the less fortunate FELDA settlers which was not directly related to the actual loan advanced by FELDA. Under this New Loan Repayment system, for example, the settler with a 2.8-hectare (7-acre) rubber holding is obliged to repay M$79.97 monthly, compared with a settler with 4 hectares (10 acres) of oil palm who is expected to repay M$259.75 monthly. Ibid., pp. 78–84, for an outline of the complexities involved in working out what FELDA considers to be equitable loan repayments.

9. MacAndrews, *Mobility and Modernisation*, pp. 105, 131, 155 and 179, gives the following results from his sample surveys of settlers' monthly incomes before entering a FELDA scheme:

	average M$
Bilut Valley, Pahang (settlers arrived 1959)	175
Jengka 12, Pahang (1975)	125
Ulu Jempol, Pahang (1965)	128
Bukit Besar, Johore (1968)	118

10. *Third Malaysia Plan 1976–80* (Government Printer, Kuala Lumpur, 1976), p. 160.

11. MacAndrews, *Mobility and Modernisation*, p. 27, n. 27, derives this definition from Sudhir Anand, *The Size and Distribution of Income in Malaysia* (World Bank 1975), who based his analysis on data from the *Post Enumeration Survey of the 1970 Population Census* (Department of Statistics, Kuala Lumpur, 1973).

12. Shamsul Bahrin and Perera, *21 Years*, p. 75.

13. The Jengka Triangle is also FELDA's largest regional project, embracing 40,470 hectares (100,000 acres). Two-thirds of the total area has been planted with oil palm, one-third with rubber. Ulu Jempol was settled between 1965 and 1967 by 377 settlers who by 1975 tended 2,347 hectares of oil palm. MacAndrews, *Mobility and Modernisation*, pp. 145–6.

14. Ownership: in 1974 the national average for cars was 4.7%, for motor cycles 32.6%, for television sets 22.4%. *Economic Report 1974/5* (The Treasury, Kuala Lumpur, November 1974), p. 102.

15. The details of settler income and expenditure in Ulu Jempol are taken from MacAndrews, *Mobility and Modernisation*, pp. 158–63.

16. Shamsul Bahrin and Perera, *21 Years*, p. 5 state that this principle was established at FELDA's first meeting on 8 August 1956.

17. Ibid., p. 41.

18. Ibid., p. 18.

19. For example, see Amir Baharuddin, 'FELDA land schemes' in Cheong Kee Cheok, Khoo Siew Mun and R. Thillainathan (eds.), *Malaysia: Some Contemporary*

Issues in Sociological Development (Persatuan Ekonomi Malaysia, Kuala Lumpur, 1979), pp. 215–24.

20. The external 11% was loaned by the World Bank, the Asian Development Bank, the OECF (loan from Japan), the Kuwait Fund and the Saudi Development Fund.

21. Shamsul Bahrin and Perera, *21 Years*, p. 145.

22. See n. 8 above.

23. Shamsul Bahrin and Perera, *21 Years*, p. 151, point out that a study done by FELDA on Lepar Hilir, Klau-Krau, Bukit Sagu and Serting in 1976 showed an economic rate of return of 14.6% for a rubber project. Another study by FELDA in 1976 for the oil palm project in Lepar Utara showed an economic rate of return of 12.5%. The two studies indicate that, though FELDA's cost of development is high, the economic returns more than compensate the investment.

24. By the mid-1970s, FELDA records show that 1 hectare of 7-year-old oil palm yielded 23.05 tonnes FFB. This compares well with figures provided by Unilever for 1982, which gave a yield of 26 tonnes per hectare, in good conditions.

25. Youth unemployment is a major problem on FELDA schemes. A FELDA survey in 1975 estimated that 36.7% of FELDA dependents on the 27 FELDA schemes surveyed were unemployed. See MacAndrews, *Mobility and Modernisation*, p. 148, n. 18. By stipulating that oil palm and rubber lots may not be subdivided on the death of the original settler, FELDA implicitly acknowledges its responsibility for helping to provide other members of a settler's family with employment. Initially, such jobs will be found in agro-based industries or local service industries, but later FELDA must take steps to promote the establishment of urban-based industries in the larger establishments. Shamsul Bahrin and Perera, *21 Years*, p. 155.

26. BAI is a subsidiary of the British company Booker McConnell which, until its assets in Guyana (formerly British Guiana) were nationalised in 1976, produced some 80% of that country's sugar. After 1945 Bookers initiated a programme for the improvement of the sugar industry that included not only capital investment and the modernisation of practices in field and mill but also the introduction of welfare services for its workers, the creation of a small core of independent farmers and the promotion of Guyanese to management positions wherever possible. With the approach of independence, Bookers sought to redeploy its expertise in tropical agriculture in a new consulting and management company, Booker Agricultural and Technical Services (BATS), which later became BAI. For a detailed account of Bookers' operations and initiatives in Guyana see Brian Scott, 'The Organisational Network: A Strategy Perspective for Development', unpublished PhD thesis, Harvard University, 1979, pp. 107–208.

27. For example, in 1979, the outgrowers achieved an average 150 tonnes of cane per hectare compared with the estate's 154.8 tonnes:

	Outgrowers				Nucleus Estate			
Crop	Ha	tch	tchm	Ave Age Months	Ha	tch	tchm	Ave Age Months
Plant cane	223.9	176.4	6.02	29.3	323.3	171.0	5.68	30.1
1st Ratoon	1,691.6	138.4	5.28	26.2	395.4	148.9	5.43	27.4
2nd Ratoon	1,166.0	118.9	4.64	25.6	389.3	150.0	5.09	29.5
3rd Ratoon	198.4	134.4	5.46	27.5	36.1	125.5	5.97	21.0
Overall	5,295.0	150.0	5.45	27.5	1,144.1	154.8	5.39	28.7

Notes: tch = tonnes cane per hectare
tchm = tonnes cane per hectare month

Source: W.D. Ware-Austin, 'Mumias Sugar Company and Mumias Outgrowers' Company: a Brief History and Description', CDC mimeograph, 1981, p. 2.

28. In 1977 MSC controlled 9,710 outgrowers, by 1978 11,346; by 1979 the number had risen to 13,110, and a year later to 15,140; by the end of 1983 MSC had contracted 23,000.

29. George R. Allen, 'Mumias Sugar Company', a paper presented to the Mohonk Conference in April 1980 and sponsored by the Fund for Multinational Management Education, New York, p. 8. The Nzoia scheme was begun in 1978 under French management, and the Sony scheme in 1980 under Indian management; both are much smaller than Mumias, and will produce 50,000–60,000 tonnes p.a. to begin with.

30. Kenya first recorded a small surplus of production over consumption in 1979.

31. Allen, 'Mumias', p. 4, points out that famine or hunger have occurred about every ten years in the Mumias area — 1907, 1918, 1931–2, 1943, 1953, 1961, 1964–5, and most recently 1980–1.

32. See Ware-Austin, 'Mumias, a Brief History', p. 2, and also his 'Report on a Visit to the Mumias Sugar and Mumias Outgrowers' Companies, 1979', CDC mimeograph, September 1979, p. 6.

33. See W.D. Ware-Austin, 'Report on a Visit to the Mumias Sugar Company and the Mumias Outgrowers' Company, 1980', CDC mimeograph, August 1980, Appendix 2. This very small margin was the result of escalating field costs set against a price of KShs133 per tonne of cane, which had been fixed in 1977 and which in that year yielded a margin of KShs50.41 per tonne (roughly ten times more). Using the 1980 exchange rate of US$ 1 = KShs7.57, the margin of KShs5.84 was the equivalent of US 83 cents.

34. Outgrowers' yields dropped sharply as a result of the severe drought in 1980 and 1981, when farmers paid more attention to their food crops. The following estimates for outgrowers' yields 1978–83 were provided by BAI:

	Yield (tonnes per ha.)	Comment
1978	70	Good season plus high proportion of plant cane.
1979	66	—
1980	60	—
1981	48	The worst effects of the drought.
1982	50	Some improvement after the drought.
1983	55	Provisional estimate.

35. The following figures for the price per tonne of cane were supplied by BAI:

	Kshs	
1977	133	
1981	147	
1982	170	
1983	203	Provisional estimate.

I am indebted to Bruce Campbell, Director, Agricultural Services (Sugar Division), BAI for providing much detailed information about Mumias.

36. Ware-Austin, 'Report 1979', p. 3, and 'Report 1980', p. 4, describes the pressures that were building up in 1979 as farmers who had cultivated 3,000 hectares of non-contract cane within the 21-kilometre radius and a further 11,000 hectares outside it were insisting that MSC transport and mill it. In 1980 the government ordered MSC to process 67,000 tonnes (MSC actually accepted 83,000 tonnes); this upset those contract growers who were forced to delay their own harvests, besides reducing by at least 50% MSC's replanting programme for registered growers. By undertaking to harvest and mill non-contract cane for a specified period, MSC was able in its turn to bring pressure to bear on the Ministry of Agriculture, which undertook to ensure

that only food crops would be grown on the land which had not been contracted to cane in future.

37. Brian Scott, 'The Organisational Network', pp. 290-3.

38. Ibid., Exhibit 4. By comparing Exhibit 4 with Allen, 'Mumias', Table VII, it appears that the K£598,000 was made up as follows:

	K£
Fixed fee	311,000
Commission	101,000
Dividend	65,000
Expansion agreement	121,000

Note: K£1 = KShs20. In 1977 US$1 = KShs8.2766 and UK£1 = Kshs14.4468.

39. For references to Gezira, see n. 14 of Chapter 10. For the KTDA see n. 14 of Chapter 5. For the Niger Project, see W.A. Hance, *The Geography of Modern Africa* (Columbia University Press, New York and London, 1964), pp. 224-6; J.C. de Wilde, 'Mali: The Office du Niger — an Experience with Irrigated Agriculture' in *Experiences with Agricultural Development in Tropical Africa*, vol. 2, *The Case Studies* (Johns Hopkins Press, Baltimore, 1967); J. Suret-Canale, *French Colonialism in Tropical Africa 1900-1945* (Hurst, London, 1971); Office du Niger, 'The Niger Development Corporation 1932-1982', unpublished document, Ségou, Mali, December 1982; K.M. Baker, 'Problems of Food Production in West Africa: the Case of Rice in the Office du Niger, Mali', unpublished paper, School of Oriental and African Studies, London University, 1984. Briefly, the Office du Niger was launched by the French in 1932 to undertake the development of the Central Inland Delta of the Niger. The aim was to irrigate over one million hectares so that cotton might be grown, to supply the French textile industry as Gezira supplied Lancashire. But the physical environment proved unsuited to cotton cultivation, which was finally abandoned in 1970. Rice is now the main crop; there is sound reason to believe that the farmers will respond to the three-phase programme initiated in 1981/2 to raise production, provided they are assured of a higher paddy price, a more abundant and steadier supply of inputs, and better guidance. The infrastructure exists to irrigate 150,000 hectares; in 1980/1 over 5,000 settler families (total population some 55,000) were farming 38,000 hectares. For references to the two cotton-based projects in Mali and Upper Volta, see n. 3 of Chapter 6; J.C. de Wilde, 'Mali: The Development of Peasant Cotton Production by the CFDT' in *Experiences with Agricultural Development*; P. Jacquemot (ed.), *Le Mali, le paysan et l'état* (Editions L'Harmattan, Paris, 1981), pp. 34-72. These two 'operations' cover a wide area, centring in Mali-Sud on the southernmost region of Bougouni-Sikasso-Koutiala, and in West Volta on the neighbouring districts of Bobo and Dedougou. Both projects have achieved substantial increases in cotton production during their first four years 1976/7 to 1979/80 — increases of 40% for West Volta and 22% for Mali-Sud. Yields have been remarkable for rain-fed cotton: about 1,000 kg/ha in Upper Volta and 1,150 kg/ha in Mali — twice the average recorded for Sub-Saharan Africa as a whole.

8 CANE SUGAR: FACTORS AFFECTING THE MARKET FOR AND THE PRODUCTION PROCESSES OF THIS COMMODITY

Ingrid Floering

Mumias's example notwithstanding, Kenya is unlikely to emerge as a consistent sugar exporter in the immediate future. For the country with the highest birth-rate in Africa, its aim must be to achieve as efficient a sugar industry as possible in order to meet rising domestic demand and save scarce foreign exchange. A producer such as Mumias might be described as insulated from world economic forces to the extent that government intervenes to protect it and guarantees a market for the end product; within limits this is no bad thing, particularly during the initial stages of a project. Yet any advocate of the modern plantation would consider that such protectionist policies, if pursued to the point where they amount to feather-bedding, risk becoming counter-productive — too costly in terms of the best use of limited resources, and too damaging to the industry. The forces that prevail in the free world as a direct result of the residual world market and low world prices affect therefore not only those producers dependent upon sugar exports for a sizeable proportion of their foreign earnings, but also those supplying their domestic market since they too, unless protected by tariffs, are exposed to the chill wind of competition. This chapter concentrates on delineating the broader economic framework against which the case studies of Chapter 9 may be set. It looks first at those features of world trade that particularly concern developing countries, and then outlines the production processes of growing and milling cane, identifying those stages where problems are most likely to occur.

The International Sugar Market

When cane and beet sugar are considered together, as they generally are in statistics which refer to world centrifugal sugar production, the developing countries[1] appear as the dominant group, accounting for almost 60 per cent of world production, as Table 8.1 shows.

128

Table 8.1: World Production and Consumption of Centrifugal Sugar by Developed and Developing Countries, 1951–5, 1961–5, 1971–5 and 1980/1 to 1982/3 (000 tonnes, r.v.)

	Developing Countries		Developed Countries		World Total		Developing Countries' Percentage of World Production & Consumption	
	P.	C.	P.	C.	P.	C.	P.	C.
1951–5	19,700	11,400	17,200	24,300	36,900	35,700	53	32
1961–5	29,200	20,000	27,600	35,300	56,800	55,300	51	36
1971–5	42,400	33,500	34,200	43,800	76,600	77,300	55	43
1980/1–1982/3	55,000	45,800	38,800	43,600	93,900	98,400	59	51

Note: P. = Production, C. = Consumption
Sources: Data for 1951–5 and 1961–5 from G.B. Hagelberg, *Outline of the World Sugar Economy* (Institut für Zuckerindustrie, Berlin, 1976) Forschungsbericht 3, Table 4, p. 37.
Data for 1971–5 taken from International Sugar Organisation (ISO) *Sugar Year Books* for 1975 and 1980.
Data for the 1980s derived from ISO Memo (81) 24 Restricted, 18 May 1981, ISO Memo (82) 26 Restricted, 13 May 1982 and ISO Memo (82) 61 Restricted, 10 Nov. 1982.

In spite of the upsurge in beet sugar production by the developed countries, notably the European Economic Community (EEC) in recent years, the developing countries have considerably raised their proportion of total production over the 1951–81 period. This is substantiated by Table 8.2, which shows that cane sugar, in which the developing countries have specialised (together with the southern states of the USA, South Africa and Australia) has increased its edge somewhat over beet sugar during the same period.

Table 8.2: World Production and Consumption of Centrifugal Sugar Derived from Beet and Cane, 1951–81 (000 tonnes, r.v.)

	Beet Sugar	Cane Sugar	Total	Cane as Percentage of Total	Consumption
1951	14,022	19,407	33,429	58	32,002
1961	23,252	31,505	54,757	57.5	53,229
1971	30,924	43,035	73,959	58.2	74,386
1981	35,676	56,255	91,932	61.1	87,749

Sources: ISO, *Sugar Year Books* for 1956, 1966, 1975 and 1981.

Yet, while raising their output in step with world production which has increased by some 250 per cent over the period under discussion, the developing countries have increased their consumption at a much faster rate. Their proportion of consumption has risen from 32 per cent to 51 per cent. This pronounced shift in the distribution of world consumption has taken place because *per capita* consumption in the developed countries (notably North America and Western Europe) has stabilised at around 40 kg p.a. and is accompanied by negligible population growth, whereas in the developing world *per capita* consumption is rising rapidly and so is population. The greatest increase in demand in the years ahead may be expected in those areas where there is most room for expansion: in Asia, for example, where current *per capita* consumption averages a mere 8 kg (national range 1–50 kg), and in Africa which averages 14 kg (national range 1–42 kg).[2]

Since many developing country sugar producers have expanding domestic markets, these are likely to be their first priority with exports a secondary consideration — though notable exceptions include Cuba and Brazil. Over the years in fact there has been a steady decline in the proportion of sugar entering world trade, as Table 8.3 illustrates.

Table 8.3: World Exports of Centrifugal Sugar as a Proportion of World Production, and the Contribution of the Developing Countries, 1951–81

	Total World Production (000 tonnes)	Total World Exports (000 tonnes)	Exports as a Percentage of Production	Developing Countries' Percentage of World Exports
1950/1	33,427	11,753	35.2	85.2
1956	40,039	12,197	30.5	87.6
1961	54,714	22,355	40.9	71.0
1966	64,189	21,109	32.9	68.0
1971	73,959	20,957	28.3	72.0
1976	82,400	22,756	27.6	72.6
1981	91,932	28,953	31.5	62.2

Sources: International Sugar Council (ISC), *Sugar Year Books* for 1951 and 1956; ISO, *Sugar Year Books* for 1966, 1968, 1975 and 1981.

Already, most sugar is consumed where it is produced, and this tendency will become more pronounced as both developed and centrally planned[3] economies strive for greater self-sufficiency. This tendency creates two areas of difficulty for those developing countries which have traditionally been the major sugar exporters and which, as Table 8.3 indicates, still account for approximately 65 per cent of world exports. The first concerns a shrinking free market and the problems it gives rise to, which are discussed below; and the second the type of sugar the developing countries should aim to export in future. The traditional exporters have always produced raw sugar[4] and continue very largely to do so, sending much of it to the refineries of Europe, North America and Japan; the developed countries in fact absorb approximately half the world's raw sugar exports, and the socialist countries of Eastern Europe a further quarter. However, the developed countries — chiefly the EEC — are reducing their refining capacity for raws as they step up their own production, and now also export sugar in the form of refined sugar (a proportion of it raws refined for export) amounting to one-quarter of the world's total sugar exports. Much of this refined sugar is imported by developing countries; their preference for it is marked, and their rate of absorption on a strong upward curve. As with the further processing of edible oils (palm oil and coconut oil, e.g. in Malaysia and the Philippines, see Chapter 5) it is a natural next stage in the development of the sugar industry that the raws be refined in the country where they are produced, thus retaining the added value of the refining process in the country of origin. A few major exporters have already set out on this road. In 1981, for example, one-third of Brazil's and one-quarter of the Philippines' exports were in the form of refined sugar. Cuba is exporting some refined sugar, and so is Thailand, and the new producers of central and southern Africa are equipped to do so.[5] The producers probably least able to make the switch are those smaller exporters historically and heavily reliant on raw sugar for their foreign exchange, and exporting a very high proportion of their sugar production.[6]

The problems arising from a shrinking free market are those of securing price stability, and developing a new pattern of international trade as the markets for sugar shift from the former metropolitan powers to the developing countries. Exporters and importers continue their search for a formula that will give them more stable prices. The market appears prone to recurrent cycles of boom and slump from which, by reason of the producers' somewhat sluggish response, it appears unable to escape, with bull markets occurring every eight years or so and very low prices prevailing in between.[7] Moreover, as the proportion of sugar entering international trade shrinks, so the effects of any slight seasonal imbalance between supply and demand are magnified and the volatile character of the market underlined yet again. The inherent problem of price fluctuation is also exacerbated by the structure of the market, which is essentially a residual one because of the large volume of contract sales. Under one agreement — the Sugar Protocol to the Lomé Convention of 1975 — the EEC undertakes to import each year 1.225 million tonnes from 13 African, Caribbean and Pacific (ACP) countries and a further 83,000 tonnes from five other beneficiaries.[8] In the socialist bloc, Cuba is committed to exporting over 5 million tonnes to the USSR and Eastern Europe, and a further 900,000 tonnes to China, the Democratic People's Republic of Korea and Vietnam.[9] Further, since the bull market of 1974 many exporters and importers have sought the security of bilateral agreements, and long-term contracts are proliferating.[10]

In the hope of introducing an element of stability, an International Sugar Agreement (ISA) — the fourth since the Second World War — came into effect on 1 January 1978 for a period of five years, with provision for renewal for a further two. Its main objective is 'to stabilize conditions in international trade in sugar at price levels which would be remunerative and just to producers and equitable to consumers by promoting equilibrium between supply and demand'.[11] Price stabilisation is based on a combination of a quota system for national producers with nationally held but internationally co-ordinated special stocks. The mechanism is designed to maintain a free market price for sugar within an agreed range of US 13-23 cents per lb.[12] These prices are subject to periodic reviews by the Council of ISO, which may adjust them if the difference between the minimum and maximum remains 10 cents. The Agreement also provides for percentage adjustments of the global quota in accordance with the level of prices. However, in spite of these provisions, the Agreement was unable to hold prices within the agreed range at the end of 1979, so that on 11 January 1980 all quotas and other limitations on exports under the provisions of the Agreement were suspended, and traders could follow their market impulses. Quotas became operative again on 14 May 1981, after prices had fallen below the stipulated US 16 cents per lb for five consecutive trading days. Criticism there has been by members of the ISA, but acceptance too that fluctuations in price might have been greater without the Agreement. Members have agreed to extend the current agreement until 1984 while freezing national Basic Export Tonnages (BETs) at 1982 levels. However, given the restricted membership of the Agreement (the EEC is not an exporting member,[13] and many developing countries with expanding markets are not importing members) and the present restrictions imposed by the USA on imports, there is no assurance a new Agreement can work without major changes in attitude among these various groups.

The free market is further complicated by recent events in the United States, which remains the largest single market outside the Soviet bloc. The United States is the world's fifth largest sugar producer, growing cane and beet sugar in roughly equal proportions, and it has two separate and well-developed sugar industries; none the less, domestic production falls short of consumption, and an important refining sector dependent upon imported raws has developed to make up the difference. However, as Table 8.4 illustrates, while production has remained fairly stable, imports and consumption have declined since the mid-1970s; imports fell by almost 3 million tonnes over the six years 1977–82, while consumption dropped by more than 1 million tonnes.

Table 8.4: USA: Production, Imports and Consumption of Centrifugal Sugar, 1974–82 (million tonnes, r.v.)

	Production	Imports	Consumption
1974	5.399	5.250	10.325
1975	5.955	3.515	9.142
1976	6.433	4.228	9.999
1977	5.764	5.291	10.361
1978	5.133	4.257	9.954
1979	5.435	4.436	9.876
1980	5.313	3.802	9.330
1981	5.789	4.646	8.958
1982	5.418	2.393	8.475

Sources: ISO, *Sugar Year Book 1981*; ISO, *Statistical Bulletin*, vol. 42, no. 4, April 1983.

The significance of these trends must be judged against the background of what has been happening in the wider sweetener market. The demise of the Sugar Act in December 1974 — after a legislative life of precisely 50 years during which the domestic market was controlled by a system of quotas for both domestic and foreign suppliers — ushered in a series of changes. The US became a participant in the world sugar market, and corn sweeteners have become a major sugar competitor. One in particular — high fructose corn syrup (HFCS),[14] or isoglucose as it is called in Europe — appears to have made serious inroads. This substitute sweetener is already in direct competition with the syrup forms of sugar that are used in the soft drinks, baking and canning industries; although the problem of crystallisation remains to be solved by further research, it is probably only a matter of years before it will emerge as a commercially attractive alternative to granular sugar. In 1975, sugar accounted for 75 per cent of the total US caloric sweetener market, and corn sweeteners for 23 per cent. By 1982, the corn sweeteners' share had jumped to 39 per cent of total caloric sweeteners, with HFCS accounting for nearly 22 per cent.[15]

There is no doubt that the rapid advance of HFCS, coupled with the dramatic turnround in sugar prices after the 1974 boom, forced the US administration to act once again on behalf of its domestic sugar producers. In 1977 a price support programme was introduced, and import duties on raw and refined sugar raised; in early 1978 these were supplemented by the imposition of differential import fees; but these measures proved insufficient to protect the minimum price targets for domestic sugar, and so in early 1982 a system of quotas was reintroduced, from which it appeared none of the 30 developing countries normally exporting to the USA would be exempt. With a total quota of 3 million tonnes it was inevitable that some exporters would be hit unusually hard: they tended to be those who over the years have become heavily dependent on sales to the USA, as well as others whose recent exports showed a rising trend — countries such as Argentina, Brazil, the Dominican Republic, Honduras, Swaziland, Thailand and Zimbabwe.[16]

The manufacture of HFCS has been taken up by several countries since 1975, and world production has increased eightfold in as many years to reach a total of 3.925 million tonnes in 1982. The USA is responsible for three-quarters of the total, and eleven other countries for the remaining quarter. Its further expansion, and penetration of sugar markets, are expected by 1985 to boost world production of all corn sweeteners to some 11 million tonnes, and of this HFCS may represent approximately 5.6 million tonnes which would otherwise have been sugar. The equivalent estimate for the world production/consumption of sugar in 1985 is of the order of 95–100 million tonnes. This puts the HFCS threat into perspective, but a threat it nevertheless remains. However, it may be argued that for the foreseeable future HFCS poses a more serious threat to the highly subsidised beet sugar producers of North America and Europe[17] than to the more efficient among the cane producers in the developing world, who are able to produce good quality sugar more cheaply. What cane sugar exporters everywhere have greater reason to fear is the continuation of the large EEC sugar surplus, which has a more pervasive effect on all aspects of the free world market than HFCS; from their point of view, the emergence of HFCS has served to emphasise the pressing need to search for new markets in the Third World.

The Economics of Sugar Production

Field Operations

Turning now to the factors which make for an efficient cane sugar industry, it is logical to begin with the plant itself. Cane, a perennial tropical plant rather like a huge grass, is tolerant of a wide variety of terrains and soils. It grows best between latitudes 25 degrees north and south and requires some 2,000 mm of rainfall, or the equivalent in irrigation water. It yields more sucrose when there are distinct wet and dry seasons, ripening well in the drier, cooler season when night temperatures fall to around 18°C, or just below. It is normally cut at around eleven months, though first-year plants are frequently cut at 14–16 months, depending upon the season of planting. After the cane harvest, the roots are fertilised and the banks in which they grow reformed and cleaned; and the next crop — known as a ratoon — sprouts within a few days. When it is necessary to replant, a segment of cane with an 'eye' or bud is planted, covered and fertilised. The importance of establishing a good plant crop from quality seed cane suited to local conditions, so that high-yielding ratoons are assured, is recognised by research institutes and competitive farmers everywhere.

Though a handful of regional industries have successfully mechanised every field operation of the crop cycle — Queensland, Hawaii and Louisiana spring to mind — the majority pursue a diverse combination of modern and labour-intensive methods. In general, almost everywhere today the preparation of the seedbed is mechanised. In many areas the cane setts continue to be planted by hand; mechanised planters have been developed, and are used in some industries, but they have not as yet improved the rate of germination beyond that which can be achieved by hand. The use of fertilisers, herbicides and insecticides varies greatly as to type, quantity and method of application and many industries would benefit from more applied research in this area. Cutting the cane, however, remains a task that is done by hand in most parts of the world; it is arduous, hot work and increasingly disliked, so mechanical harvesters of various designs are now being widely tested. At this stage in harvester development the cane is frequently burnt beforehand to make the machines' task easier, but it is a practice that is not necessarily a good one since the danger of fires getting out of control is ever-present, while the mills for their part are forced to accept cane with a higher proportion of extraneous matter than in the days when the cane was cut, topped and cleaned by hand. A great deal of cane is still manually loaded into roadside trucks for transport to the mills, though in the more modern industries this job is being rapidly mechanised. Ratoons are normally started by tractor-drawn disc-cultivators. Given the cost of clearing the old stools and preparing the ground thoroughly for the new setts, ratoons are sometimes taken annually for up to ten years; generally, however, in those industries where the law of diminishing returns is readily understood, the cost of replanting is accepted as the lesser of two evils and farmers work a three to five year cycle in the certainty of higher ratoon yields.

The sequence of field operations calls for investment in materials and machinery on the one hand, and for a well-organised but none the less flexible routine on the other, whether the production unit is a Cuban smallholding of less than 10 hectares, a Thai farm of 10–50 hectares, a Queensland owner-operated farm of 20–60 hectares, a Barbadan estate of 100 hectares, or Swaziland's Simunye project with 8,500 irrigated hectares. In every cane industry yields can be raised. Even the most technically advanced can benefit from further research into and development of higher-yielding and disease-resistant varieties. In the Third World, where cane cultivation is more often than not extensive rather than intensive, yields can be raised by more careful husbandry at all stages; by the irrigation of more land, especially by the water-conserving drip method; by the optimum application of fertilisers and by better control of pests and weeds. Mechanisation alone is not the answer, except in those situations where it replaces costly, reluctant or absent labour. The real solution to the need for greater output lies in the application of new knowledge, intelligently adapted to meet local requirements and fully utilised.

Mills

As the mills represent the most capital-intensive sector of any sugar industry, regardless of how mechanised the field operations may be, the unit costs of milling demand close attention. Costs will be lowest in those cases where factories can operate for long periods without a break, at full capacity. To do this they require a steady supply of clean, ripe cane throughout the whole of the period during which ripening is possible, in quantities determined by their grinding capacities. Growers should aim to cut their cane at optimum ripeness, and transport it to the mill within 24 hours of cutting, before it deteriorates and the sucrose content drops. Those better-organised industries concerned with the efficiency of the extractive process recognise the importance of this stage in the sugar cycle by paying growers on the basis of sucrose delivered. All too often, however, growers are still paid on the basis of the quantity of cane delivered, which does not give them any incentive to improve their field practices. To get their cane to the mills in good time, growers need either to employ additional, temporary labour or to invest in harvesters and tractor-trailers, besides managing their work-load in such a way that cutting, loading and transporting dovetail so that bottlenecks in cane deliveries can be avoided. If the harvest period could be extended, both groups would benefit, the mills by operating for periods during which they presently stand idle and the growers by spreading the work-load for men and machines.

The object of many research programmes is therefore to discover whether, and if so by how many weeks, the natural harvesting season may be extended beyond the present average of five months. Varietal work with early maturing canes indicates that, if a proportion of the cane area were planted with such varieties, they could extend the harvest period by perhaps three weeks: not a very long time in itself, but in certain situations amounting to an extension of the order of 15 per cent. Another line of research lies in the development, evaluation and correct application of what are called 'growth-regulating chemicals', which by raising sucrose levels at the beginning and end of the season are able in effect to lengthen harvest time. Basically, these chemicals are of two kinds: growth promoters,[18] and growth inhibitors which reduce stalk growth so that the plant's energy may be channelled into increasing sugar storage, i.e. ripening. By encouraging what the climate cannot, growth inhibitors are proving most effective in areas where seasonal changes in temperature and soil water are normally too slight or too extreme to permit optimum ripening.[19] The correct selection of cane varieties, growth promoters and growth inhibitors makes possible in any one area the better programming of the mills and the better use of their capacity. In sum, such selection brings cane cultivation closer to the ideal plantation situation in which all the operations can be smoothed out over a longer period, levelling out peaks and troughs in the demand for labour.

Artisan Production

Broadly speaking, the growing and harvesting of cane at the present time remain labour-intensive operations, while the large-scale processing of cane is clearly capital-intensive and is discussed below. Yet alongside the centrifugal mills in some countries an older form of processing survives that in its essentials pre-dates the Industrial Revolution, offering small cane farmers an alternative market for their cane[20] and producing a type of sugar by the open-pan technique that is popular. It is a low-cost, cottage industry, characterised by small mills employing not more than 15 people scattered among the cane fields. Because it remains a village industry, and its product a sticky brown substance of poor keeping quality, governments have not paid it much attention until recently when the 'small is beautiful' concept gained ground and it appeared to hold out the promise of providing the basis for an intermediate type of sugar industry. Whatever its ultimate future, artisan sugar does not yet appear to be in any danger of being supplanted by centrifugal. In six countries (India, Pakistan, China, Colombia, Bangladesh and Burma) artisan production either exceeds or more or less equals centrifugal production; considerable quantities are also produced in Thailand, Indonesia and Brazil, and the countries of Central America also rely on it for a proportion of their consumption.[21] Estimates for the decade 1964–74 suggest an annual increase in world artisan production of approximately 3.5 per cent; if this has been maintained since, world output probably amounted to about 18 million tonnes in 1982/3, equivalent to one-quarter of the world's centrifugal cane sugar. Expressed another way, at least one-fifth of the world's cane is still processed the old-fashioned way.

Comparative Efficiency

Although the development costs of the agricultural sector are increasing disproportionately as sugar schemes are being promoted for political and socio-economic reasons in more marginal areas than in the past, the factory still represents the largest single block of expenditure in any enterprise. Within the 1970s the f.o.b. cost of new capacity, expressed first per tonne of cane handled daily, rose from £1,875 to £6,000 (see Table 8.5); for the complete decade the range was of the order of £1,500 to £7,000. Looking at Africa, the cost therefore of a project with a total capacity of 2,000 tonnes of cane daily (TCD) was £3.75 million in 1971; by 1975 the cost of a similar project had risen to £8.5 million; a year later it was up to £11 million. Although the figures are not strictly comparable, costs rose as steeply in Asia and Latin America.

Table 8.5: Estimates of Contract Prices for New Sugar Projects, 1971–8

Project Location	Date of Contract	Capacity (TCD)	Cost (£ million)	F.o.b. Cost per Tonne Cane Handled Daily (£)
Africa	1971	2,000	3.75	1,875
Asia	1972	400	8.60	2,150
Africa	1973	3,500	7.00	2,000
Latin America	1974	3,000	12.50	4,200
Africa	1975	5,000	15.00	3,500
Africa	1975	2,000	8.50	4,250
Africa	1975	6,500	23.00	3,500
Asia	1976	2,500	9.00	3,500
Africa	1976	4,000	18.00	4,500
Africa	1976	4,500	20.00	4,500
Africa	1976	2,000	11.00	5,500
Africa	1977	3,500	15.00	4,300
Latin America	1977	4,000	20.00	5,000
Asia	1978	2,000	12.00	6,000

Source: I. Carmichael and B. Newton, 'Cost Economics of Production Capacity Expansion', a paper presented to the International Sweeteners and Alcohol Conference, The Future of Sugar, London, 1–3 April 1980.

Investment capital of this magnitude imposes terms which can only be met if the project is well managed, operating close to the capacity for which it was designed. Clearly, less is expected of the older plantation-mill complexes which may not grow cane under irrigation or employ the latest techniques in the field, and possess mills of limited capacity built to handle only a few hundred tonnes of cane daily. Nevertheless they can be low-cost producers if they get the balance right between inputs and outputs, within the limits set by their particular circumstances. However, most producers today are aiming for high sugar yields per hectare, and these are normally associated with modern production techniques in field and mill; of course, other factors such as the local cost of inputs and labour are significant, which means that high yields may not necessarily guarantee a low-cost operation though the two usually go together in a well-run enterprise.

Given the spectrum of factors influencing production costs, and the lack of strictly comparable data, any attempt at categorizing producers in terms of cost-effectiveness should be viewed with caution. The British Ministry of Overseas Development (MOD) has drawn up an index of producers devoid of any figures (see Table 8.6) which is as good a starting-point as any. Australia and South Africa are placed in the low-cost group, their performance reflecting the astuteness of their farmers, highly mechanised field operations and relatively new processing facilities; but so too are the Philippines, Thailand and India where mechanisation is limited. Many developing countries, possessing some modern mills and cheaper labour in all sectors, can achieve some cost advantages over developed countries; these in turn, where labour has become scarce and more expensive, will seek to regain their competitive edge through greater capital investment and better management.

Table 8.6:   The Division of Cane Sugar Producers into Five Cost
             Categories

Low-cost	Low/average	Average	Average/high	High-cost
Australia	Dominican	Continental	West Indies	Middle East
Fiji	Republic	Asia	Europe	West Africa
S. Africa	Egypt	Central	Part of	North America
Mauritius	Some East	Africa	USA	Japan
Thailand	Africa			
Philippines	Some Latin			
India	America			
Some Latin				
America				

Source: Lloyd Chilvers and Robin Foster, *The International Sugar Market: Prospects for the 1980s*, Economist Intelligence Unit Special Report no. 106 (London, 1981), p. 74.

An attempt to augment these general descriptions is summarised in Table 8.7. The costs of production are given in US cents per lb, and relate to the mid-1970s. They support, as far as they go, the definitions given by the MOD: South Africa, the Philippines and Brazil are placed at the lower end of the scale, registering costs of

9.5, 8.5 and 6–8 cents respectively; the Dominican Republic lies midway with 10 cents, and the West Indies near the top with 10–15 cents.[22] A more recent American survey, presenting data for 1979 and 1980, states that costs ranged from 8.7 cents per lb in Brazil to 33.7 cents in Japan's highly subsidised industry; the average for the 25 countries studied was 17 cents per lb, which drops to 15.7 cents if the very high figures for Nigeria and Japan are excluded.[23] This survey makes the further comment that 'the estimated production costs of Australia, Brazil, Kenya and South Africa tend to fall well below the average, and we believe Swaziland and Colombia also fall into this category'. There appears to be a fair measure of agreement between the three sources.

Table 8.7: Costs of Sugar Production for Selected Countries (US cents per lb)

West Germany[a]	21.0
Netherlands[a]	21.0
Guadeloupe	'high cost'
Martinique	'high cost'
Benelux[a]	17.0
Trinidad & Tobago	15.6
USA	15.0
Nicaragua	13.7
Panama	13.5
Jamaica	13.3
Belize	13.2
India	11.4
Australia	10–12
Barbados	10.6
Dominican Republic	10.0
Guatemala	9.6
South Africa	9.5
Costa Rica	9.5
Taiwan	9.4
Mexico	8–10
El Salvador	8.9
Honduras	8.8
Philippines	8.5
Brazil	6–8

Note: a. EEC beet producer, for comparison.
Source: D.H.N. Alleyne, *The International Sugar Industry and the Third World*, Third World Forum Occasional Paper No. 9, 1979, p. 64. No date is given for these figures, but they appear to relate to the mid-1970s.

The 1970s have seen costs rising fast for developed and developing countries alike. Data for the USA, which tend to be the most comprehensive and accessible, suggest that costs in the early 1970s rose by about 6 per cent and thereafter by about 10 per cent a year; the most marked increases were in cane production costs — which in general make up roughly 70 per cent of the total cost of sugar production — rather than in milling and refining. Australia and South Africa registered similar increases. The costs of cane sugar production in developing countries are harder to assess: labour tends to be cheaper, but the increasing use of fertiliser and pesticides, the higher consumption of oil as partial mechanisation progresses, and the interest on loans earmarked for new projects, irrigation schemes and modern agricultural equipment are all contributing to a steady increase in costs. In certain high-cost areas like Jamaica and Trinidad increases in recent years have been running as high as 15 per cent a year. It would appear that only those producers with cheap labour and little mechanisation — as in the less developed African and Central and South American countries — have been able to register single figure increases.[24]

Overall, with very few exceptions, yields do not appear to have increased in 1979 and 1980 over what was recorded for the mid-1960s and mid-1970s by Connell Rice (see Table 8.8). Argentina, Brazil and Kenya showed a small improvement, while yields in Peru, Indonesia and Thailand were lower partly as the result of drought. The average yield for all countries studied by Connell Rice was 6.40 tonnes of sugar per hectare. If this is compared with the average 10.20 tonnes achieved by six of the most efficient low-cost producers — namely Australia, Brazil, Kenya, South Africa, Swaziland and Colombia — then there is considerable room for improvement. As very few if any of the national sugar industries are presently running at peak production, the more efficient use of existing capacity will provide the quickest and most likely source for an increase in production in the immediate future.

Conclusion

The general significance of this overview of the international sugar market for developing countries may be summarised as follows. Tropical sugar cane producers are now in intense competition with both beet sugar and synthetic sweeteners in a market which is normally over-supplied. To make it worth while for developing countries to produce sugar at all, whether for home consumption or

Table 8.8: Cane and Sugar Yields for Selected Countries for the Crop Years 1966/7 and 1976/7 (tonnes per hectare)

		1966/7		1976/7	
		Cane	Sugar	Cane	Sugar
N. America	USA	89.91	9.33	83.43	9.12
C. America	Antigua/St Kitts	50.92	5.96	62.20	7.19
	Barbados	86.44	10.03	57.84	–
	Belize	50.30	5.39	57.14	6.79
	Costa Rica	54.23	4.87	50.00	4.32
	Cuba	62.85	5.78	53.97	4.17
	Dominican Rep.	57.98	6.76	64.35	8.22
	El Salvador	73.45	7.73	76.19	7.89
	Guatemala	62.76	5.95	67.50	6.75
	Honduras	95.83	6.01	66.00	6.26
	Jamaica	73.33	7.68	56.45	5.81
	Mexico	60.32	6.46	65.85	6.59
	Nicaragua	70.40	6.67	n.a.	n.a.
	Panama	51.53	2.40	n.a.	n.a.
	Trinidad/Tobago	58.69	5.52	60.27	5.75
S. America	Argentina	41.88	5.41	48.00	4.80
	Bolivia	29.14	2.97	36.92	3.31
	Brazil	52.66	5.23	49.50	4.83
	Colombia	100.10	10.83	117.30	12.54
	Guyana	78.80	7.08	74.77	6.36
	Paraguay	37.07	1.43	35.38	2.15
	Peru	156.70	16.24	160.00	18.18
	Uruguay	30.00	1.71	30.00	3.33
	Venezuela	80.34	7.19	74.50	6.40
Asia	India	40.34	4.02	51.07	5.39
	Indonesia	82.59	7.19	80.00	10.67
	Japan	60.90	7.17	69.00	8.59
	Pakistan	33.84	n.a.	32.59	3.15
	Philippines	53.35	5.63	56.00	5.40
	Taiwan	66.38	7.41	80.00	8.30
	Thailand	43.33	4.25	49.40	4.22
Africa	Kenya	65.79	5.25	67.50	6.67
	Malagasy	53.26	6.44	54.00	6.70
	Malawi	76.30	6.43	100.00	10.81
	Mauritius	58.56	7.17	74.07	8.83
	S. Africa	81.09	8.48	91.00	11.05
	Swaziland	119.10	14.33	110.00	13.64
	Zaire	54.61	5.88	95.49	10.37
	Zambia	n.a.	n.a.	107.00	12.84
Oceania	Australia	75.13	10.85	87.14	11.78
	Fiji	51.40	7.13	48.00	6.67

Source: *World Sugar — Capacity, Cost and Policy* (Connell Rice and Sugar Co., New Jersey, 1977), Section II.

export, one or both of the following conditions must be satisfied. First, a country must have a comparative advantage in growing cane sugar. Even if domestic production is intended to substitute for imports, it must constitute a more efficient use of indigenous factors than some other activity might be, including food or other export commodities. Alternatively, the sugar must be competitive at realistic rates of exchange with foreign sugar, so that it can sell in the world market and earn foreign exchange.

Tables 8.6 to 8.8 show very wide contrasts in prices and yields in different countries; and, though there is no direct correlation between costs or yields and regions, low costs are usually associated with either high levels of mechanisation or with very low wages. What is needed is to raise yields as well as incomes in the poorest countries, while ensuring that they can still compete internationally; and this is where the plantation may have something to offer. This is the main theme in the case studies in Chapter 9, which suggests ways in which the modern plantation system may be an asset to Third World countries engaged in sugar production.

Notes

1. Countries are classified as 'developing' in this chapter in accordance with Article 2 of the International Sugar Agreement (ISA) of 1968, which defined as 'developing' any member in Latin America, in Africa (except South Africa), in Asia (except Japan), and in Oceania (except Australia and New Zealand), and included Greece, Portugal, Spain, Turkey and Yugoslavia. In addition, the United States offshore area, Puerto Rico, is here included in the 'developing' category. Beginning in 1963, data for the French overseas department are consolidated with those for the EEC and from that point on no longer included among 'developing' countries. Taken from G.B. Hagelberg, *Structural and Institutional Aspects of the Sugar Industry in Developing Countries* (Institut für Zuckerindustrie, Berlin, 1976), Forschungsbericht 5, p. 54. Using this definition, the USSR and the satellite countries of Eastern Europe are defined as developed.

2. One model for the period 1976-90 projects an annual increase in consumption for the developed countries of 1.5% compared with 4.1% for the developing countries. E.M. Brook and D. Nowicki, 'Sugar: Econometric Forecasting Model of the World Sugar Economy', prepared by the Commodities and Export Projections Division of the Economic Analysis and Projections Department of the World Bank, March 1979, Table 8, p. 68; Annex I and p. vi of Summary and Conclusions.

3. World Bank studies frequently divide the world into three groups of developing, developed and centrally planned economies; within the ISA definition, the USSR and Eastern Europe are classed as developed, while China and the other centrally planned economies such as North Korea and Vietnam are classed as developing.

4. This is the traditional pattern that has grown up over the past three centuries. Raw sugar, or 'raws' as it is sometimes referred to, is the impure centrifugal (i.e. factory-produced) sugar of commerce, a light brown crystalline substance containing at least 96% sucrose, together with inorganic material, various forms of insect life and numerous microbial flora some of which are harmful. Cane raws therefore require

refining. White sugar with a sucrose content of 99.9% is the end product. It is unusual for white sugar to be exported from the tropical cane sugar areas, chiefly because of the difficulty of transporting it under hygienic conditions, and partly because the loading is much less mechanised than for raw sugar which is handled in bulk. Cane raws are normally refined at or near the ports of importing countries. Sugar statistics normally refer to raw sugar and are given in tonnes raw value (r.v.), unless otherwise stated.

5. Several of the new industries in Africa have been designed to produce high-quality direct-consumption sugars which current technology can produce cheaply without the need for remelt refining. Zambia and Zimbabwe are good examples.

6. The material for this paragraph is drawn largely from a report prepared by the UNCTAD Secretariat in December 1982 for the Permanent Sub-Committee on Commodities titled 'Marketing and Processing of Sugar: Areas for International Co-operation', Ref. TD/B/C. 1/PSC/29, paras. 99–112.

7. This argument, which also dismisses as over-rated the effect of adverse weather on sugar prices, is advanced by M. Attfield, 'Outlook for World Supply and Demand', *Sugar y Azucar*, April 1983, pp. 27–31.

Since the Second World War there have been five bull markets: 1951, 1957, 1963, 1974 and 1980. In 1974, when the average ISA daily price for the year was US 29.66 cents per lb, the highest monthly price recorded was 56.16 cents in November. In 1980 the average ISA daily price for the year stood at 28.69 cents, and the highest monthly figure was 40.55 cents in October.

8. Under the Protocol, any sugar within an agreed quota which cannot be marketed in the Community at or above the price negotiated annually would be purchased by the Community at the guaranteed EEC intervention price. Though the Sugar Protocol, unlike the Lomé Convention, is of unlimited duration, the Community may ask for its revision at two years' notice. This is a source of concern to the ACP countries who regard the large EEC surplus as a potential threat to their future quotas. It is apposite to recall that the Commonwealth sugar exporters were selling 500,000 tonnes more to a guaranteed (British) market under the former Commonwealth Agreement than they now may under the Protocol which replaced it when Britain joined the Community.

The quota allocations are as follows (tonnes, white value):

Barbados	49,300	Carried forward:	
Congo	10,000	All ACP states	1,230,500
Fiji	163,600	Other beneficiaries	
Guyana	157,700	Belize	39,400
Jamaica	118,300	St Kitts-Nevis)	
Kenya	5,000	Aguilla)	14,800
Madagascar	10,000	Suriname	4,000
Malawi	29,000	India	25,000
Mauritius	487,200		
Swaziland	116,400	Total	1,313,700
Trinidad & Tobago	69,000		
Uganda	5,000		
Tanzania	10,000		
All ACP states	1,230,500		

Source: Text of Protocol No. 3 of the Lomé Convention, as printed in the UNCTAD report 'Marketing and Processing', p. 9.

9. In 1982 the exports under Special Arrangements totalled 7.645 million tonnes, as follows:

To EEC	1.410 million

From Cuba
  to USSR &
  Eastern Europe
	5.219

From Cuba
  to China
  Albania
  Korea
  Vietnam
  Yugoslavia
	0.972

From USSR
  to Bulgaria
  Mongolia
  Vietnam
	0.044

Source: ISO Memo (83) 17 (Restricted), 22 April 1983, Table 6.

10. See 'The Development of Long Term Contracts in the International Sugar Trade', an unpublished article by Simon Harris, Consulting Editor of *World Sugar Journal*.

11. ISO, *Annual Report for the Year 1977* (ISO, London, 1978), p. 11. This Report carries a useful précis of the main features of the Agreement, the fourth in the last 30 years; the others were signed in 1953, 1958 and 1968.

12. Under the original terms of the Agreement, the price range was set at US 11 to 21 cents per lb. This was raised 1 cent on 1 April 1980, and again on 19 November 1980 by another cent, to bring prices in the range of 13 to 23 cents per lb.

13. Since the Agreement was signed in 1977, the EEC has become the largest exporter to the free market, providing more than a quarter of the sugar entering it. In the crop year beginning September 1981, even with 1.8 million tonnes taken off the market as planned, the community had a potential export availability of some 5.25 million tonnes, which must have had a depressive effect on prices. Low prices throughout 1982 were in the main the result of three factors:

(1) a surplus of supply over demand, brought about partly by record production in the Community (over 16 million tonnes for 1981/2) coupled with exceptional crops in India, Thailand and Cuba;

(2) the increased exports by ISA members after their quotas were suspended in January 1980; and

(3) the 1982 BETS and related quotas for ISA members being insufficiently low to have a real impact on world prices. It would be logical to restrict supply, but all exporters are reluctant to accept restrictions when one exporter, with much greater financial resources than any one exporting member of the ISA, remains outside the Agreement. For more details see W.K. Miller, 'The International Sugar Agreement: a Status Report' (ISO, London, 1982). W.K. Miller is the Executive Director of the ISO, and presented his paper first to the Conference of the Queensland Cane Growers' Council in Brisbane in March 1982, and subsequently to the Sugar Club, New York, on 24 March 1982.

It appears that EEC exports were 5,580,020 tonnes in 1982, against 5,343,752 tonnes in 1981 (ISO, *Statistical Bulletin*, vol. 42, no. 4, London, April 1983).

14. Two kinds of HFCS are in general use: HFCS42, which is a first generation product used in the baking, canning and food processing industries; and the more

widely used HFCS55 (55% HFCS, 40% dextrose, 5% higher saccharides), a second generation product used by the soft drinks industry. The most comprehensive analysis of world production and consumption of HFCS is to be found in a paper given to the 1981 World Sugar Research Organisation Annual Meeting held in Buenos Aires in March: S. Vuilleumier, of McKeany-Flavell Co. Inc., 'World Corn Sweetener Outlook', *F.O. Licht's International Sugar Report* (usually referred to simply as *Licht's*), vol. 113, no. 12, 15 April 1981.

15. J.D. Sullivan, 'The US Sugar Market 1983-1985', *Sugar y Azucar*, April 1983, p. 38. There is a sound commercial reason for the direct substitution of HFCS for sugar: it is cheaper. Towards the end of 1981 US wholesale refined sugar prices stabilised at US 27 cents per lb, which permitted HFCS manufacturers to maintain a discount against sugar of approximately a quarter but still price their product at 20 cents per lb dry weight (production cost 12-15 cents per lb). By July 1982 the discount was reported to be 40%. See ISO PRC (82) 1 (Restricted), 17 September 1982 — Data presented to the Price Review Committee for consideration on 12 October 1982, Table 1 and comments p. 2.

16. For a discussion of recent US policy and its impact on sugar exporters, see the UNCTAD Report 'Marketing and Processing', paras. 34-44 and Table 4; Sullivan, 'US Sugar Market', pp. 35-8.

17. Just how seriously the EEC Commission takes the threat to sugar from HFCS may be gauged from its policy since the mid-1970s. In the early 1970s there were significant plans afoot among manufacturers to expand HFCS production. But by 1977 the Community was faced with a growing beet surplus, so a levy on HFCS was introduced on HFCS production which changed the competitive price relationship between sugar and HFCS. As a result, HFCS production and usage was stymied. In 1979 the levy was replaced by a production quota system. By 1981 the policy-makers in Brussels were seeking once again to equalise prices for refined sugar and HFCS rather than permit HFCS to carry on being sold at a lower price. The outlook, with slow population growth rates and a continuing surplus of beet sugar, for HFCS production in Europe is therefore very limited. Vuilleumier, 'World Corn Sweetener Outlook', pp. 18-20.

18. Recent trials in South Africa, Hawaii and parts of Central and South America with growth promoters 'indicate an increase in stalk mass of up to 30% which is accompanied by an increase in the size and number of sugar-storing internodes'. The compound used was Ethrel. T.A. Bull and G.R. Cullen, 'Chemical Products Applied to Sugar Cane Fields', *Sugar y Azucar 1981 Yearbook* (Palmer Publications, New York, 1981), pp. 48-68.

19. In South Africa, for example, the general use of a relatively low-sucrose variety NCo 376 coupled with the widespread development of irrigation has highlighted the need for an artificial ripener at the beginning and end of the milling season, and Ethrel when applied in the correct amounts and at optimum time was found to be successful as a growth inhibitor too. Other chemicals in commercial use are Polaris (glyphosine), used in Hawaii, the Philippines and the Americas; Embark (mefluidine), used in the Philippines, Thailand, Taiwan, Brazil, Mexico and South Africa; and Roundup (glyphosate), which is now replacing Polaris in Hawaii, South Africa and Brazil. Bull and Cullen, 'Chemical Products', p. 65. An indication of the scope of recent research into chemical ripeners is provided by the proceedings of the International Society of Sugar Cane Technologists (ISSCT). At the ISSCT XVII Congress of February 1980 in Manila 10 of the 33 papers presented to the Plant Physiology section dealt with chemical ripener trials. Four in particular may be mentioned briefly:

(1) In Jamaica trials with Polaris and Mon 8000 suggest that of the two Mon 8000 will allow for greater flexibility in harvesting schedules, particularly when applied to B51129. T. McCatty, 'A Review of Sucrose Enhancer Trials in Jamaica in 1974-78' (3 vols. ISSCT, Manila, 1980), vol. 1, pp. 630-43.

(2) In Trinidad, glyphosate ripeners proved more effective than Polaris in bringing about sugar enhancement in B41227, and have permitted more flexible harvesting during the first six weeks when previously juice quality had been poor and harvesting not always possible. G.F. Mason, 'Chemical Ripening of Variety B41227 in Trinidad', vol. 1, pp. 663–75.

(3) In Hawaii, which has a very variable climate, a harvest period of about ten months, and the presence of miniature suckers in two-year-old crops, chemical ripeners were found to improve juice quality throughout the year. H59-3775 proved the most responsive to Polaris. Chemical ripening induced by Mon 8000 was found to be a very precise function of dosage, time and the juice quality of the cane at the time of application. H.W. Hilton, R.V. Osgood and A. Maretzki, 'Some Aspects of Mon 8000 as a Sugarcane Ripener to Replace Polaris', vol. 1, pp. 652–61.

(4) In South Africa, the salts of glyphosate (Mon 8000 and Roundup) were able to increase the yield of sucrose when applied to mature sugar cane with juice purities in excess of 80% at the time of spraying, both early and late in the milling season. M.St.J. Clowes, 'Ripening Activity of the glyphosate salts Mon 8000 and Roundup', vol. 1, pp. 676–93.

Plant response to these growth-regulating chemicals varies, reflecting differences in environment, cane types, rates of application and their timing. However, yield increases in excess of 2 tonnes of sugar per hectare have been recorded, though the average improvement is of the order of 0.5 to 1.0 tonne of sugar per hectare.

20. For example, in India the farmers are the backbone of both artisan and centrifugal industries. It has been estimated that India harvests an average 2.63 million hectares each year to produce 125–135 million tonnes of cane. There are probably more than 5 million farmers growing cane. This number, and the small quantities they grow, make scheduling the harvest a very complicated matter over which the factories can exert little control. As a result of the freedom of choice the growers are able to exercise, the portion of the Indian cane crop delivered to the centrifugal mills in the ten years 1963–72 ranged from 22.6 to 33.9%. D. Smith, *Cane Sugar World* (Palmer Publications, New York, 1978), p. 104.

In Thailand, on the other hand, it appears that in many areas the owners of small artisan mills now prefer to plant cane for the centrifugal factories instead of working their mills which yield small profit. Thailand's cane farmers have been well paid for their cane in recent years (see Chapter 9). Amara Pongsapich *et al.*, *Chonburi Project: Institution and Human Resources Development in the Chonburi Region* (Chulalongkorn University Social Research Institute, Bangkok, 1970), p. 200.

21. The artisan production of selected countries may be compared with their centrifugal output for 1974:

Country	FAO estimate artisan output (000 tonnes)	ISO figures centrifugal output (000 tonnes)
India	8,110	4,489
Pakistan	1,422	607
China	826	950
Colombia	700	895
Mexico	560	2,838
Bangladesh	517	107
Thailand	290	985
Brazil	280	6,931
Indonesia	281	1,025
Burma	140	80

Countries producing less than 100,000 tonnes

Costa Rica
Ecuador
El Salvador
Guatemala
Nicaragua
Panama
Peru
Philippines
Taiwan
Venezuela
Vietnam

World Total 1974   13,542

Note: FAO estimated World Average Annual Artisan Production for 1961/5 to be 10,400 tonnes.

Sources: The artisan estimates were taken from Lloyd Chilvers and Robin Foster, *The International Sugar Market: Prospects for the 1980s*, Economist Intelligence Unit Special Report no. 106 (London, 1981) and G.B. Hagelberg, *Structural and Institutional Aspects of the Sugar Industry in Developing Countries* (Institut für Zuckerindustrie, Berlin, 1976), Forschungsbericht 5, Table 1, p. 14. The centrifugal figures from ISO, *Sugar Year Book 1980*.

22. The conclusions of this survey are supported by Report no. 1894, 'World Sugar Economy: Review and Outlook for Bank Group Lending', World Bank, Washington DC, 2 February 1978, para. 17: 'The financial cost of production (in 1977 constant dollars) of major producers of raw sugar ranges from about 9 to 17 cents per lb.'

23. W.A. Cromarty, 'World Sugar Supply-Demand Outlook for Two to Five Years', *Sugar y Azucar*, April 1981, pp. 46-56. At the time of writing, W.A. Cromarty was the Executive Vice-President of Connell and Company, a subsidiary of Connell Rice and Sugar Co., Inc., of Westfield, New Jersey, USA. He was one of three co-authors of *World Sugar — Capacity, Cost and Policy* (Connell Rice and Sugar Co., New Jersey, 1977) referred to as the Connell Rice Report. Some of the figures he gives for 1979–80 are based on conclusions presented in the Connell Rice Report.

24. L. Chilvers and R. Foster, *The International Sugar Market: Prospects for the 1980s*, Economist Intelligence Unit Special Report no. 106 (London, 1981), pp. 74-5.

9 CANE SUGAR: THREE CASE STUDIES

Ingrid Floering

Contrasting Government Attitudes to Sugar Production: An Overview

Before discussing the three case studies — the Dominican Republic, selected industries in Africa, and Thailand — it is necessary to make the point that government attitudes towards the plantation model, and the modern management principles that guide it, are crucial to the success of this economic institution. An overview of the 70 or so countries that make up the world's cane sugar industry reveals that, though similarities exist between some of them, there are almost as many structures for the industry as there are countries producing sugar — each one shaped by its particular physical, economic and political environment. The more successful industries possess some if not all the characteristics associated with modern management, and their structures range from an almost total reliance upon the plantation system (e.g. Brazil, the Dominican Republic, Zimbabwe) to the kind of loose association of highly professional farmers described briefly in Chapter 6 (e.g. South Africa, Queensland). Yet favourable physical conditions and sound management practices cannot by themselves guarantee success. It may be stating the obvious, but a political environment sympathetic to the require-ments of the industry is also essential. By this is meant, at its simplest level, approval of the structure that operates in the country in ques-tion; it may be the capitalist approach of Brazil, which supports the efforts of the entrepreneurs so long as they deliver in terms of out-put, regardless of the social costs accruing from the continued dependence on an underprivileged labour force; it may be the socialist approach of Cuba, which emphasises the importance of central planning (of industrial rather than agricultural inputs, as the former appear easier to control) to meet production targets; or it may be the approach of a developing country such as Kenya, where the state joins with private enterprise in developing new projects. Whatever the structure, it is important that government believes in a strong sugar industry. It may go further, and express its support through economic means — credit facilities, subsidies, tariffs, etc. — but these are not inevitable concomitants, nor are they always necessary for success.

On the other hand, where government adopts an ambivalent attitude, the industry usually fails to prosper. The results of an inconsistent policy since the Second World War may be seen in a rather extreme form in four of Britain's former sugar colonies in the Caribbean — Barbados, Guyana, Jamaica and Trinidad. Here, post-colonial government resistance (though to varying degrees) to modernisation owes much of its vigour to the historic fact that the plantation system, which took root early in these lands, has been associated throughout with colonialism.[1] After reaching peak production in the late 1960s/early 1970s[2], they have displayed the classic symptoms of decline. As a group their production during the decade 1969/71 to 1979/81 dropped by 31 per cent, with Trinidad falling 49 per cent and Jamaica 38 per cent. This overall decline is the result not of a deliberate policy to cut back production, but of a general inefficiency attested by the deteriorating yield of sugar per hectare. In the seven years 1975–81 their average yield has dropped from 6.24 to 4.86 tonnes per hectare, i.e. by almost a quarter.[3] Many reasons have been advanced for this poor performance, ranging from careless cultivation practices, unplanned burning of pre-harvest cane, insufficient labour at harvest time, badly organised transport and too much extraneous matter in the cane delivered to the mills, to the existence of too many small and uneconomic mills and stoppages in the mills due to equipment failure and labour disputes. All these are in part to blame, but they are symptomatic of rather than the cause of the industry's malaise, which may be traced back to the countries' political, cultural and social environment.

At the end of the Second World War output was low but so were production costs, chiefly as the result of very low wages which made for miserable living standards that to this day have left a legacy of resentment towards anything to do with sugar. The companies that then controlled the mills and a large part of the cane production made a sustained effort to improve output through research into better cane varieties, insisting upon better cultivation practices and extending mechanisation wherever possible, and through updating their mills and keeping them in good repair. Conditions in the industry improved, and strong unions won higher wages and better conditions for their members. But it was a case of too little too late to eradicate bitter memories, and inherited attitudes towards what is still regarded as slaves' work (though royal assent was given to the parliamentary bill abolishing slavery in 1833) survived. The approach of independence brought to the fore political parties, backed by the unions, which were determined to gain control of the economy. Acquisition of foreign assets took place gradually in Trinidad and Jamaica, but in one swift move in Guyana.[4] Whatever the methods applied, the governments found themselves masters of an institution that colonialism had used to develop the land, and were perplexed as to how to proceed. In the event, they changed little and the structure and functioning of the industry continued as before: in Trinidad and Guyana the plantations have survived; only in Jamaica was an attempt made to create workers' cane-growing co-operatives, but even there a substantial part of the acquired land was soon leased back to the now-nationalised mills to continue growing cane under the plantation system.[5] Moreover, though ownership had passed from the 'foreign exploiter' to the national government, the bad image of the plantations persisted, with the result that governments have not been willing to provide the necessary capital for improvements or encourage the unions to adopt a more realistic attitude to mechanisation, while insisting on keeping prices down in the domestic market. The sugar industry has become the Cinderella of politics and, though there is now an awareness that the future of the industry on which so many people depend for their livelihood is in jeopardy, these governments have yet to resolve the central dilemma of what position to give it within their economy.

In all four countries sugar is no longer the major earner of foreign exchange. Petroleum products account for at least 90 per cent of Trinidad's earnings, bauxite and alumina lead in Jamaica and Guyana, and tourism leads in Barbados.[6] These capital-intensive industries (notably bauxite and alumina) pay high wages, which serve to push up wages in the labour-intensive sugar sector where they are not accompanied by increased productivity. Largely as the result of higher wages, but in part also the result of a sharp increase in the cost of fuel and fertiliser, the costs of sugar production have risen threefold in Jamaica and Trinidad and by two and a half times in Guyana in the decade 1965–75.[7] Having become high-cost producers, not all the Caricom industries may be able or wish to continue in their traditional role of sugar exporters.[8] Of the four, only Barbados — with its industry still largely in private hands — appears to possess the political will to maintain production at mid-1970s levels.

Government support for the sugar industry is nowhere more evident than in Brazil, the world's foremost producer,[9] which would suggest that here is a country deserving further study. Yet, though Brazil's industry is structured along plantation lines, and the units are big (some are reported to extend beyond 35,000 hectares),[10] the practical details of how the principles of plantation agriculture are being applied are unknown. This has something to do with Brazil's sheer size, but more to do with the ambitious targets set by the Figueiredo regime for the production of sugar for export and fuel alcohol, derived from cane, for the domestic market: by 1985, if all goes well, the country should be producing some 14 million tonnes of sugar (compare this with Cuba's target of 10 million tonnes for that year) and 10.7 billion litres of fuel alcohol.[11] If these targets are to be met, the area planted to cane must be doubled between 1981 and 1985, from approximately 3.2 million hectares to approximately 6.44 million.[12] An expansion of such proportions and in so short a time can only be effectively handled by large units working under pioneer conditions, and the result for Brazil, the country where the plantation system has survived to an extent unmatched anywhere else in the world, must be an intensification of control in the hands of the big mill and distillery owners. According to São Paulo's Secretary of Agriculture, 'the figure of the independent sugar cane planter who supplied raw material to the distilleries is disappearing, and in his place the big mill owners are establishing themselves'. He added that many of the mill owners were hiring former small farmers as sharecroppers to promote the planting of 100 per cent of the land round their distilleries.[13]

Forceful leadership, whether by government or by the industry itself (as in Australia and South Africa), is a necessary adjunct of any successful sugar industry today, and Brazil is well provided for in this respect by the Instituto do Acucar e do Alcool (IAA),[14] a semi-autonomous body, which interprets national policy and lays down the guidelines to which the wholly private industry must adhere; it produces an annual crop plan, allocating quotas to mills and distilleries; it co-ordinates the country's research programme and runs five major research stations which carry out varietal work besides propagating good seed for their localities; it handles all sugar exports, and all sales of fuel alcohol; any new venture, be it mill or distillery, must be vetted by the IAA before funds can be released by central government. In this way, government and the entrepreneurial sector work closely together.

The significance of the Proalcool programme (which aims by 1985 to meet 2 per cent of Brazil's energy requirements and thereby reduce oil imports) may eventually be recognised as lying not so much in agricultural developments and their subsequent social repercussions but rather in the South/South exchange of technology and management expertise. In September 1983 the millionth alcohol-driven car rolled off the assembly line in Brazil, and 90 per cent of all new cars had alcohol-powered engines. Moreover, 7 million vehicles already on the roads used gasohol (a 20:80 mixture of anhydrous alcohol and petrol). This achievement reflects the R and D work that has been directed towards producing an alcohol free from corrosives, engines resistant to corrosion, and a safe storage and distribution system; it also indicates that the country's capital goods sector has expanded to the point where it can provide almost all the equipment needed by the distilleries, mills and plantations. At a time when world interest in the energy potential of biomass — which may be derived from a wide variety of tropical crops besides cane, such as bananas and cassava — is increasing, Brazil is in a strong position to export its alcohol technology, together with a range of related industrial goods.[15]

Cuba, second to Brazil in world sugar production and the world's leading exporter, is likewise gaining a reputation in the Third World for its expertise in the milling sector of its sugar industry. In 1980 two new mills — the first to be built in Cuba for over 50 years — came on stream; another two followed in 1982, and four more will be ready by 1985. They mark the completion of a long and difficult period of economic readjustment following the exodus of American technicians after the revolution of 1959. The Cuban sugar industry has traditionally paid more attention to its milling sector than to its agricultural sector, relying heavily on outside capital and engineering skills, and upon moving from the American into the Soviet sphere of influence this tendency was reinforced by the need for Cubans to do more themselves.[16] From scratch, starting with a literacy campaign, the country set about creating its own machine industry; today it builds cane harvesters, designs its own mills and supplies 70 per cent of all their equipment, and exports computerised control systems for processing sugar.[17] In exchange for Soviet oil, capital equipment and machinery, Cuba sends the greater part of its sugar surplus to the Soviet bloc; yet it has continued to export about one-third of its surplus — and more in those years when prices were high — to the free world, which means that it is also able to take part in the exchange of new technology which goes on outside the Soviet orbit.

Pride in the fact that Cuba now possesses one of the most thoroughly overhauled milling sectors among traditional exporters, supported by a complex mill-rail network, has encouraged the authorities since 1979 to be more open about the country's industrial progress and declare their plans for the 1980s, which envisage an output of 11 million tonnes by the end of the decade. Yet the country, which remains dependent for 85 per cent of its export earnings on one agricultural commodity, continues to reveal little of its agricultural sector, probably because techniques remain extensive rather than intensive and cane yields below the average for the Caribbean.[18] A few facts are known. Improvements that have had the greatest impact are those connected with the harvest; in-field loading is fully mechanised, and at least 45 per cent of the cane — a quantity greater than the entire harvest of Australia — is now harvested by machine. Cuba is also making progress in plant research: from 1980 to 1982 approximately 40 per cent of the entire cane area was replanted with Cuban disease-free varieties, replacing B4362 which had succumbed to rust in 1980 and pulled sugar production for that year down by almost a million tonnes. More interesting, there remains a place in this socialist economy for the small farmer. There are 35,000 of them, who own about 250,000 hectares and grow some 13 million tonnes of cane, equivalent to 1.4 million tonnes of sugar (rather more than the total output of the Dominican Republic). Their yields are acknowledged to be higher than those of the large state farms, which is contrary to the relationship between farm size and cane yields commonly found elsewhere.[19] However, a more thorough comparison of the private smallholdings and the state farms, which control 80 per cent of the cane land, is not possible because objective reports about the size and organisation of the latter are not yet available. For this reason Cuba, like Brazil, cannot become the subject of a case study for the purposes of this book.

Turning now to the three case studies for which ample documentation exists, the first analyses the modern plantation in the Dominican Republic, where it has successfully evolved from earlier plantation antecedents. Studies by members of the World Bank and an economist seconded to the International Labour Organisation have shown that for discussion purposes the Republic's sugar industry can usefully be divided into two sectors, one public and one private.[20] The performance of both sectors is evaluated with reference to the criteria outlined in Chapters 1, 4 and 8; the poorer results of the state sector may be explained by the fact that political considerations appear to outweigh economic. The second case study looks at eight industries in central and southern Africa, paying particular attention to the introduction of plantations and related smallholder activities in Zimbabwe, Malawi, Zambia and Swaziland. In the past 25 years several African governments have adopted the plantation system, regarding it as a most useful tool for the promotion of economic and social change. The third concentrates on Thailand, which became a major sugar exporter only in the mid-1970s. Thailand's industry is not based on the plantation estate nor does it appear to possess many of the characteristics that reflect modern management; yet, if it is to remain competitive in the world market, it would benefit from a more consistent government policy, and from the acceptance of the need for as well as the application of more rigorous standards at every stage of production.

The Dominican Republic

The Dominican Republic has maintained an unusually steady output for the past 20 years. During the 1960s production averaged 790,000 tonnes, and there was little annual variation. Then it rose from 886,200 tonnes in 1969 to 1,014,075 tonnes in 1970 and has stabilised at around 1,200,000 tonnes since. Sugar plays a major role in the Republic's economy, employing 167,000 people and a further 40,000 during harvest. It earns US$250–300 million in foreign exchange annually (roughly 25 per cent of the total value of exports in the late 1970s). Until and including 1981 the Republic relied on sending 80 per cent of its exports to the USA; in 1982 exports to the USA halved, and the Republic was successful in finding other outlets in Africa and Europe. The Republic's industry is structured on the plantation system, with 16 mill-estate complexes producing the country's sugar but supplementing their own cane with supplies from about 8,300 outgrowers (*colonos*).

For an analysis of their comparative performance, the plantations can be divided into two groups. The public sector comprises twelve complexes that the government inherited when Trujillo was overthrown in 1962. In the turbulent period that followed, when several of these enterprises which the ex-dictator had personally acquired were proving uneconomic, the government had little alternative but to assume management. It did so for economic rather than doctrinaire reasons at the time, but in the years that followed it was perhaps inevitable that this public sector, theoretically free from political interference, should have come under the sway of the politicians. The twelve enterprises were grouped into one organisation known as the Consejo Estatal del Azucar (CEA) and account for some 65 per cent of output. The private sector consists of two separate organisations, La Romana and the Casa Vicini. The Central Romana Corporation (La Romana) is a wholly owned subsidiary of Gulf and Western Industries (G & W), an American multinational. The Central Romana is the largest mill in the Republic (and one of the largest in the world) with a capacity of 17,500 tonnes of cane daily (TCD), and it forms the nucleus of a large agro-industrial complex which includes livestock production and the manufacture of furfural[21] from cane bagasse. La Romana is acknowledged the most efficient sugar company in the country, although it is located in the eastern part where rainfall is low and the soils relatively poor. The second private enterprise, Casa Vicini, runs three mill-plantations and accounts for 7 per cent of production. Small though this proportion is, the Vicinis, who are Dominicans of Italian extraction, have been pioneers in the industry; they were the first to use chemical fertilisers and herbicides, and to irrigate by aerial aspersion; they are the only group using mechanical harvesters; they were the first employers to sign a collective agreement with a recognised trade union, in 1963.

The quality of cane cultivation has an important bearing on the overall efficiency of the industry which, in statistical terms, is dominated by the state sector. As elsewhere in the Caribbean, cane yields per hectare have tended to decline. For example, average yields fell between 1969 and 1973 by 13.6 tonnes per hectare.[22] The explanation for this appears to lie not with the plantations, where yields may vary from estate to estate, depending largely upon physical conditions, and yet remain relatively stable over the years, but with those *colonos* who have extended their control over cane lands. The general picture at the end of the 1970s showed the CEA mills administering 40 per cent of the Republic's cane land, the private sector managing about 30 per cent, and the *colonos* the remaining 30 per cent.[23] More than two-thirds of the *colonos'* cane went to CEA; in fact, those *colonos* supplying CEA have expanded their production by almost 650 per cent between 1968 and 1978.[24] How they succeeded in doing this provides yet another illustration of the potent force of the political environment, which has a pervasive influence throughout the Republic's sugar industry.

With very few exceptions, most *colonos* have taken up cane farming since the mid-1960s. Those — and they are the majority — who supply CEA are in the main senior military officers or high ranking civil servants who have acquired their land through a process of illegal privatisation, taking over little by little much of the land that had originally passed to the state upon Trujillo's demise. Because many of these individuals wield political power, the state mills are unable to refuse to grind their cane; moreover, several mills near the capital are no longer in a position to refuse, since they are the ones which have lost control over most of their lands in recent years and are now dependent upon the *colonos*. There are risks for CEA in relying for one-third of its supplies on the *colonos*, who are speculative by nature and respond quickly to world sugar prices; at times of rising prices the area of cane expands rapidly, often to the wasteful extent of large areas being left unharvested, only to contract as quickly when prices drop so that some mills may be faced with shortfalls. It has also been estimated that the yields from CEA's *colonos* are 20 per cent lower than the average yield for CEA's twelve estates.[25] It is generally agreed that the *colonos* do not cultivate carefully: land preparation is inadequate, the use of fertiliser scant, the number of ratoons allowed per plant excessive, and harvesting poorly organised — all of which result in headaches for the mills and a lower yield of sugar per tonne of cane processed.

A second much smaller group of *colonos* supply about one-third of La Romana's cane; a few of them are long-established land-owning families who provide the bulk of La Romana's *colono* cane; the majority however are former G & W employees and the beneficiaries of a deliberate programme of land redistribution initiated by the company in order to divest itself of a potentially embarrassing asset, i.e. its cane land. Initially, the company sold off plots of land to individual workers; but on finding that subdivision at death was resulting in a reduction of cane area, the company devised a new scheme in 1977 whereby land has been made over in a large indivisible block to a special company in which the beneficiaries (normally field-workers of long standing) hold stock rather than titles to land. While these prospective *colonos* learn their managerial skills, La Romana continues to manage the land as an integral part of its cane programme. G & W's ultimate aim is the expansion of *colonos*' cane production until it matches the supply of its own cane; in time this will mean the transfer of 12,000 hectares (i.e. about

30 per cent of its cane land) to this worker-owned company and also, it is hoped, ensure substantial local support for the company's continued presence.[26] Yields from the worker–owners' land are lower than those from company land, but that is considered a small price to pay for survival.[27]

An analysis of the relative performance of the state and private sectors suggests that in every respect the private sector performs better, with the sole exception of cane yields per hectare. Here the state sector does better; in 1974 the very high yields from CEA's two totally irrigated plantations raised its average yield to 54 tonnes per hectare, compared with 42 tonnes for Casa Vicini and 40 tonnes for La Romana. Limited water supplies and inferior soils and topographical conditions in the private sector account for the difference.[28] Yet it would appear that CEA could do better: for, while both sectors follow similar field practices, with mechanised land preparation and the widespread use of identical fertilisers and herbicides, one expert has stated that in the state sector 'this apparent homogeneity does not necessarily imply that the precision and timeliness of such tasks is either optimal or identical', citing the use of nitrogeneous fertilisers which are frequently applied too late to secure optimal response.[29]

The most relevant indicator of efficiency is the sugar yield given as a percentage of cane, because it is the sum of all the agricultural and processing stages. La Romana had the highest sugar yield in 1974, with 12.50 per cent (i.e. obtaining 12.50 tonnes of sugar from 100 tonnes of cane); CEA followed with 11.63 per cent and Casa Vicini with 11.41 per cent.[30] However, because production at La Romana is so much greater than at the three Casa Vicini complexes, the weighted average sugar yield of the private sector was well above that of the public sector. La Romana's performance is the result of the precise timing of harvesting and the careful scheduling of cane deliveries, as well as the very low proportion of grinding days lost during the sugar campaign (*zafra*) — all the function of good management.[31] One example of the private sector's edge in this respect is to be found in a comparison of the various transport systems. The system generally prevailing is for the cane to be carried by ox-cart to the rail-sidings, and by rail to the mill yard, though in some cases — usually from more distant outgrowers' land — tractor-drawn carts deliver direct to the mill. Though manual loading is the normal practice, mechanical loaders are sometimes used, and transloading by crane is the rule for La Romana and the Vicini estates. So much for system; what matters is how well it operates. La Romana's rail system is efficient because it has been properly maintained. The same may be said for Casa Vicini, which in 1978 completed the modernisation of the rail system on its largest estate, and has since completed improvements on a second. The condition of CEA's system, however, has been severely criticised. The shortage of rail wagons to hold cane for overnight grinding, insufficient standardisation of wagons and spares between estates and within individual estates, and obsolete repair facilities are cited as contributing to its general deterioration. The consequent delays cause the sucrose content to drop. But the damage does not stop here. In order to compensate for poor quality cane, it appears that the state mills frequently process quantities in excess of their capacity; breakdowns occur, a mill's performance declines; then unit costs of sugar production go up, and the sugar recovery factor goes down. According to FAO estimates for the 1971–7 period, the total amount of cane milled by CEA rose by 18 per cent, but was accompanied by a drop in the overall yield of sugar from cane from 11.81 per cent to 10.84 per cent.[32]

Behind this picture of lower performance in the public sector lies a difference in the quality of management, for which four reasons may be advanced. First, CEA's management is significantly less well qualified because the state corporation uses less strictly professional criteria in recruitment, and makes many of its senior appointments for political reasons. Second, managerial salaries and fringe benefits are lower in the state sector. Third, partly because political considerations introduce an element of uncertainty, the state sector offers less attractive long-term career prospects. And fourth, CEA offers less managerial job satisfaction owing to the inferior level of its technology in the mills compared with the private sector, which has recently undertaken large reinvestment programmes at Central Romana and at the Vicini's largest mill.

With a management attuned to broad political considerations rather than those economic considerations that have a specific bearing on the sugar industry, the state sector is at a disadvantage when government policy conflicts with its own requirements. One such occasion occurred in the mid-1970s when the government, attempting to make more jobs available to Dominican nationals, did not renew its traditional agreement with Haiti covering the annual migration of Haitian cane cutters. Since slavery was abolished, the Dominican *zafra* has depended almost totally upon Haitian labour.

At least 40,000 out of the 45,000 cane cutters employed are Haitians, many of whom have settled since the late 1960s in the Republic, forming a pool of labour that employers like to call upon: disenfranchised, often present in the country illegally and not well organised as a group, they are in a weak position to demand higher wages though it is acknowledged that their productivity is greater than that of the Dominican cutters. One-quarter of the Haitian cutters employed by CEA are migrant workers, yet in 1977 CEA's management — apparently toeing the government line — announced that no Haitian workers would be imported for the 1977/8 *zafra*. This was disastrous for the public sector: Dominican cutters were not forthcoming and the army was ordered into the cane fields; even so, much CEA cane was left standing. The private sector was able to circumvent the government because it employs fewer migrant workers, and pays higher wages (including fringe benefits) than the state sector.[33]

Chapter 4 stressed the importance of plant research in raising yields and agronomic standards generally, and here too there are important differences in the emphasis and direction given to this work at the Republic's two research stations. At La Romana, more resources are allocated to the production of new varieties through genetic crossing with cane fuzz than at Duquesa, CEA's experimental station, where the primary emphasis is on the selection of promising varieties from a genetic pool produced largely elsewhere. Because La Romana's research station has been in existence since 1948, is stronger on basic research, receives more funds and has a larger and more highly qualified staff than Duquesa (established in 1965), it is able to make a greater contribution to the industry as a whole. It has produced two new cane varieties CR-6101 and CR-67400 which are being grown commercially, and three other promising strains are at the pre-commercial stage. It has also provided Duquesa with the canes to start its varietal work, has trained several CEA agronomists, and employed two scientists who subsequently became Directors of Duquesa. In effect, Duquesa relies on La Romana for much of its inspiration and practical guidance. As for the Vicinis, they run a small experimental station which concentrates on testing known varieties. Yet, true to their reputation for innovation, one of their top executives has become the first president of the Dominican Association of Sugar Technologists.

The foregoing comparison of the performance of the state and private plantation sectors indicates how standards can slip even within the plantation system if political considerations are allowed to come between management and its monitoring role. For almost 20 years the Dominican government has put political rather than commercial considerations first in its dealings with the sugar industry, and these have taken their toll of both sectors. The state sector, because it is the larger of the two and because its yields are lower than they need be, is in the stronger position to improve national output immediately by adhering more rigorously to accepted practices at every stage in the sugar cycle. Meanwhile the private sector (La Romana in particular) remains uncomfortably aware that the pressures for a partial redistribution of cane land and the creation of more jobs operate against achieving greater efficiency through further mechanisation.

But CEA is short of funds, and to put this right requires a change of attitude from government. Since 1965 the industry as a whole has had to sell sugar for the domestic market to the Government Price Stabilisation Institute (INESPRE) at a price below cost, after which INESPRE has sold to the consumers at a price which includes a tax used to subsidise electric power.[34] Moreover, CEA's constitution provides that any profit remaining after deduction of export duties, corporate income tax, production costs and a small reserve for maintenance be divided among government and workers in the proportion of 60:40. Inevitably, with profits a low priority and the high incidence of taxes eroding both management initiative and the supply of capital funds for investment, factories and the transport system have deteriorated and low productivity is the final outcome. CEA is widely recognised as the Republic's highest-cost producer. If the government were willing to re-examine its policies, it has a tool in the Dominican Sugar Institute (INAZUCAR) which formulates domestic sugar production targets, directs product and marketing research, assists government in negotiating export sales through bilateral agreements, and sets export quotas for the various mills. Then, having put its own house in order, if CEA were to take the lead in the mechanisation of harvesting, in-field transport and short-haul transport as a recent report recommended,[35] the private sector would surely follow, secure in the knowledge that it could no longer be pilloried for shedding part of its work-force on to an already crowded labour market. The smaller private sector has always given the industry stimulating professional leadership, there is no doubt of that, but in certain respects it has discovered that it too must fall into line.

Africa

Since 1961 the sugar industry of Africa has more than doubled its output, and 32 countries now produce centrifugal sugar. This expansion owes much to the appearance of new producers, though higher yields, an extended area to cane and greater milling efficiency in the older industries have also contributed. However, Africa remains a net importer and is likely to remain so for many years in view of continuing population growth and rising *per capita* demand. The countries that stand to benefit most from this state of affairs are those operating a profitable industry capable at least of ensuring self-sufficiency in sugar in step with their own rising demand, and preferably producing a surplus for export. South Africa and Mauritius have been traditional exporters for decades and rely on the sugar industry for a proportion of their export earning;[36] the new producers, on the other hand, making self-sufficiency their first priority, cannot become exporters overnight and, though some of them have reached this point, others have some way to go before foreign exchange earnings will help offset the high capital costs of investment. In this African case study, it is proposed to comment briefly on the two exporters of long standing, South Africa and Mauritius, and on recent developments in the new industries of Kenya and Sudan, before considering in more detail four countries whose governments have enthusiastically espoused the modern

Table 9.1: Africa: Productivity of the Sugar Industry in Eight Selected Countries, 1977–81

	Tonnes Cane per Hectare 1977–81	Tonnes Sugar per Hectare 1977–81	Production (tonnes r.v.) 1979–81	Exports (tonnes r.v.) 1979–81
Kenya	91.03	9.19	355,573	3,351
Malawi	93.45	10.98	148,987	101,337
Mauritius	74.87	8.51	614,289	584,755
S. Africa	80.68	9.50	1,969,890	801,938
Sudan[a]	71.03	6.82	180,000	—
Swaziland	104.31	12.15	318,083	299,073
Zambia[b]	106.91	11.77	105,022	1,888
Zimbabwe	107.56	13.32	354,359	212,962

Notes: a. Sudan has yet to become an exporter; during the three years 1979–81 Sudan imported an average 170,816 tonnes p.a.
b. Zambia exported for the first time in 1981.
Source: ISO, *World Sugar Economy: Structure and Policies*, vol. 2, *Africa* (ISO, London, 1983), from the various country sections.

plantation, namely Zimbabwe, Malawi, Zambia and Swaziland.

When the industries in the eight countries selected for discussion (see Table 9.1 for their productivity data) are analysed, it readily becomes apparent that the same three factors must usually be present for sound development as elsewhere: good relations between government and industry, modern management and irrigation where necessary. A strong combination of the first two can overcome the absence of the third, as in South Africa; but if the combination is weak, as it is in Sudan, then however well the project has been planned its chances of future success are limited.

Looking first at South Africa and Mauritius, they are well ahead of the field with regard to the quantities of sugar produced and exported, yet in terms of yields they lag behind because their cane is largely rain-fed.[37] For South Africa this drawback is offset by a highly organised and efficient industry which, should a drought occur,[38] appears able to recoup its losses over a period and remain highly profitable. But in Mauritius the modest cane yields achieved by smallholders are coupled with a milling sector that needs rationalising, consisting as it does of 21 small and frequently outdated mills with an average throughput of just under 3,000 tonnes a day. The Mauritian economy remains heavily dependent on sugar (cane occupies over 90 per cent of the cultivated land and the industry employs one-third of the working population), and the government is concerned that output be maintained so that it may finance the island's social and economic programmes. Yet over the last 20 years output has barely increased[39] and the target of 800,000 tonnes by 1985 is unlikely to be met in view of the government's other plans for steady urbanisation and crop diversification. Even the comparative advantage among developing country exporters of holding the largest quota allocation (487,200 tonnes) under the Sugar Protocol of the Lomé Convention, plus access to US markets, does not appear to provide a sufficient incentive to halt the decline in profitability that has characterised the industry in recent years.

In contrast to Mauritius, South Africa has doubled its output since 1961; and, by paying attention to the more fundamental issues of research,[40] yields and mill modernisation, now possesses one of the most highly organised industries in the world. The 17 mills are privately owned, with control of twelve of them split between two groups.[41] Cane is supplied under three systems: some 20 per cent is grown on estates associated with the factories, 72 per cent by approximately 3,000 commercial farmers and the remaining 8 per cent by 17,000 subsistence farmers. Growers and millers are equal partners in the South African Sugar Association which is responsible for determining sugar policy covering all aspects of planning, production, marketing and research, leaving to the Department of Industry only the regulation of domestic sugar prices.

Such freedom of action is normally denied the sugar industries of developing countries, whose governments usually insist on being involved in any new project; indeed, for all projects developed since the early 1970s this must be so, since the investment sums are now so great that they require both international and domestic capital. Furthermore, neither multinationals nor international agencies wish to shoulder the burden alone, and look for a financial commitment from government — just as government today when awarding a management contract looks for a financial commitment from the company concerned as evidence of its goodwill. Progress then depends on the level of co-operation between the two parties, who may not necessarily share the same priorities. In Kenya, for example, co-operation will be crucial to the future well-being of an industry which sugar technologists view with some concern, noting the serious impact of recent drought on a crop that is not irrigated, and the escalating costs of fertilisers, pesticides and other inputs. From the outset, the Kenyan government made self-sufficiency its goal, and accepted that large mills run on modern management lines were necessary to this end; but in looking for social benefits too, it insisted that the mills receive the bulk of their cane supplies from thousands of small farmers; faced with the prospect of declining yields in the coming decade, government will in future have to tread more carefully in shaping a policy that will meet both the economic need for profitability and the social need for rewards with which to maintain the morale (and thereby the productivity) of the cane growers.[42]

The modern plantation system has been adopted by several new nations struggling to establish procedures and standards where none existed before, and the exceptional yields obtaining in Malawi, Swaziland, Zambia and Zimbabwe show what may be achieved under tightly controlled conditions. Yet other nations which likewise do not possess the resources required to achieve success on their own — finance, skilled and experienced manpower, physical and social infrastructure all being in short supply — have adopted equally ambitious schemes only to find them falling far short of expectations. Sudan is a case in point, and its efforts to develop an agro-industrial alternative to cotton illustrate how badly things can go wrong when elaborate projects go forward unsupported by the necessary management skills.

Sudan has yet to achieve its long-intended goal of becoming a sugar exporter, with an eye on Middle East markets. To this end it initiated Kenana, which it claims is one of the largest sugar complexes in the world today. The Kenana Company was incorporated in March 1975 and the first phase of the factory was commissioned in 1979; when fully operational it should handle 17,000 tonnes of cane in 24 hours, and is expected to produce 330,000 tonnes of sugar per year. The mill will draw all its cane supplies from its surrounding estate of 34,000 hectares of irrigated land that ten years ago was scrubland, used intermittently to grow sorghum. At 1977 estimates the total cost of this integrated complex was given as US$500 million, which is greatly in excess of the standard costing for such projects put forward by the World Bank.[43] Sudanese sources including government put up 40 per cent of the capital, and all but 8 per cent of the remainder was raised in the Middle East.[44] Lonhro were originally awarded the management contract, but lost it in 1978 when the Sudanese government took over.

Whether the hopes vested in this colossal project will be fully realised remains to be seen. Kenana is admirably situated with regard to climate and water supply, and has a terrain and soils that lend themselves to extensive irrigation and mechanisation. But to these natural advantages, all else must be added, including the infrastructure to support a future population of around 60,000 in what was until very recently an almost empty land. Though planned to be fully operational by 1982, Kenana's delayed start-up was perhaps inevitable given the need to transport all the machinery and equipment overland to a site 240 kilometres south of Khartoum. But if the project's up-to-date field layout, irrigation network, mechanised field equipment and modern mill[45] are eventually to be put to good use, then much will depend on the management team which must deal not only with the problems posed by Kenana's size but also with the problems of training and supervising a work-force to carry out all the skilled operations of an irrigated sugar cycle.

The Sudanese government's record as manager of its other sugar schemes is not a particularly proud one. Besides Kenana, Sudan has four other mills, two commissioned in the 1960s, a third in 1976 and a fourth in 1980, with a total designed capacity of 390,000 tonnes of sugar per year. However, none of these mills has yet worked at full capacity; crippled by the problems of inadequate cane supplies and mechanical breakdowns, their joint production amounts to approximately 130,000 tonnes p.a.[46] Sudan's sugar production will probably be sufficient to satisfy a home market of some 350,000 tonnes by the mid-1980s if all goes well; but, as the country's total sugar capacity is of the order of 720,000 tonnes, it has a long way to go before it approaches cost-effectiveness. In Kenana the government has a well-planned scheme capable of helping it achieve self-sufficiency and a surplus for export; the final measure of its success will be a reasonable pricing policy that reflects the efficient use of indigenous resources. But success may prove elusive, if Sudanese management continues to cut itself off from the mainstream of modern management practices, as it seems to be doing.

Zimbabwe, Malawi and Zambia

The problems besetting the industry in Sudan are not found in Zimbabwe, Malawi and Zambia because the new sugar industries of these countries are firmly structured along the lines of the modern plantation estate to which, without a doubt, they owe their swift success. This, in turn, has encouraged a readiness on the part of the governments of Malawi and Zambia to introduce smallholders to cane growing; with the help of the CDC, they have recently established two schemes which are heavily oversubscribed. This suggests that here is another formula for future agricultural development, alongside the plantation-mill complex which — for sugar — provides both central processing facilities and the latest technical and scientific information.

Zimbabwe has emerged as one of the most efficient sugar producers in the world despite undergoing years of domestic instability, international trade sanctions and an exodus of capital. A favourable climate and access to sufficient water for irrigation provide the right physical conditions, to which may be added the benefits of an extensive cane research programme. But the most important contributory factor has been the type of organisation chosen by the two companies responsible for sugar's development since the early 1960s. A private Zimbabwean group owns Hippo Valley (10,560 TCD) and the Tongaat-Hulett Group owns Triangle (8,000 TCD). Together the two plantation-mill complexes produced a record 401,316 tonnes of sugar in 1982, supplying raw sugar for the export market and the country's two refineries besides operating in conjunction with ethanol plants which have made Zimbabwe self-sufficient in alcohol production. The Ministry of Trade and Commerce determines production levels and domestic and export sales. In 1980 sugar earned Zimbabwe US$75 million in foreign exchange.

Malawi's industry has also been developed by private enterprise; production began in 1966, expanded steadily until a sizeable surplus was produced for export in 1973 and continued to expand further to reach a record 182,876 tonnes in 1982. Sugar is now, with tea and tobacco, a major source of foreign exchange. The industry is dominated by Lonhro. The Lonhro Sugar Corporation (LSC) controls the Sugar Corporation of Malawi (SUCOMA) which owns and manages Nchalo mill (5,040 TCD); LSC also holds shares in the new Dwangwa mill (3,600 TCD) which began processing in 1980 under management provided by Lonrho Ltd (the parent company of LSC). SUCOMA is largely responsible for the country's marketing and export structure, and exports from Malawi are co-ordinated by LSC with only superficial involvement by government. All in all, apart from administering wholesale and retail sugar prices for the domestic market, government has been content to allow private industry exceptional freedom of action.

The government of Malawi has recently demonstrated a willingness to encourage sugar smallholders, by co-operating with the CDC to establish a scheme for 300 farmers on land adjacent to the Dwangwa complex. CDC began to plan the Dwangwa Smallholder Sugar Project soon after becoming financially involved in the Dwangwa complex — it originally loaned over £2 million to the government to subscribe for shares, and this was followed by a further £2.9 million in 1980. The scheme began to take shape on the ground in 1978, and by the end of 1982 294 farmers and their families had been settled on 2-hectare cane plots, with a further 1.2 hectares each on which to grow food. The yields already recorded for the fertile Dwangwa Delta are among the highest in Africa, averaging 122 tonnes cane per hectare and approaching 14 tonnes sugar per hectare. The combination of an ideal physical environment, intelligent and industrious farmers, and good management appear to have secured the future of this particular project.

Whereas Malawi's industry has thrived under a policy of government support without direct involvement, in neighbouring Zambia the Zambia Sugar Company went ahead as a joint venture by government and private capital from the outset, shortly after independence in 1964. In 1968 the Nakambala mill and estate were established under Tate and Lyle management; by 1982 the country was virtually self-sufficient, with Nakambala (7,200 TCD) providing all the raw sugar required by Ndola refinery — at the time of independence Ndola relied upon imported raw sugar — as well as the newer Nakambala refinery. The mill has, however, been pre-.vented from reaching its full production capacity of 150,000 tonnes of sugar p.a. by limited cane availability, its estate of 10,000 hectares not being large enough to meet its requirements. In response to this problem CDC created the Kaleya Smallholders Company in 1981 with a view to developing a further 1,900 hectares of irrigated cane land; two-thirds of the area will be settled over four years by some 300 farmers with 4 hectares of cane each, and the remainder will be developed and managed by CDC as a nucleus estate.[47] Zambia should therefore soon be in a position to meet rising domestic demand.

Swaziland

To this group of highly successful producers must be added a fourth, Swaziland, which shares with one or more of them the following features: an industry organised around large mill-estate units; government holding shares in these enterprises; high yields; all questions relating to production and sales (domestic and export) the prerogative of an independent body; and a productive smallholder sector. Possessing not only the most advanced smallholder project in southern Africa, but also one of the latest mills to come on stream, Swaziland's sugar industry provides an excellent example of the economic and social benefits that can accrue from good management, applied here to units that vary considerably in size.

Swaziland exported sugar for the first time in 1965, and by 1982 was exporting almost 350,000 tonnes, having raised production in that year to a record 402,471 tonnes. The industry is the major productive user of the country's natural resources of land and water, and is crucial to the country's well-being. It employs more than 13,000 people; probably 80,000 people — or 14 per cent of the population — are wholly or partly dependent on it. Three mills account for the total production of sugar and molasses, of which approximately 95 per cent is exported to earn for Swaziland more than half its foreign exchange. This has been achieved in the 25 years since 1958, when sugar was first manufactured at a small mill by the Usuthu river.

Until Simunye (6,000 TCD) had completed its first full year of production in 1981, Swaziland's production rested with Mhlume and Ubombo, two mills which came into production in 1960 and which have been enlarged on several occasions since until they reached their present capacities of 7,000 TCD and 6,000 TCD respectively. Ubombo was established in the south by Lonhro, and Mhlume in the north by CDC.

CDC's involvement with Swaziland dates back to 1950, when it purchased 42,500 hectares in the Low Veld from the descendants of John Thorburn — in 1889 he had acquired 45,000 hectares from King Mbamdzeni — and thus found itself in possession of what has remained the largest tract of land under its control. The first priority was to bring water to the land, the second to determine by trial and error what crop held the soundest commercial prospects for development. By 1955 CDC management was convinced that sugar held the key to future prosperity, but, as events turned out, rice was to provide the bread-and-butter revenue until the doubling of Mhlume's capacity to 3,800 TCD in 1966 made sugar the undisputed major crop.[48] It is worth making the point here that CDC's rationale is a commercial one, for it sees its initial task as that of any commercial organisation, investing its funds in development schemes for the promotion of economic projects that will not only help to increase the wealth of the territory concerned but will also yield a reasonable return on the money invested. It insists that its projects should prospectively pay their way. At this juncture, however, CDC's thinking parts company with that of a typical commercial enterprise, because its ultimate objective — having brought a scheme to fruition and trained local people in managerial, supervisory and technical skills — is to work itself out of those schemes in which it has a controlling interest by transferring them to the government concerned. By 1982 CDC had come closer to this stage in Swaziland, having transferred 50 per cent of its interest in the Swaziland Irrigation Scheme (SIS), the parent organisation that manages the 30,500 hectares remaining from the block originally purchased, to the Ngwenyama in trust for the Swazi nation. The significance of this transfer lay in the fact that SIS controls the water supplies via the Mhlume Canal to the various CDC irrigated projects (some 11,700 hectares in total) in the country, and also to neighbouring private estates and smaller farms (3,000 hectares). This transfer brought the ownership of SIS into line with that of the Mhlume Sugar Company (mill and 4,800-hectare estate) which was already jointly owned.

Undoubtedly the most interesting and significant unit spawned by SIS is Vuvulane Irrigated Farms (VIF), which began to take shape in 1960 as soon as Mhlume mill was successfully launched. With a processing plant within easy reach and the routine for cultivating a staple crop established, CDC judged this the moment to proceed with a smallholder/settlement scheme. Dispersal of land to local citizens was firm CDC policy by the late 1950s but — ever-mindful of cash-flow requirements — the scheme that CDC originally adopted incorporated three types of landholding: ten farms of 41.5 hectares (100 acres) for people of all races, five farms of 24.3 hectares (60 acres) for Swazis, and sixty 3.2-hectare (8-acre) smallholdings for Swazis. Since that time, the ten large farms have been reduced to three and are independent of VIF;[49] the five 24.3-hectare (60-acre) farms have flourished, and four have paid off their mortgages; and the number of settlers has increased to 263, with leaseholds varying in size from 3.25 to 6.5 hectares, of which about three-quarters is planted to cane, and the remainder to cotton and vegetables.

As at Mumias in Kenya, the management team schedules the routine tasks and ensures that those requiring careful timing and/or the use of heavy machinery are carried out by its own services. The farmer's job is to see to the maintenance of his own crop, that it is weeded, fertilised and irrigated; sometimes he may pay others to do the work, and to grow his vegetables; he may decide to accept (and pay for) CDC's assistance in spraying his cane with chemical ripeners to raise sucrose levels by the beginning of harvest on 1 May. As growers are paid according to the sucrose level of their cane, they are keen to shorten the harvest season by cutting out the last five to six weeks, when the onset of heavy rain causes the sucrose level to drop sharply from the 16 per cent obtaining mid-season (August-September) to around 11 per cent. In recent years Mhlume mill has complied, shortening its crushing season from 33 to 28 weeks. Under CDC supervision the Swazi farmers have achieved cane and sucrose yields which match those of the estate and private farmers. In 1980/1, for example, VIF averaged 107.53 TCH, compared with SIS's average of 111.16 TCH and Mhlume's 98.24 TCH; sucrose levels for the same period were 14.15, 14.43 and 13.44 tonnes per hectare respectively.[50] For other years a random check suggests that VIF yields lie midway in the overall range. The satisfying result for the farmers has been an income which, even in those years when world prices were unusually low, has made it well worth their while to plant again.[51]

Eyebrows were raised when a third sugar complex for the Low Veld was mooted in the early 1970s. Swaziland already possessed two efficient mills, and was exporting over 90 per cent of its total production. These mills could be expanded with a further minimum capital outlay, as they subsequently were in the late 1970s to a capacity of 140,000 tonnes each; so many economists considered a third mill would be a grave financial risk because an erratic world market prone to periodic slumps would be its only outlet. But government saw in the expansion of sugar production a way to increase foreign exchange earnings, create more jobs, train more Swazis in new skills and stimulate economic activity in rural areas; and a pre-investment study, carried out with CDC's assistance, convinced it that a third venture similar in size to the first two was feasible. The detailed planning and development study was entrusted to Tate and Lyle Technical Services (TLTS), and completed in June 1975. The limiting factor appeared to be water. The amount that could be drawn with certainty from the Black Umbuluzi river would support an estate of 8,500 hectares, which at full production would be able to supply Simunye (6,000 TCD) with 88 per cent of its cane requirements. It was decided to organise the estate on a plantation basis, at least during the period of major development while loans were being repaid. Thereafter it would be possible for small farmers to join the scheme.[52]

The financial package that was finally put together to permit the incorporation of the Royal Swaziland Sugar Corporation (RSSC) — sole proprietor of Simunye Sugar Estate (SSE) — in December 1977 reveals an unusually diverse provenance. As Table 9.2 shows, the Swaziland government and the Swazi nation (Tibiyo Taka Ngwana) together hold E26 million of the total equity of E40.1 million (US$47.6 million at 1977 prices), representing 64.8 per cent. The rest was subscribed by public and private groups in Africa, Europe, Asia and America. Swazi sources have also advanced almost half the loan capital totalling E91.2 million (US$108.6 million). An analysis of the application of funds during the development period 1978–81 (see Table 9.3) shows what a high proportion the factory and infrastructure absorbed between them; it also underlines the cost of establishing an irrigation and drainage network on which the productivity of an enterprise rests. The planning team devoted considerable effort to resolving whether to adopt a higher capital cost system of overhead irrigation or a lower cost furrow system, and eventually chose overhead sprinklers for 80 per cent of the cane area in the belief that it would lead to higher cane yields. The construction of the all-important Mnjoli dam and supply canal was the separate responsibility of the Swaziland government, which raised three-quarters of the total E22.5 million (US$26.8 million) in the form of a soft loan from Germany. Tate and Lyle Engineering (TLE) were awarded the contract for the construction of the overall project, and TLTS the contract for the management of the completed project.

Table 9.2: Swaziland: Financial Sources for the Simunye Sugar Estate, 1977

	Equity (E million)	Loan (E million[a])
Swaziland Government	13.0	29.0
Swazi Nation (Tibiyo Taka Ngwana Fund)	13.0	13.0
Nigerian Government	4.0	—
Tate and Lyle Ltd	3.5	—
Coca Cola Export Corporation	1.7	—
Mitsui and Co. Ltd	1.5	—
Commonwealth Development Corporation	1.0	3.0
DEG (German Development Company)[b]	2.0	2.1
International Finance Corporation	0.4	7.0
EIB (European Investment Bank)	—	10.0
International Development Corporation/Credit Guarantee Insurance Corp. (SA)	—	20.5
Barclays Bank/Export Credit Guarantee Department (UK)	—	6.6
Total	40.1	91.2

Notes: a. Swaziland is a member of the Rand monetary area and its currency, the Lilangeni (plural Emalangeni), is on a par with the Rand.
b. Deutsche Gesellschaft für Wirtschaftliche Zusammenarbeit (Entwicklunggesellschaft) mbH.
Source: S.J.F. Winn, 'An Introduction to Simunye Sugar Estate', *Proceedings of the South African Sugar Technologists' Association*, June 1979.

Table 9.3: Swaziland: The Application of Funds for Simunye during the Development Period 1978–81

	Approximate Expenditure (per cent)	(E million)
Land development	8	10.0
Agricultural and harvesting equipment	9	10.0
Irrigation and drainage	19	23.0
Factory	24	30.0
Infrastructure and housing	24	29.0
Net working capital, pre-production expenses	16	20.0
Total	100	122.0

Source: Winn, 'Simunye'.

Simunye's achievement, for a complex and modern venture, is recorded in the crop performance data for 1982, its first year of operation at full capacity. Not only had all the deadlines for the various stages of field and mill development been met, but the data revealed that actual performance was in many cases better than the design parameters. While the total tonnage of cane milled and sugar made were marginally below, the sucrose content of the cane was within the acceptable range.[53] The mill extraction rate was above 95 (97.57) per cent, the overall recovery was above 84 (86.53) per cent, and mechanical efficiency was given as being 96.56 per cent. Such results have not always been evident in other parts of the world, where delays have had a very significant effect on overall costs and delayed receipt of income.[54]

The social benefits accruing from Simunye's completion are considerable. In spite of incorporating a high degree of mechanisation into the project, especially in field operations, RSSC has created jobs for 3,200 people and constructed two townships for them and their families, each with the infrastructure that is expected today — drinking water, electricity, sewerage disposal, roads, parkland and a wide range of sporting and recreational facilities. Moreover the corporation has built two schools, provided medical facilities and is running a training centre for 50 apprentices covering the whole spectrum of trades in the company. As the community grows so a radically new way of life becomes more firmly established.

All decisions regarding Swaziland's industry are taken by the Swaziland Sugar Association (SSA), a statutory body created by the Sugar Act of 1967 but neither administered nor financed by government. It is run by a Council consisting of equal numbers of growers' and millers' representatives, with an independent chairman having a casting vote (which has never been used); all decisions are in fact made jointly, and where there is no unanimity there is no decision. Sucrose quotas, which permit the cultivation of cane and control delivery to the mills, are issued by the Quota Board, on which growers and millers are represented. However, independent members nominated by the Minister responsible for the industry hold the majority when it comes to voting, so that public interest may ultimately control what is of public concern. As for the sales of sugar and molasses for the domestic market (which is small in spite of high *per capita* consumption[55]) and for export, these are the prerogative of the Association which also reviews the price received by the cane growers each season.

As events turned out, Swaziland was fortunate in the timing of its expansion, because the completion of Simunye coincided with a boom in the world market during which ISA quotas were suspended. When the quotas were reimposed in May 1981 Swaziland's BET — to which its annual quota is linked — had been raised just under 120,000 tonnes to 176,000 tonnes in accordance with its improved capacity and performance in the interim, and subsequent adjustments among exporting countries gave Swaziland a final quota of 220,000 tonnes for 1981.[56] If the figures for the country's domestic consumption (25,000 tonnes) and its guaranteed outlet under the terms of the Sugar Protocol to the Lomé Convention (120,000 tonnes) are added to this quota, it is evident that Swaziland has found markets for 90 per cent of its production. Moreover, as part of the Simunye package agreed when world prices were low, Tate and Lyle offered to purchase 250,000 tonnes over an unspecified period; for half the amount Tate and Lyle contracted to pay a price midway between the EEC price and the world price, and for the remainder the world price if the SSA took up the option.

Swaziland is not a sleeping partner in the sugar industry but an increasingly active one as the social and economic benefits spread in widening circles. The government has benefited from the normal taxation of company profits, and also since 1973 from a levy imposed on sugar export proceeds which yielded nearly E70 million (approximately US$85.4 million) in eight years. More important politically for a developing country, the government has recently become the major partner in the industry; in addition to its original stake of 65 per cent in the RSSC, it has acquired 50 per cent of the equity of the Mhlume Sugar Company and 40 per cent in Ubombo. These assets have brought it a dominant interest in the cane land as well: Simunye grows 88 per cent of its cane requirements; Ubombo grows 47 per cent of its supplies, and takes 12 per cent from the Tibiyo Taka Ngwana estate which it also manages; and Mhlume controls 72 per cent of its supplies, growing 38 per cent, receiving 25 per cent from SIS (jointly owned since 1982 by CDC and the Ngwenyama representing the Swazi nation) and a further 9 per cent from VIF. VIF's progress from being a direct CDC project to becoming a limited company wholly owned by the Swazi nation is fitting, final comment on a small country's determination to become economically independent; it has created a smallholder community within the traditional tribal system of land tenure, and has convinced its farmers of this new way forward.

Thailand

Thailand entered the world market in the early 1960s but made its real impact only after the sharp price rise of 1974. By expanding its production eightfold during the period 1963/4 to 1977/8[57] it now stands fourth in the developing world's league of sugar exporters, and intends to hold this position by continuing to export approximately 1.2 million tonnes a year. Thailand's reputation is therefore of recent origin and is all the more remarkable for a country that likes eating sugar and depends for about 40 per cent of its consumption on artisan sugar. Whether, however, the centrifugal industry can survive without government protection, given its present methods of operation, is uncertain. This case study differs from the preceding two in describing an industry which does not embrace the modern plantation — the milling and cane-growing sectors are entirely separate, with the mills taking all their cane from independent farmers — but concludes that, if Thailand is to become more competitive in the world market, both the government and the industry would do well to pay more attention to the principles of modern management as defined in Chapters 1, 4 and 6. What is required from the government is a more consistent long-term policy which relates prices to area and production in such a way that the industry as a whole will be forced to reduce its costs relative to world prices by adopting standards for each stage in the sugar cycle that are more in line with accepted modern practices, and by monitoring its own performance.

The reasons for the conspicuous increase in production that turned Thailand so swiftly into a world exporter are to be found in a combination unique to Thailand of, on the one hand, government initiative and, on the other, the response to that initiative from the private sector represented by certain entrepreneurial families[58] able to raise the necessary capital to build mills and by those farmers quick to grow more of the crop that promised good returns. The interaction between the government and the private sector has been close throughout. Determined to reduce the country's dependence on imported white sugar, the government took the first step in 1937 when it built Thailand's first centrifugal mill at Lampang in the North Region, and a second at Uttaradit in the north of the Central Region four years later; both factories were situated in artisan sugar areas where cane was an established crop, and both employed the sulphitation process so that raw sugar might be refined into white for local consumption. Because they believed it would be profitable, private companies followed government example, and moved into the sugar industry on a large scale in the post-Second World War years. Farmers in the vicinity of the new mills turned their backs on the artisan mills, and by the late 1950s the production of centrifugal sugar matched rapidly rising demand. Thailand entered the 1960s with a sugar surplus, which coincided with a very low price on the world market (roughly half the millers' production costs); so in 1962 the government banned the construction of new mills and introduced a cess on sugar production with a view to supporting domestic prices and encouraging greater productivity among farmers and millers. No control on sugar production was imposed, however. The cess was used to subsidise the export of surplus sugar and proved so successful, though unintentional, an incentive to further production that it was abandoned in 1966 when the government confirmed that its priorities remained a steady supply for the domestic market and the reduction of production costs. Again, the government did nothing to limit cane area and sugar production, and this fact, coupled with the attractive price paid for cane relative to other crops, encouraged the farmers to continue overproducing. The millers/exporters then brought pressure to bear, and in 1969 Thailand became an exporting member of the ISO in the hope that secure export sales would relieve the pressure on domestic prices. But the volume of exports permitted by the ISO was insufficient to absorb Thailand's surplus, and after 18 months the millers had persuaded the government to withdraw its membership so that they might look for additional markets. Then came the 1974 boom; whereupon the government reversed its earlier policies by imposing an export premium which, with the exception of six months in 1980 when all exports were banned in the wake of an exceptional drought, it has maintained on a sliding scale since.[59]

For the industry as a whole the upshot of these alternating, *ad hoc*, policies has been considerable protection, since at no point were effective measures taken to control output. No doubt such implicit protection has its attractions for the government, in view of the capital sums invested and the large number of farmers involved; but it has not been beneficial for the industry where inefficient practices have tended to become accepted procedure and the impetus for improvement has stultified. None the less, steady expansion has resulted in Thailand posessing an exceptionally modern milling sector: out of 44 mills, 15 have a capacity of 8,000 TCD or more, and a further 22 range from 2,000 to 7,900 TCD, a situation which may usefully be compared with Cuba's, where only 18 of 151 mills are reported as having a capacity of 7,000 TCD or more. With a total capacity of 200,000 TCD, the country can process up to 22 million tonnes of cane with ease during a 120-day season.

Sugar production is concentrated in a few localities. Though soil suitability and water availability are important factors for an upland crop that cannot tolerate the periodic flooding of the central plain, within these parameters a water supply sufficient to meet the needs of the large modern mills rather than the requirements of the crop itself appears to have been the decisive factor in determining where sugar is produced in quantity. Of the 15 mills mentioned as having a capacity of 8,000 TCD, eleven are situated in the two adjacent provinces of Kanchanaburi and Rajburi, along a short (and heavily polluted) stretch of the Mae Klong.[60] According to the 1978 Agricultural Census, these two provinces, together with the neighbouring provinces of Suphanburi and Nakhon Pathom, produce 54 per cent of the country's sugar. A further 16 per cent is produced in the two provinces of Chonburi and Rayong. All six (four in the west and two in the east) lie in the Central Region, which accounts for three-quarters of the country's centrifugal output.

Milling and cane growing have always been separate activities organised independently of each other. Loose reference is sometimes made to 'plantations' when the larger farms are discussed, but the modern plantation system as defined in Chapter 1 does not exist. It may be, given the structure of Thai society, that some of the entrepreneurs with a large stake in the mills also own large tracts of land where cane may be grown by tenant farmers, but the managerial supervision that would normally stem from an integrated organisation centred on the mill is absent.

Essentially, Thailand's cane-growing sector is a mixed one. There are three categories of farmers: the traditional farmers of the central plain who usually grow cane as well as other crops, and who themselves supply most of their labour, perhaps calling on mutual arrangements with neighbours at busy periods; the small farmers who have cleared and settled land in forest reserves,[61] who tend to be specialist cane farmers; and the large landholders who farm 50–200 hectares apiece and produce a range of upland crops besides sugar, relying solely on hired labour.[62] The large farmers exert a decisive influence in matters concerning the organisation of cane supplies and the annual agreement of cane prices, since they grow more than half the country's cane on holdings of 60 rai (9.2 hectares) upwards, though there are only 7,500 of them. Even so, the small farmers still dominate production, some 100,000 of them growing the remainder (46 per cent) on holdings of less than 60 rai, with more than 70,000 on holdings of less than 20 rai (3.2 hectares).[63] These labour-intensive farms make for a cane-growing sector in which mechanisation is not an issue; as wage rates are low throughout the industry,[64] most agricultural tasks are done everywhere by hand.

An account of the agronomic practices in Thailand should begin by pointing out that in many parts of the country cane is grown alongside other crops such as paddy, cassava and maize; these are short-seasoned intercrops which can be reduced in area to make way for cane should it offer in any one year a higher return. Normally, one plant and two ratoon crops are taken, though on the lighter, poorer soils of Chonburi the farmers take only one ratoon before replanting. The most commonly planted varieties are those from Australia, Taiwan and Hawaii, because Thailand has done little as yet to develop its own varieties to suit local conditions. Tractors are widely used to prepare the land for planting, the larger farmers hiring them out to the smaller farmers, but from this point on through the cane cycle very little mechanical equipment is used until trucks are brought in at harvest to transport the cane to the mills. Planting, weeding and the application of chemical fertiliser are all done by hand, though on a few of the larger farms and on some of the irrigated smallholdings in Suphanburi sprayers are used to apply herbicides. Harvesting too is done by hand, frequently by women who use special knives to cut the cane a few centimetres above the ground; piles of ten to twenty stalks are tied into bundles with green leaves from the tops, and later loaded into trucks, usually owned and driven by individual farmers, though smallholders may call in a neighbour or truck operator.

While labour remains abundant and cheap, the fact that cane growing is labour-intensive is not in itself a disadvantage, provided that agricultural tasks are properly carried out. By the agronomic standards presently prevailing in Thailand, they are. Yet cane yields are low, roughly 45–50 tonnes per hectare,[65] and ought to be a greater cause for concern than they appear to be. Clearly more attention needs to be paid to those measures that are accepted by more efficient producers elsewhere as part of their overall responsibility. In Thailand no serious effort has yet been directed by either the government or the industry towards raising yields by research into

better cane varieties, studying soil deficiencies and crop requirements and identifying the appropriate fertiliser, by providing
cheaper fertiliser and easier credit, by extending irrigation to reduce
the moisture stress that lowers both cane yield and sucrose content in
the dry season, or by expanding extension services so that farmers
might understand the need for more careful husbandry at certain
stages. The delivery of immature and/or stale cane to the mills is a
case in point. Plant cane is usually sown in the spring months before
the onset of the monsoon in May, to be harvested either after eleven
months at the end of the dry season or after 18 months, having
grown through another wet season; ratoons get seven to eight
months of active growth and time to mature if not cut before the
middle of the dry season. But the temptation on occasion has been to
cut immature plant and ratoon crops at the beginning of the dry
season, when sucrose content is still rising. The delivery of stale cane
causes a further reduction in sucrose content and is a serious
problem. Failure to schedule deliveries means that trucks may queue
for as much as 24 hours before unloading their cane directly on to the
feed conveyors, while cut cane lies in the fields. One study by the
FAO reported in 1970 that the period between cutting and grinding
averaged 66 hours, with a range from 34 to 98 hours. Another report
conducted in 1978 mentioned delays of two to fifteen days.[66]

Turning to the milling sector, it appears that, modern though the
mills are, they could operate more efficiently. At each stage of the
extraction process delays occur which could be put right with better
supervision. The production line is frequently interrupted by irregular cane supplies, machine breakdowns, a shortage of spare parts
and inadequate maintenance. A report submitted by Colombo Plan
experts to the Sugar Institute, Bangkok, in 1978 stated that on
average the mills lose 10–15 per cent of their operating time as the
result of such stoppages — a loss 'incomparably higher than any
other major producing country'.[67] The result for the industry as a
whole is a sugar yield that is well below average, for low cane yields,
low sucrose content and a poor extraction rate together give a final
figure of 4.6 tonnes sugar per hectare. One tonne of cane produces
only 84 kg of sugar, as compared with Cuba's 108 kg and Australia's 137.5 kg.

What Thailand's sugar industry evidently lacks is a unitary
approach that would tie mill and farmer together and hold them to a
common goal. It needs an overall system of organisation that must
stem from the mill where the large investment in machinery requires

an operational programme which cannot ever be as flexible as that obtaining out in the fields. What Thailand has got, however, is an untrammelled market system in which each unit, group or sector fights for itself with little thought for the consequences for the industry as a whole. The tenuous links between the mills and the farmers illustrate this well. The two are linked by intermediaries called quotamen, usually either headmen of the villages where cane is grown or big farmers in upland areas. Their task is to ensure that the mills receive all the cane they require. They are assigned quotas of 1,500 tonnes or more, which they may distribute as they wish among local farmers. They are normally expected to deliver 80 per cent of their quota before receiving payment from the mill, and from this they deduct their fee of Baht 10-20 (in January 1981 Baht 20.50 = US$1.00) per tonne before settling up with the growers. The arrangement is primarily a commercial one. From the mills' point of view it reduces the number of growers they each have to deal with from approximately 2,300 farmers to about 400 quota holders, and in effect it also serves to exempt them from any responsibility for scheduling cane deliveries or initiating extension services. While it is claimed with some justification that the quotamen play a small part in supplying inputs such as fertiliser and seed cane, in deciding the timing of the harvest and helping to organise the transport of the cane, these are all subsidiary to their chief activity which is to supply the cane for which they have contracted. From the small farmers' point of view it is a costly system. The quota fee, the interest charged on any credit advanced, the payment for cultivation and transport services, and the fact that payment for their cane is usually withheld until the end of harvest, add up to more than Baht 50 per tonne of cane. 'Although firm evidence is lacking, it is safe to assume that of the Baht 650 per tonne which the smallholder ought to receive in 1980/1 less than Baht 600 is usually paid and that the difference goes to the quotaman.'[68]

The sole point at which the government becomes directly involved with the farmers is in establishing the cane price at the beginning of the milling season. Relations between the government and both sectors of the industry have been described by one authority as more like those between business partners than between government and governed;[69] this goes some way towards explaining why the price is usually settled only after protracted negotiations between government officials, the millers and the farmers, represented by their trade associations.[70] In recent years the farmers have argued their case well, winning for themselves a quadrupling of the cane price between 1971 and 1981.[71] It is, in fact, widely accepted that the successful organisation of farmers into pressure groups led by the quotamen has contributed to the expansion of cane more than any other factor. Yet such freedom to negotiate has a negative aspect; it leads — on the industry's part — to a proliferation of interested parties whose vociferousness has contributed to the general absorption with short-term gain at the expense of any long-term plans for improvement.

On the government side matters are complicated by the fact that there is no central policy, no one body with responsibility for the sugar industry. Various government departments control certain functions, and if there is an overlord it is the Deputy Prime Minister with Special Responsibility for Economic Affairs. The ministry most involved with sugar is the Ministry of Commerce; on a year-to-year basis it decides what proportion of total output shall be reserved for the local market, and how much millers may produce for export; more important, it appears to have the final word on prices, though the Ministry of Industry shoulders the burden of renegotiating the cane price. The Ministry of Commerce also attempts to maintain fixed prices for white sugar on the domestic market at both wholesale and retail levels, though these price controls are not completely effective since there is some movement in relation to world prices; and finally it settles the price the two export organisations must pay the mills for their raws, and the level at which the export premium comes into operation. As for the Ministry of Agriculture, it plays a subsidiary role with its various activities divided between departments which overlap very little; its function seems to be to cushion the impact in the countryside of decisions taken by the Ministry of Commerce, rather than to initiate real change. The Sugar Institute, financed from export premium proceeds, was established in 1968 to superintend the activities of millers and farmers, to collect statistical material, and to organise research and extension services, but to date its influence upon the industry has been slight.[72]

The prices agreed by the government, unsupported by any effective measures to limit production, have permitted cane to emerge as one of the most profitable crops — if not the most profitable — in recent years.[73] Both the mills and the farmers have done well for themselves. In spite of the quotamen, the farmers in 1980/1 were able to make a profit ranging from Baht 32,655 (US$1,600) per hectare on the smallest, irrigated holdings in Suphanburi to Baht 7,015 (US$342) per hectare on the poorer soils of Chonburi. Such profits would be in order if they reflected a productivity that matched or was close to that achieved by other exporters, but they do not. In their critical report the Colombo Plan experts highlight the reality with this example:

> In 1977 an Australian grower received Baht 277 per ton of cane which yielded 140 kg of sugar. A Thai farmer received Baht 300 per ton of cane which yielded only 83 kg of sugar. To be competitive with Australia in the raw sugar market, the Thai farmer ought to have been paid only Baht 223 per ton. As it was, the Australian mill paid Baht 2,693 of cane cost per ton of sugar and the Thai miller Baht 3,614.

Since it would appear that the mills have never been allowed to suffer any real loss, the ultimate loser must have been the government through its subsidies.

> To illustrate the sums involved, consider the year 1980. Due to an exceptionally bad crop only 450,000 tons of raw sugar was exported. The average price was Baht 6,584 per ton, or Baht 658 per bag. Average production costs are not known but are estimated at Baht 964 per bag, including a 15 per cent profit for the mills and deducting receipts from molasses. Excluding the profits the costs would be Baht 837 per bag or a loss of Baht 178 per bag, amounting to a total loss for the country of over Baht 800 million.

As government subsidies are given on spot sales, not on forward contracts, the total loss would have been less. Nevertheless, the fact remains that the mills (and the growers) profit in good years and do not have to take the losses in bad.[74]

Thailand's agriculture stands at the crossroads. The contribution of the agricultural sector has until very recently rested on the farmers' ability to apply familiar techniques to a steadily expanding area. As it appears that most of the cultivable land has now been brought into production, any further improvement in output can only come about through raising yields. But yields for all crops remain low across the board compared with those in other countries, and there is little sign of improvement. Sugar yields for example have remained static for the past 20 years. For a country like Thailand, in which agriculture still forms the backbone of the economy, generates at least one-quarter of GDP, employs three-quarters of the working population, and provides more than half the export earnings, this low productivity is a serious matter. It is generally agreed that the farmer responded marvellously to external demand once he had been brought into the exchange economy.[75] But the farmer has now reached the point where, if he is to increase his output, he has to change his techniques; and to do this he needs guidance to sustain his dynamism. As Muscat has pointed out in discussing the farmer's contribution to the post-Second World War expansion of upland crops, of which sugar cane is one,

> the farmer can respond only to the technology presented to him within the limitations of economic rationality as determined by the market; he cannot compensate for the ignorance still prevailing about problems of agriculture on Thailand's poor soils or for the weakness of institutions charged with educating him.[76]

What Muscat wrote in the mid-1960s is very relevant to the situation in which the sugar industry finds itself today.

The government has recently shown signs of wanting to grasp the nettle of stable production. It intends to tackle the problem on two fronts, through a national production plan linked to a policy for cane prices that will reflect world market conditions, and by setting an example through the four state mills in helping the small farmers improve their performance. A five-year plan, beginning in the crop year 1982/3, is intended to bring farmers and millers into closer and therefore more competitive contact with the world market. Production will be divided into three parts, roughly 600,000 tonnes of refined white sugar for the domestic market, another 600,000 tonnes of raw sugar for export under long-term contracts negotiated by a new company in which government, farmers and millers are equally represented, and any additional raw sugar (most probably never less than another 600,000 tonnes except in bad years) for export through the existing private channels. Under the new scheme to be promoted by the new company — the Thai Cane and Sugar Corporation — the farmers will be paid a preliminary price of Baht 350 per tonne of cane; at the end of September in each year the price will be reassessed, and the farmers will be paid any balance due once the income from all sales in domestic and foreign markets are known. The income will be divided on a 70:30 basis between farmers and millers. As a spokesman for the Ministry of Commerce commented:

The past practice was often plagued with problems and disputes, but the new system will ensure full fairness. Planters will now have to bear the adverse consequences of a world price slump or enjoy the benefits of a price boom as much as the millers.[77]

The government also intends that stronger links should be created between the four mills it controls and the farmers delivering to them. All four already buy cane according to sugar content instead of weight and there is evidence that the farmers have begun to respond, delivering cane with a sucrose content about 10 per cent above the national average. The Suphanburi mill has gone a step further, giving assistance to those farmers nearest the mill with holdings of less than 100 rai (16.1 hectares); it deals directly with them (doing away with the quotamen), offers them extension services, and also provides them with cheap credit which is tied to specific field operations and may not be used for any other purpose. The results have been impressive, for these assisted farmers have grown cane from which 130 kg per tonne can be extracted, compared with the 105 kg from each tonne delivered by the big farmers further away from the mill, who do not receive assistance and generally rely on quotamen.[78] Doubtless the government has in mind the extension of this system to its other mills. To underline its commitment to a better way of doing things, it has announced plans to extend the Suphanburi mill from 3,500 TCD to 10,000 TCD.[79]

Whether the government's plans will bring about a noticeable improvement in productivity remains to be seen. There has been no mention of establishing measures to control production (the absence of which negated so many government initiatives since the late 1950s), merely a statement about how production is to be allocated. Clearly the government hopes that its new pricing policy will bring about some contraction in cane area, and that the private mills and those farmers supplying them will follow the example set by the government mills. It may yet prove necessary for the government to impose its views more firmly before the industry will improve its performance. The energies that originally found expression in commercial initiative and market acumen need now to be channelled in a more productive direction, before a formula that is right for Thailand, in which modern management principles play their part, comes into its own.

Conclusion

Since the Second World War the cane producers of the developing world have demonstrated an ability to meet rapidly rising domestic demand, and some of them have also produced a surplus for export. The traditional producers have been joined by a large number of countries keen to establish a viable import-substitution industry. The routes to success are diverse but most share one feature — a unitary approach that co-ordinates both sides of industry (cane production and processing) without necessarily organising them under common ownership. This is fundamental to the formation of a structure within which all parties can operate constructively, which in turn fosters an environment congenial to new ideas. Such a structure need not necessarily be based upon the plantation system, but inevitably it will depend in the broadest sense upon a system such as that outlined in Chapter 6, in which all participants are agreed on a common goal and conform to the rules and quotas laid down by the body as a whole. The final measure of success is to be found in the acceptance of standards and adherence to practices that maximise the output of the production unit. It may be a capital-intensive mill complex established in southern Africa within the last decade, which must aim for high yields in order to justify its costs. Or it may be a small Belizean farm no bigger than 6 hectares, operating a low input/low output system, which none the less provides a sound route to viability within its national framework.

Sometimes state policies create an environment in which it becomes difficult for producers to operate efficiently. Where government is ambivalent towards the sugar industry, as in Jamaica and Trinidad, production has slumped. Where government has allowed political considerations to override economic, as in the state sector of the Dominican Republic, performance cannot match that obtaining in the private plantation sector. In both cases, if government were to adopt a more positive approach, the application of modern management techniques to current practices would bring about an improvement in output. And this holds true for almost every situation where low yields presently prevail.

Though this book is primarily concerned with the contribution that large agricultural units can make, it envisages a continuing role for the small farmer. Indeed his role, operating in a range of contrasting political and economic situations, is increasing. In Cuba, for example, alongside the dominant state farms and in spite of political propaganda that has threatened their existence for the past 20 years, the farmers in the private sector have thrived and are more productive than the state farms. In Jamaica and Trinidad, where the state plantations are no longer pulling their weight, small farmers grow a surprisingly large proportion of the cane.[80] In the Dominican Republic, outgrowers are steadily increasing in number; while those who supply the state mills may be described as speculative farmers from whom high yields are not expected, those supplying the private sector are achieving satisfactory results. In southern Africa most of the new producers that rely on the modern plantation estate for the bulk of their sugar output have also established smallholder schemes that are proving very successful. And in Thailand the industry which depends entirely on independent farmers buys almost half its cane from small farmers with less than 10 hectares each. What most of these farmers are learning, though as yet to varying degrees, is the importance of operating in groups rather than as single units, and conforming to a set of practices which have proved to yield good results.

There are, however, situations in which the unitary system is largely absent; both sides show very little awareness of the problems faced by the other, and yields are lower than they need be. The lack of a co-ordinated structure for Thailand's industry has provided the millers and farmers with the opportunity to make large profits, and these in turn have encouraged the rapid expansion of the industry to its present size; but it has done very little to increase productivity. Thailand's industry has now reached the stage in its development where some mechanism is required to link the two sectors, so that together they may adjust to a common goal and work to agreed standards that will ensure greater productivity. While an expanding population and a disproportionately large agricultural sector continue to shape Thailand's economic policies, its cane farmers cannot aspire to become owner–operators like those who underpin Queensland's highly efficient industry,[81] but they can progress part of the way given an organisational framework that promotes co-operation.

In other parts of the Third World, where population pressure is less extreme than in South East Asia, the modern plantation, which guarantees uniformity of production on a large scale, has become a necessary and important feature of the economy. There are three environments to which it is particularly suited. The first is where physical conditions dictate a measure of control over the environment that is beyond the scope of the individual farmer, usually over water whether for drainage or irrigation. Guyana's industry could not have developed without the plantation system,[82] nor could more recent ventures such as Kenana in Sudan. The second is in frontier conditions where 'empty' lands and a policy of fast development demand heavy investment, much mechanisation and the introduction of additional labour. Brazil offers many examples of modern frontier plantations which are being created with a measure of old-fashioned ruthlessness that disregards the social cost. The third is in Africa, where the need to improve the quality of life in many rural areas has led governments to insist that well-defined social and economic objectives have their place in every new project. Almost every African country setting up its own sugar industry may be mentioned in this context, though developments in Kenya, Malawi, Swaziland, Zambia and Zimbabwe provide some of the best examples to date.

Arguments are now being advanced that urge the adoption of smaller units rather than monolithic enterprises, of which Kenana is but the latest example. Development experts are also coming round to the view that the pace of progress should be set with reference to sure foundations rather than to any breakthrough that cannot be sustained. What matters most is that the production unit should enjoy proper management and have effective access to up-to-date technology. This applies with equal force to the smallholding and the large modern venture; both have their place in the further development of the cane sugar industry.

Notes

1. This is not the place to examine the early history of plantations and the parallel institution of slavery which were developed from the sixteenth century onwards in the Caribbean, and southwards into South America, to produce sugar for the metropolitan powers of Spain, Portugal and Britain. But it is relevant to point out that political independence came much earlier to some sugar colonies than to others. For example, Brazil became independent in 1822, having been ruled since the sixteenth century by Portugal; the Dominican Republic in 1821, having been ruled by Spain since 1492; Cuba in 1898, following intervention by the USA, having been ruled by Spain for over 300 years. But Jamaica and Trinidad became independent only in 1962, and Barbados and Guyana in 1966.

Three works are helpful: N. Deerr, *The History of Sugar* (2 vols., Chapman and Hall, London, 1949 and 1950); A. Hugill, *Sugar and All That: a History of Tate and Lyle* (Gentry Books, London, 1978); B. Scott, 'The Organisational Network: a Strategy Perspective for Development', unpublished PhD thesis, Harvard University Graduate School of Business Administration, 1979. Hugill and Scott provide valuable information about company activities in the twentieth century (Tate and Lyle in Jamaica and Trinidad, Bookers in Guyana, respectively).

2. Peak production for the four were (tonnes, raw value):

Barbados	1967	211,862
Guyana	1971	394,540
Jamaica	1966	508,247
Trinidad	1965	254,608

Source: ISO, *World Sugar Economy: Structure and Policies*, vol. 1, *Central and South America* (ISO, London, 1982).

These figures may be compared with the 1979–81 averages in n. 3 below.
3. Caricom yields 1975–81 (tonnes sugar per hectare) were as follows:

	1975	1976	1977	1978	1979	1980	1981
Barbados	6.38	6.63	7.50	6.50	7.31	7.09	6.06
Guyana	7.59	6.39	4.96	6.11	5.54	5.02	5.52
Jamaica	5.90	5.62	5.80	6.95	6.19	4.82	4.53
Trinidad	5.09	6.03	5.56	4.35	4.24	3.35	3.32

Source: ISO, *World Sugar Economy*, vol. 1.

For a comparison with other producers mentioned in the Western hemisphere, the production and yields 1979–81 for selected countries were as follows:

	Tonnes cane per hectare 1979–81	Tonnes sugar per hectare 1979–81	Production (tonnes) 1979–81	Exports (tonnes) 1979–81
Barbados	67.15	7.25	116,490	95,690
Belize	39.63	4.23	105,600	98,493
Brazil	54.80	4.96	8,119,356	2,424,517
Cuba	50.85	5.53	7,510,000	6,843,983
Dominican Republic	56.97	6.12	1,106,803	897,243
Guyana	69.66	5.36	307,604	275,090
Jamaica	58.35	5.18	243,808	150,983
Trinidad and Tobago	43.70	3.64	116,806	75,128

Source: ISO, *World Sugar Economy*, vol. 1.

4. *Barbados* left the estates in private hands, but in 1970 brought all the mills, which had in the majority of cases been owned by groups of estate owners, under the control of one company Barbados Sugar Factories (BSF) Ltd; shares in BSF are held by all sections of the industry, with 18% for the owners of cane lands.

Guyana nationalised Bookers, who controlled more than 80% of the country's production, in 1976.

Jamaica in 1971 acquired the lands of the island's three largest plantation-mill complexes accounting for over 50% of production, and in 1976 created the National Sugar Company (NSC) to take over all Jamaica's factories. (The two largest complexes — Frome and Clarendon/Monymusk — accounted for 33% of the island's output and represented Tate and Lyle's investment in Jamaica.)

Trinidad made an offer in 1972 for 51% of the shares of Caroni Ltd (a Tate and Lyle subsidiary, processing 88% of the estates' and small farmers' cane, and producing 90% of the island's sugar) and in 1976 acquired the remaining 49%.

5. In Jamaica the Labour Party bought the lands of the three largest estates in 1971, but leased them back to the companies pending their future subdivision. Under

the People's National Party 23 cane-growing co-operatives were eventually created in 1976; but they were considered an economic failure by the incoming Labour Party in 1980, and disbanded in November 1981. The mills have since resumed all management and investment functions for cane production along traditional plantation lines. See W. Higgins, 'Worker Participation in Jamaican Sugar Production', *Rural Development Participation Review 1980* (United Sugar Workers' Co-operative Council, Jamaica), vol. 1, part 2; *Sugar World* (GATT-Fly, Toronto), vol. 4, no. 5, December 1981; *F.O. Licht's International Sugar Report* (hereafter referred to as *Licht's*), vol. 113, no. 35, November 1981, p. 752.

6. In *Barbados* the importance of tourism makes the services sector dominant, contributing 67% of GDP; mining and manufacturing account for 12.2% and agriculture 12.4%. Sugar, molasses and rum account for 52% by value of exports (sugar alone for 45%).

In *Guyana* agriculture remains the largest sector of the economy, contributing 16.5% to GNP, with mining accounting for 12.5% and manufacturing 9.7%. However, bauxite and alumina account for 49% of exports, sugar for 28% and rice 10%.

In *Jamaica* the industrial sector contributes 37% of GNP, and alumina and bauxite account for 72% of all exports; sugar accounts for about 8%.

In *Trinidad* oil and gas have pushed the industrial sector's contribution up to 62% of GNP, leaving services with 35% and agriculture only 3%. Sugar accounts for about 6% of export earnings.

Third World Diary 1981 (Third World Foundation, London 1980).

7. I. Smith, 'Can the West Indies' Sugar Industry Survive?', *Oxford Bulletin of Economics and Statistics*, 1976, Part 2, pp. 134-7.

8. *Barbados* is making every effort to restore sugar production to 150,000 tonnes and relies on the estate sector (estates range from 4 to 800 hectares, though 100 hectares is the average, and provide 85% of the cane) to improve field operations and mechanisation at harvest when labour is in short supply. Barbados is recognised in the Caribbean as the leader in cane technology. A new refinery opened in 1982. *Licht's*, vol. 113, no. 27, 14 September 1981, p. 577.

Guyana, given its massive investment in the drainage and irrigation infrastructure for sugar and the low returns from its second major crop, rice, must continue to use its sugar assets wisely in the face of low world sugar prices. It sends about 50% of its surplus to the EEC, and sells the rest on the free market. In 1982 the EEC paid the ACP countries £235 per tonne; the price the ACP countries received on the free market was £93 per tonne. Yet the cost of producing a tonne of sugar in Guyana was estimated to be £230. See 'Britain's bitter role in sugar's failure', *The Times*, 31 August 1982, and subsequent correspondence on 3, 7, 10 and 14 September.

Jamaica had to import sugar from the USA in 1981 and 1982 in order to meet domestic demand and its commitment to the EEC which for the present it is unwilling to relinquish. Unaided, the industry on its present showing is unlikely to make the progress the government hopes for, which means that government must choose between further subsidies and fundamental reorganisation. Several proposals have been put forward. Tate and Lyle have suggested that several estates switch to more profitable but equally labour intensive agricultural production. Gulf and Western have offered to purchase the Frome mill, at 6,500 TCD the largest in the country. Government is considering these proposals, as well as remedial measures of its own ranging from total divestment of the sugar mills to private industry to the closure of one or two sugar complexes in the hope of stabilising the rest. ISO, *World Sugar Economy*, vol. 1, p. 39.

Trinidad, alarmed at the industry's swift decline, is seriously considering radical plans to restructure the industry which centre on reducing mill capacity by 25% and breaking up the state plantations into private farms which would go in for mixed farming and cattle rearing besides growing cane. *Licht's*, vol. 113, no. 27, 14 September 1981, p. 577.

9. In 1981 the leading cane sugar exporters were (tonnes, raw value):

	Production	Exports
Cuba	7,925,634	7,071,445
Australia[a]	3,508,551	2,982,057
Brazil	8,726,381	2,670,049
Philippines	2,376,064	1,277,593
Thailand	1,702,192	1,154,858
Dom. Rep.	1,107,609	864,034
South Africa[a]	1,987,241	736,768
Mauritius	609,144	458,640
Swaziland	367,485	344,892
Guyana	320,168	281,622
Zimbabwe	391,320	164,226
Malawi	177,323	131,354
Jamaica	204,010	124,512
India	5,991,237	105,882

Note: a. Classified as developed producer, included for comparison.
Source: ISO, *Sugar Year Book 1981*.

10. For example, the Sao Martinho mill, owned by the Ometta family, is reputedly the largest mill in the world with a throughput of 24,000 tonnes daily. Almost half the cane processed is grown on its own 37,000 hectares where 7,500 workers are employed. *Sugar y Azucar*, June 1980, p. 15.

11. The original programme to reduce oil imports by raising alcohol production (one of several measures) was launched in 1975 and given additional momentum after President Figueiredo was elected in March 1979. Progress has been good, but not as fast as envisaged. Sugar production rose from 6.9 million tonnes in 1974 to 8.8 million tonnes in 1977; for the five years 1977–81 it averaged 8.0 million tonnes, edging up again in 1982; the estimate for the crop year 1983/4 (June-May) was 9.4 million tonnes. Alcohol production stood at approximately 0.660 billion litres for the years 1972/3–1976/7, then doubled in 1978/9 to 1.47 billion litres; by 1982/3 it had reached 5.2 billion and the estimate for 1983/4 was 7.2 billion litres.

12. In 1981 sugar production was 8.726 million tonnes and alcohol 4.1 billion litres. Cane occupied 3.2 million hectares or 6% of total crop land, and of this sugar accounted for 1.73 million hectares. By 1985 sugar is scheduled to increase by a further 5.275 million tonnes (by 60%) and alcohol by 6.5 billion litres (by 154%). Assuming yields remain much the same (an average 55 tonnes cane per hectare 1979–81) the percentage increases in output will require an additional 3.243 million hectares.

(In November 1981 the Minister of Industry announced that the target of 10.7 billion litres of alcohol had been put back by up to two years because of a shortage of government funds.)

13. *Sugar y Azucar*, December 1981, p. 18.

14. The IAA comes under the budgetary control of the Ministry of Industry and Commerce, but otherwise it is run independently by its Deliberative Council, a small body consisting of members from the Cabinet of the President, from the mills and plantations, with its president appointed by the President himself. R.F. Colson, 'The Proalcool Programme: a Response to the Energy Crisis', *Bank of London and South American Review*, vol. 15, no. 11/81, May 1981.

15. Brazil's ability to export its new technology is discussed from many angles in H. Rothman, R. Greenshields and F.R. Callé, *The Alcohol Economy* (Frances Pinter,

London, 1983), pp. 51–3, 89–104 and 150–2.

16. Following the Reciprocity Treaty of 1903 (by which America and Cuba extended to the other a 20% preferential tariff) American investment flowed into Cuba, with the result that by the late 1920s it was responsible for 70% of Cuba's mill capacity. Juan Martinez-Alier, *Haciendas, Plantations and Collective Farms*, Library of Peasant Studies No. 2 (Frank Cass, London, 1977), p. 103.

Martinez-Alier provides a thoughtful analysis of Cuba's pre-revolutionary sugar industry, and goes on to argue that post-revolutionary Cuba did not turn its back on sugar. He regards the poor production of the early 1960s as reflecting the dislocation of revolution (*émigré* technicians withdrawn, mills dismantled, the hiatus of land reform, harvests disrupted because of a serious shortage of labour). Castro's rhetoric advocating diversification merely masked what he and the industrialists knew: that Cuba could only go forward from a position of strength, based on a sugar industry capable of earning the necessary foreign exchange for the development of other sectors.

17. H.D. Rodriguez, 'Cuba: Development and Building of New Sugar Mills', *World Sugar Journal* (Special Edition, Cuban Sugar Industry at a Glance), February 1982, pp. 18–20; *Licht's*, vol. 113, no. 36, 11 December 1981, p. 777.

18. See n. 3 above for a comparison with other countries.

According to the most up-to-date report, strenuous efforts in the agricultural sector (more attention to preparation of the seedbed, taking fewer ratoons, pursuing more efficient weeding and fertilisation) have helped raise yields a little — to 52 tonnes cane and 5.5 tonnes sugar per hectare. Eduardo David, 'Sugar Production in Cuba', *Sugar y Azucar*, February 1983, pp. 100–8.

19. G.B. Hagelberg, 'Sugar and the Cuban Economy', *F.O. Licht International Sugar Economic Year Book and Directory 1979*; Hidalgo L. Ariza, 'The Structure of the Sugar Sector in Cuba', Proceedings of the First World Sugar Farmers' Conference, Guadalajara, May 1981.

20. Two reports have provided most of the material for this section: E.M. Brook and W.R. Ringlien, 'The Sugar Industry in the Dominican Republic', *Licht's*, vol. 111, no. 34, 30 November 1979, pp. 659–66; C.D. Scott, *Tecnologia, Empleo y Distribucion de Ingresos en la Industria Azucarera de La Republica Dominicana* (Organizacion International del Trabajo, Programa Regional del Empleo para America Latina y El Caribe, PREALC/158, Septiembre 1978).

21. Furfural is an aldehyde which may be produced from cane bagasse (the fibrous residue left after the juice has been extracted). Before 1966 its major use was in the manufacture of nylon; once it became possible to make nylon directly from petrochemicals, furfural was increasingly used in the manufacture of resins where high temperatures and acid resistance are required. It is also used as a binder for cores of plastic moulds, and serves as a selective solvent in oil refining, pharmaceutical production and in the preparation of fungicides. Scott, *Tecnologia*, p. 15.

22. Cane yields fell from 62.1 tonnes in 1969 to 48.5 tonnes in 1973. Ibid., p. 5.

Brook and Ringlien confirm declining yields during this period: 'Overall cane yield per cultivated hectare, 45.5 tonnes per hectare, has declined by nearly 5% annually over the 1963–1965 to 1973–1975 seasons. Discrepancies in information from different sources are due to the poor quality of data reported and the fact that an increasing portion of the cane area is not being harvested.' Brook and Ringlien, 'Dominican Sugar', p. 660. Yields appear to have improved since, see n. 3 above.

23. These percentages are provided by the Federacion de Colonos Azucareros (FEDOCA), the tenant farmers' organisation to which 10 of the 11 regional farmers' associations are affiliated. According to FEDOCA, 7,000 FEDOCA farmers grow some 3.5 million tonnes of cane, producing 385,000 tonnes sugar. The farmers not affiliated to FEDOCA are the 1,300 members of the Asociacion de Colonos de Central Romana. *Sugar y Azucar*, November 1981, p. 49.

24. The supply of *colonos'* cane to the CEA mills rose from 609,126 tonnes in

1968 to 3,913,110 tonnes in 1978. Scott, *Tecnologia*, p. 6.

25. Brook and Ringlien, 'Dominican Sugar', p. 662.

26. The *colonos* supplying Central Romana may be divided into four groups: one landowning family supplies between 80,000 and 100,000 tonnes p.a.; a second group supplies between 30,000 and 40,000 tonnes each, while a third produces between 10,000 and 20,000 tonnes apiece. The smallest *colonos* supply between 5 and 1,000 tonnes each.

In 1977 there were approximately 600 *colonos* supplying Central Romana, and in addition some local employees had received stock in the new company. Scott, *Tecnologia*, pp. 46-7. If the figure of 1,300 *colonos* given by FEDOCA (see n. 23 above) is approximately correct, then G & W appears to be making progress with its land distribution programme.

27. In 1977 outgrower yields at La Romana varied between 42 and 44.5 tonnes per hectare, compared with 47 tonnes on the estate. Scott, *Tecnologia*, p. 47.

28. Ibid., pp. 20-1 and Table 8.

29. Ibid., pp. 24-5 and 34.

30. Ibid., Tables 7 and 8.

31. In 1974, when the number of grinding days was identical in the CEA mills and Central Romana (186 days), the proportion of grinding days lost by the state sector was 12.9% compared with 0.9% at Central Romana. Ibid., p. 35.

32. Brook and Ringlien, 'Dominican Sugar', p. 663.

33. A survey in 1967 showed that 72% of La Romana's work-force were Haitians (15% of its total work-force being Haitian seasonal workers) whereas only 64% of CEA's workers were Haitians (16% seasonal). More Haitians have settled at La Romana for two reasons: a greater opportunity for work in the slack season, either in the furfural plant or in the crop diversification scheme growing crops for the local market; and better pay. In December G & W paid a piece-rate to cutters of RD\$1.37 per ton, compared with CEA's rate of RD\$1.35. For a worker who remained at La Romana for the entire harvest, various bonuses and fringe benefits raised his earnings by as much as 31% of the basic wage. This would include an additional lump sum payment of 10 days' average earnings at the end of the harvest and a cash payment at Christmas. CEA paid a less generous lump sum and no Christmas bonus. Scott, *Tecnologia*, pp. 52-3.

34. In 1976 the average cost of sugar production in the state sector was US 10.7 cents per lb (at 1978 constant prices). The average price on the world market was 7.8 cents/lb; at the same time INESPRE paid the mills 6.0 cents/lb for brown sugar and 7.7 cents/lb for refined. INESPRE then doubled the price to the wholesaler (12.7 cents/lb for brown and 14.2 cents for refined) and the consumer eventually paid 14.0 cents/lb or 17.0 cents/lb respectively. Brook and Ringlien, 'Dominican Sugar', pp. 663 and 665.

In order to improve on low world prices and bring an element of stability to its trading, the Republic is looking for more long-term contracts similar to the one signed in 1979 with Venezuela to supply over 200,000 tonnes in that year at a reported price of 11 cents/lb (c.i.f.). Otherwise CEA and the Vicini group sell their sugar on a public tender basis to local sugar brokers representing international brokerage firms, while La Romana is protected to a greater degree through an integrated marketing arrangement with refiners in the USA.

35. Report by Bookers Agricultural and Technical Services Ltd., Parts I and II, commissioned by CEA in 1975.

36. Sugar exports account for 1-2% of South Africa's foreign exchange earnings, and for 58-66% of Mauritius's:

	Year	Value of sugar exports (US$ 000)	Value of total exports (US$ m)
South Africa	1979	184,133	18,397
	1980	497,262	25,680
	1981	295,280	20,856
Mauritius	1979	251,220	376.57
	1980	281,882	434.70
	1981	189,875	323.80

Sources: *FAO Trade Yearbook 1981; IMF Direction of Trade Statistics Yearbook 1983.*

37. South Africa irrigates 15% of its cane, Mauritius none.

38. South Africa suffered a severe drought in 1980 which reduced production in 1980 and 1981 to the point where South Africa had to import 21,000 tonnes from Zimbabwe to meet commitments. Production had recovered by 1982. ISO, *World Sugar Economy: Structure and Policies*, vol. 2, *Africa* (ISO, London, 1983), p. 41.

39. Average annual production for 1961-3 was 624,689 tonnes, for 1971-3 715,163 tonnes, and the estimate for 1981-3 is 692,114 tonnes. Ibid., p. 29.

40. South Africa's research station at Mt Edgecombe is renowned for its varietal work, and its research into diseases and pests affecting cane. Naturally, many neighbouring sugar industries benefit.

41. The two groups are Tongaat-Hulett and C.G. Smith Sugar Ltd.

42. See Chapter 7 for an account of Mumias — Kenya's most successful sugar venture and a good example of a nucleus estate.

43. See Chapter 8 for a brief reference to the high capital costs of new projects. In 1976 the World Bank suggested an upper limit of US$1,200 per tonne of sugar capacity: 'Adding new production capacity through new development of support infrastructure and factories in areas not previously producing sugar: investment costs for a 100,000 tonne unit is estimated at US$950-1,200 per tonne of sugar capacity depending on the extent of irrigation, transport infrastructure and maturation period of crop.' Choeng H. Chung and Ezriel Brook, 'The World Sugar Market: Review and Outlook for Bank Group Lending', Draft, 16 December 1976. Using this costing, and allowing say a further 10% for inflation, the total for a project of Kenana's size would be US$435.6 million.

44. The nominal capital of the Kenana Sugar Company, November 1978 (expressed in percentages):

Sudan government	32.21
Kuwait	18.52
Saudi Arabia	18.24
Arab Investment Co. (Riyadh)	13.69
Sudan Development Corp.	8.05
Lonhro Ltd	3.24
Nissho-Iwai Ltd	1.14
Gulf Fisheries Co., WLL (Kuwait)	1.14
Unsubscribed and unpaid	3.77
	100.00

Source: Karl Wohlmuth, 'Der Staat in peripheren Okonomien und die Transnationalen Konzerne: Interaktionen am Beispiel der Kenana Sugar Corporation, Sudan', Research Report no. 7, October 1979, University of Bremen.

45. *Sugar y Azucar* devoted the whole of its February 1981 issue to Kenana. It emphasized (1) the international array of contractors, (2) the capital and expertise required to establish the infrastructure needed to support a future population of 60,000, and (3) the modernity of the project (as exemplified by the factory equipment and the emphasis on mechanisation in the field). Water is brought by a 29-km supply channel to the project, and delivered by a network of subsidiary canals, contour channels and field furrows. All stages of cultivation are mechanised, including planting which is unusual; 75% of the cane is cut by machine; both harvesters and loaders off-load into 24-tonne trucks driven on to the fields which take the cane direct to the mill (such one-step transport from field to factory — doing away with in-field trailers delivering to roadside trucks — is rarely attempted). In the mill the designers opted for milling trains rather than diffusers, as these were considered more flexible should stoppages or appreciable changes in the rate of throughput arise. The mill operates for $7\frac{1}{2}$ months a year, but if further expansion to 500,000 tonnes capacity is undertaken, it may eventually run for 11 months.

46. The two older complexes suffer from a lack of spare parts, too few overhauls and an erratic cane supply from numerous tenant farmers. The two newer mills are experiencing trouble with some of their automated machinery. More seriously, they have been badly sited; settlement in the cracking clays has seriously affected the alignment of machines, requiring costly repairs. Moreover, cane yields in both vicinities are low as the result of poor management, irregular water supplies and insufficient field equipment. *Licht's Special Report*, 'An Outline of Expansion Plans in the World Sugar Industry', June 1978; *Licht's*, vol. 113, no. 3, 22 January 1981.

47. At Kaleya the first group of farmers arrived in 1983 after the first cane harvest. They will work as cadets for a year before being given their land.

48. For an authoritative account of CDC's involvement in Swaziland from the 1950s see Sir William Rendell, *The History of the Commonwealth Development Corporation 1948–1972* (Heinemann, London, 1976), pp. 186–200. Rendell describes the protracted negotiations that finally led to the Swaziland Administration being granted a sugar quota by the South African government in December 1957. In June 1959 the Mhlume Sugar Company was formed jointly by CDC and Sir J.L. Hulett and Sons Ltd. (the largest company in the South African sugar industry). Mhlume began as a Hulett subsidiary, but was taken over by CDC when it acquired the majority shareholding in 1965; CDC bought the remaining 10% from Hulett in 1966.

49. The original 405 hectares — 1000 acres — have since become three freehold units of 189.5, 140 and 97.5 hectares respectively. Swaziland Sugar Association, 1981.

50. Swaziland statistics refer to sucrose not sugar: sucrose figures may be converted to sugar as 1.17:1.00.

51. In 1982 the farmer's average income per hectare of cane was E696 (approximately US\$733), 14.5% down on his 1981 income. As the farmer cultivates an average 3.6 hectares, his average income in 1982 — excluding income from other sources — was E2,433 (US\$2,636). I am grateful to Joe Mulholland, CDC's Assistant Natural Resources Adviser, for so patiently providing all the information concerning CDC's activities in Malawi, Swaziland and Zambia.

52. It is interesting to note that improvements in irrigation techniques may eventually bring about a reduction in the water required by a given area for a given output. It would then be possible to expand the cane area.

It could be that as Simunye Sugar Estate develops the experience to increase the efficiency of water application to the crop, the water requirements will be reduced to the point where additional areas could be taken in, at least from a technical standpoint. Final confirmation of the potential of the area will be problematic until reliable data can be accumulated as to the irrigation run-offs of adjacent citrus and sugar estates, and their effect on the total flow in the Umbuluzi River.

(S.J.F. Winn, 'An Introduction to Simunye Sugar Estate', *Proceedings of the South African Sugar Technologists' Association*, June 1979, p. 3.)

53. The factory is designed to mill 1,050,000 tonnes cane and in 1982 crushed 1,042,262; it should produce approximately 120,000 tonnes sugar p.a. and in 1982 made 110,354 tonnes; the sucrose content was 12.06%, well within the stated range of 11.5–15.0%. From a comparison of the design parameters (Winn, 'Simunye', p. 4) with RSSC crop performance data (supplied by Tate and Lyle).

54. I. Carmichael and B. Newton, 'Cost Economics of Production Capacity Expansion', a paper presented to the International Sweeteners and Alcohol Conference, The Future of Sugar, London, April 1980, paras. 13 and 14.

55. Swaziland has a population of some 600,000. *Per capita* consumption is the third highest in Africa; Mauritius registers 42.2 kg p.a., South Africa 41.5 kg and Swaziland 39.8 kg.

56. During 1982 the ISO decided that BETs for 1982 would remain in effect for 1983 and 1984. This confirms a new and higher BET for Swaziland of 254,839 tonnes; Swaziland's quota for 1982 was 216,613 tonnes. ISO Memo (82)50 Restricted, 6 October 1982.

57. I.e. from 167,900 tonnes to 1,561,700 tonnes. K. Bot, *Employment and Incomes in Sugar Cane Cultivation in Thailand* (ILO-ARTEP, Bangkok, November 1981), Appendix Table 2.

58. A study of the information given in *Million Baht Business Information Thailand 1980-1981* (Pan Siam Communications, Bangkok) suggests that control of more than 50% of Thailand's mill capacity is in the hands of three families. The Assadathorn family (Thai Roong Ruang Group) have a controlling interest in three large (i.e. over 6,000 TCD) factories in Uttaradit and Kanchanaburi, and considerable minority interests in at least six other factories in Kanchanaburi, Chonburi and Rayong. In the majority of cases a member of the Assadathorn family manages the factory too. The Chinthammit family (Kwang Soon Lee Group) has a controlling interest in two large factories — one in Rajburi, the other in Kanchanaburi — and further interests in four factories (two in Kanchanaburi, one in Khon Khan and one in Chonburi). All six are managed by members of the family. The Wongkusolkit family (Mitr Group) has considerable minority holdings in four factories (two in Rajburi and two in Kampangpetch) and manages three of them.

59. For a fuller account of government policies see Bot, *Employment and Incomes*, pp. 15–18; Choomchai Atachinda and Prajuab Lewchalermvongs, 'Thailand' in Asian Productivity Organisation, *Sugar Cane Production in Asia* (APO, Tokyo, 1980), p. 327; J.C. Ingram, *Economic Change in Thailand 1850-1970* (Stanford University Press, 1971), pp. 126–7, pp. 139–40; D. Smith, *Cane Sugar World* (Palmer Publications, New York, 1978), pp. 121–6.

60. Deduced from a list of Thailand's mills in *F.O. Licht International Sugar Economic Year Book and Directory 1981*.

61. It appears that the farmers were not hindered in their efforts to clear virgin land in the forest reserves, which were officially protected. The Consolidated Land Act of 1908 gave people the right to take as much land as they could 'turn to profit' — normally 20–50 rai (1 rai = 1,600 sq. metres). The Land Act of 1936 specified 50 rai as the maximum which could be taken. Though this limit was confirmed in the Land Code of 1954 it was abolished in 1959 by Announcement No. 49 of the Revolutionary Party, after which presumably farmers were free to take more than 50 rai. See Ingram, *Economic Change*, pp. 79 and 267; J.H. Kemp, 'Legal and Informal Land Tenures in Thailand', *Modern Asian Studies*, vol. 15, no. 1 (1981), pp. 1–23.

62. A.J. de Boer, 'Statistical Summary of the Sugar Industries in APO member countries' in Asian Productivity Organisation, *Sugar Cane Production in Asia* (APO, Tokyo, 1980), p. 137.

63. *Agricultural Census of Thailand 1978*, Tables 3.4 and 3.5.

64. Most wages are paid by task, e.g. Baht 30 per tonne for harvesting, Baht 120 per rai for weeding. The main reason for paying by task seems to be lack of supervisory labour which is necessary if wages are paid by day. Task rates work out at Baht 30 a day. Bot, *Employment and Incomes*, pp. 36–7.

65. Ibid., p. 5; Choomchai and Prajuab, 'Thailand', p. 325, state that yields varied greatly from year to year, the range during the period 1961/2 to 1977/8 being 31–52 tonnes per hectare. Bot, *Employment and Incomes*, p. 26, states that in 1980/1 yields varied from 80 tonnes for irrigated plant cane in Suphanburi to 31 tonnes for second ratoon cane in Chonburi.

66. Smith, *Cane World*, p. 123; Bot, *Employment and Incomes*, p. 54, n. 1.

67. Bot, *Employment and Incomes*, p. 55, quoting Colombo Plan experts (JICA), 'Improvement of Raw Sugar Quality and Production Efficiency' (The Sugar Institute, Bangkok, 1978).

68. Bot, *Employment and Incomes*, pp. 38–40; Smith, *Cane World*, p. 125; Boer, 'Statistical Summary', pp. 68–9.

69. Smith, *Cane World*, p. 125.

70. The millers are grouped into two organisations which are also responsible for marketing their sugar both domestically and for export: the Thai Sugar Producers' Association with 40% of total capacity, and the Thai Sugar Manufacturing Association with 60%. Bot, *Employment and Incomes*, p. 10.
Between 1961 and 1969 the area planted to cane fluctuated greatly, depending on how well the mills treated the farmers. So the Kanchanaburi growers formed a militant organisation in 1964 and the Chonburi farmers in 1969. In 1970 the two groups joined forces. By 1977 the associations numbered five and came together as the Federation of Sugar Cane Growers of Thailand (or Thailand Sugarcane Planters' Federation). As the associations are led by the quotamen, the Federation effectively controls the entire supply of cane and therefore is in a strong bargaining position *vis-à-vis* the millers and the government. Choomchai and Prajuab, 'Thailand', p. 318. The cane growers are the only group of farmers in Thailand able to organise themselves in this way. Bot, *Employment and Incomes*, p. 18.

71. In 1971/2 the price paid to growers was US$7.50 (Baht 150); by 1980/1 the price had risen to US$32.50 (Baht 650). *Sugar y Azucar*, August 1976, p. 29 and October 1981, p. 24.

72. Accounts giving some idea of the forceful interplay of characters and arguments at government level are to be found in the *Far East Economic Review*, e.g. 9 May 1980, 26 September 1980, 21 August 1981 and 11 December 1981. See also J. Messineo, 'Thailand's Proverbial Sugar Problem', *Sugar y Azucar*, October 1981.

73. Ingram, *Economic Change*, p. 264, gives the value at wholesale prices of the average output per rai (his figures reflecting the Bangkok price and not the farm price, and thus giving no indication as to cost and net return for the farmer) of selected crops in 1965–7. These are set out below beside the profits per rai for the farmer in 1978/9, as given by Bot, *Employment and Incomes*, p. 53. Both sets of figures suggest that cane was profitable in those years, second only to cassava (in Baht):

	Ingram 1965–7	Bot 1978/9
Cassava	611	1,262
Cane	606	324
Kenaf	569	− 146 (loss)
Mung bean	414	68
Soy bean	363	284
Maize	325	35
Paddy	291	53

74. Bot, *Employment and Incomes*, pp. 56–7.

75. Ingram, *Economic Change*, pp. 261–5.

76. R.J. Muscat, *Development Strategy in Thailand: a Study of Economic Growth*, Praeger Studies in International Economics and Development (Praeger, New York, 1966), p. 93.

77. Paisal Sricharatcharya, 'Thailand tries to iron out the production bumps', *Far Eastern Economic Review*, 5 November 1982, p. 72. See also the *Standard Chartered Review*, January 1983, p. 31; the *Reuter Sugar Newsletter*, 14 December 1982, 20 April 1983 and 25 April 1983. Three international sugar firms Tate and Lyle Ltd, and E.D. and F. Man of the UK, together with the Kerry Trading Company of Hong Kong, have agreed to buy 3 million tonnes of raws from the new Thai company over five years 1983–7.

78. Bot, *Employment and Incomes*, p. 49.

79. The *Reuter Sugar Newsletter*, 3 January 1983.

80. Jamaican farmers have grown just over half the country's cane since the mid-1960s. In 1974 two-thirds of the farmers' output was grown by 176 farmers averaging 7,500 tonnes each from approximately 110 hectares. The remaining one-third was grown by about 16,000 part-time farmers cultivating hillside plots of 0.25 to 0.5 hectares. ISO, *World Sugar Economy: Structure and Policies*, no. 6, *Argentina–Barbados–Jamaica* (ISO, London, 1980).

In Trinidad successive British governors since the 1870s encouraged small farmers to supplement estate supplies. They now produce 40% of the island's cane, and more cheaply than the estates. Hugill, *Sugar and All That*, p. 124; S.N. Girwar, 'The Place of Government and Factory owned Plantations in the Sugar Industry', Proceedings of the First World Sugar Farmers' Conference, International Federation of Agricultural Producers, Guadalajara, May 1981.

81. The Queensland cane farmers are widely admired for their professionalism, capital-intensive farms and yields. In the sugar world they provide an excellent example of the independent farmer who monitors his own performance, as described in the section 'Direct Planning Systems' in Chapter 6. They have the education and the capability to solve most of the problems that arise on their 20–70 hectare farms, but they do not work in isolation. The sugar industry is highly regulated, and very largely self-controlled; it works closely with the Queensland government which buys all the raw sugar produced and is also responsible, through contracts with Australian refiners, for the distribution of raw and refined sugar. The mills are allocated quotas, and farmers must deliver their cane to the mill to which their land has been assigned; in this way output is controlled. The methods of payment for cane and raw sugar, which include premiums on quality, play an important part in promoting farming and milling efficiency. The industry's international reputation owes much to a wide range of research programmes, development projects and technical field services. Fifteen of the 33 mills are co-operatively owned by cane growers, the remainder by proprietary companies. This interlocking structure has evolved over the years; it may be traced back to the end of the nineteenth century when the Federation of Australian states decided to break up the plantations and repatriate the South Sea islanders. The sudden shortage of labour forced the new owner–operators to devise their own ways of solving the problem; self-help, capital investment and strong associations rapidly became — and remain — the linchpins of their competitiveness.

82. Guyana's sugar lands lie along a narrow coastal plain below sea level, and require much capital expenditure and managerial effort to maintain an elaborate system of sea-walls, low-level drains and high-level irrigation and navigation channels along which the cane is punted to the mills.

10 GENERAL CONCLUSIONS AND SUMMARY

The discussion began with the need for more agricultural produce to meet the growing gap between what is now produced and what is needed to meet the rapid increase in the world's population.

In the preceding chapters many difficulties have emerged in the face of each approach to agriculture. Most have a very real validity. Social questions — of employment, standard of living, changes in life style, participation in responsibility for development and the changes that it brings — have an importance which transcends a doctrinaire or narrowly political examination. They raise questions of the most basic of values and every attempt to move development forward in the Third World must be compelled to take account of them.

Nevertheless the most urgent imperative of all is to feed and keep alive the population of every country; it would be difficult to plead that there is anything more important than the cure of starvation and the raising of the standard of nutrition universally above the bare minimum. If production of more food (or other agricultural products which can be traded for food) requires change, then surely change should be accepted. Moreover, it is here that the concepts of efficiency and productivity for which, in a Western sense, the price may be thought too high in the case of other aspects of development, can without demur be seen to justify themselves. More leisure, or a non-industrial pattern of life, might well be preferred to the attractions of a consumer-goods orientated society; a socialist pattern of state organisation may well look more attractive than the profit motive for most economic activities, without any call to judge between them as to productivity and efficiency. Indeed a pattern of the minimum of change for some societies may well be the most attractive of all options; but it can hardly be adopted when any part of the population is underfed. Greater production from the land is a problem which should be judged on very pragmatic criteria.

This is often forgotten. The desirability of a project to increase productivity from the land is often assessed and discussed as if it were a general development or welfare project. Schemes are condemned because they might favour particular sectors of the population, or call for a different pattern of work and employment. Even ventures which are already producing tangible quantities of the product for which they were formed are criticised because they have not given birth to a particular form of society or community.

Social engineering can become the determinant of policy to the detriment of greater agricultural production. It is a constant attraction and indeed temptation for the planner and the politician. Those who try to frame production schemes must therefore take account of it, allow for it and try so to frame the institutions they build that they can be adapted to social considerations as well — with the minimum of interference with their prime objective of productivity.[1]

Detailed comparisons of the efficiency of different agricultural systems are difficult. Soil fertility, water supplies and rainfall, drainage and sunshine are constantly varying factors. After them come the questions about the thoroughness and efficiency with which systems can be applied. It is possible to produce records over the years which will suggest that particular projects and organisations have a good record and thus make possible comparisons with other systems. But, if only because two agricultural organisations are never exactly the same, it is impossible to take one type of organisation, whether it be co-operative smallholdings or a plantation system, and claim automatic superiority for it merely because it is that particular system.

It is, however, possible to claim from certain broad figures over a period of years that the institutionalisation of agriculture and the steady application thereby of international technology and recognised management skills will lead to greatly increased production. Conversely, failure to make change come about in the rural scene will not only produce stagnation, but even lead to a considerable drop in existing production, as more attractive developments outside agriculture draw labour away from it. Countries whose governments have encouraged the growth of corporate agricultural ventures, usually associated with an international network of management and technology, have prospered in their agricultural production, while those who have not encouraged their growers in the same way, or have even set their face against it, have produced a very different result. Again, from the nature of the subject, it is impossible to produce figures which will substantiate a universal verdict, but the figures for palm oil, as an example of a crop which has had an outstanding history since the war of managerial and technical development, show dramatically what can be done (see Table 10.1).

Table 10.1: Palm Oil Exports from Selected Countries in 1960 and 1976 (tons)

	1960	1976
Nigeria	186,000	0
Indonesia	109,000	406,000
Malaysia	92,000	1,335,000
Ivory Coast	0	91,000

Source: T. Forrest, 'Agricultural Policies in Nigeria 1900–1978' in J. Heyer, P. Roberts and G. Williams (eds.), *Rural Development in Tropical Africa* (St Martin's Press, New York, 1981), p. 251. Forrest comments that 'historians with a taste for conjecture may feel that the long-standing argument that a peasant oil palm industry would give way to international competition from plantations has finally been resolved by [these] figures'.

There is moreover a deeper significance behind the figures themselves. As has already been said, palm oil is the crop which, with rubber, has had the most intensive development effort world-wide. It has had a large research effort devoted to it, especially since the 1950s, both as to its managerial methods on plantations and the agronomy and technology that is thereby applied. It has also seen a striking adaptation of a management system and technology to a desired social pattern in the achievements of FELDA, which has succeeded in combining plantation methods with a system of smallholdings, and has thereby played a very large part in the enormous increase in production shown above for Malaysia.

The figures are also a tribute to consistency of government policies. Malaysia and the Ivory Coast have not hesitated in their faith in institutionalisation and plantation methods. In Indonesia, though the achievements in the same direction have been considerable, the single-minded consistency on the part of the government has not been as great.[2] In other words, by according proper priorities, adopting suitable approaches and institutions and using international networks of know-how and technology, it is possible to bring about a basic and lasting change and a considerable betterment in what the land can produce. Is it possible to identify, from what has gone before, the critical features behind these successes and suggest programmes which could lead to similar success elsewhere?

Government Policies

During the last 30 years, most Third World governments have, from time to time, aimed in a general way at increasing production from the land. What is needed, however, is something more specific — schemes which have as their clear and main aim the increase of productivity. General development and improvement should follow if the increase in production is achieved, but the planning and choice of the institutional system should be guided first by the need for production rather than by the preference for a particular social or communal pattern. The two are usually not mutually exclusive, but it is important that the pattern be laid out with production in mind and the adaptations only then made to take in the social considerations. If the increase does not come about because the institution set up to achieve the project is not an efficient one, there will be no beneficial outcome in terms of social patterns anyway, and no progress will have been made against food shortages.

Plantations are a particularly apposite case here. The Government of Malaysia, for instance, in spite of the sort of prejudices which have been examined in earlier chapters, encourages an economy which depends on plantation systems and has been able to adapt them very successfully to reflect its social policies, as instanced in the way that FELDA, on the back of a growing production success, was able to induce change in living patterns and social organisation and do it purposively and in accordance with a long-term plan.[3] It is, however, vital to recognise that this sort of change could never have come about if the original organisation had not first been successful in building up the production on which to base the social pattern. To establish a system first for bringing about the change in life style would have been to set up a project which would have been bound to fail because there was no base on which it could build. In other words, the need for production was made paramount, in spite of the prejudice attached to the idea of a plantation system; once adopted, the system was successfully adapted — but this could only be done once there was a system on which to build. In Nigeria, no such solution could be possible; the dislike of the plantation idea, common to all Nigerian governments since the beginning of the twentieth century, has meant that there has been no extra wealth created from increased supplies of palm oil, no increased availability for its use as a basic food in the country, and no opportunity to build a changed rural society based on it.

This is not an argument for the adoption of the plantation system; but it is an argument for choosing, after proper examination of the different alternatives, a management system or an institution which is designed to increase agricultural production, either for internal consumption or export, single-mindedly and without other objectives at this stage. Only if and when this system has proved successful, should its adaptation to suit other aims and social targets be tackled as the next part of the project. If these other objectives cannot be realised, it is of course possible to abandon the plan. The cost of abandonment in terms of lost production will then be clear, but if the initially chosen system is altered in its essentials, the production will be lost in any case and the desired social aim, in so far as it rests on the wealth created from the crops, will not be achieved either.

Once the importance of the need has cleared the way to open-minded choices of suitable ways to proceed, the possibilities are greatly enlarged. If they can be applied properly, there are both techniques and technologies which can steadily improve output through new ventures, and produce better results than those which already exist.

New Crops

It was remarked at the beginning of Chapter 1 that, although in his history man has used 3,000 plant species for food, the world's population today depends upon about 20 crops, and that some of these have been developed much more intensively than others. The choice of the products for this intensive treatment has been largely determined by the interest of the developed countries. There is, then, an immediate area where further work should produce comparatively quick results — by applying the methods that have been successful with the developed crops, both in terms of plant research and agronomic system, to crops which, though familiar and widely grown, have not had the intensive development that has been seen in the case of oil palm, rubber, etc. This is discussed more fully later.

It may well be, however, that major increases could also come from plants which, through accidents of history or geography, have not been so thoroughly examined and exploited; their potential has not been properly evaluated, nor has it been possible to begin to estimate the advantages or difficulties of cultivating them. Work has already started on identifying them; international bodies and private corporations have become interested, but their individual abilities to carry the enquiry forward must be recognised as very different. This emerges clearly if we take as an example the work done in 1974 at the National Academy of Sciences in the USA. They set up a high-level panel which was widely international and representative of developing as well as developed countries to consider 'under-exploited tropical plants with promising economic value' and identified 36.

All of these can be grown in the tropics, have a significant potential as a source of food, forage or industrial raw material and are thought to be of help in making developing countries, or at least areas within them, more productive. But the panel found it could go no further. It comments:

> The task of weighing the technical details against the economics, needs, resources and capabilities of a particular country or area is perforce left to interested, competent authorities . . . This report does not detail how to introduce the plants to new areas. Readers should appreciate that achieving this goal may be complex and difficult . . . Even if all these problems are overcome, the plant will be successful only if a market exists or can be created for its products. The information in this book is only a starting point for what may prove to be laborious and troublesome projects.[4]

This means in practice that there must be a well-qualified organisation or institution to do the development and the evaluation. Initial work, whether in the laboratory or the field, can only be of value when it is followed by a carefully managed scheme to increase the scale of the development, to test what has been done again in a different climate and different soil conditions, and with different cultivation techniques, perhaps with the use of different machinery. All this, if it is to advance steadily and be checked at every stage, needs an institution which is linked to an international research and scientific network; there must be a constant crossfeeding of information from different disciplines concerned not only with the scientific aspects but the commercial and marketing possibilities as well — along the lines of the actual examples described in Chapter 4.

Once production has grown to commercial quantities, processing and storage and distributing become equally important — with control of quality and grading throughout. Indeed the questions of processing and storage/distributing can themselves destroy a project even when all the problems of growing and collection can be solved. The Babassu nut, for instance, with an excellent high oil content and few agronomic problems, is so hard that it is difficult to crack and extract the oil on a commercial scale — and so it has been very little exploited.[5] Indeed, even with as well-established a crop as bananas, failure to provide a carefully controlled grading, transport and ripening system, vertically integrated right through to the final point of sale, has spelt disaster when it could not be provided by co-operatives who were perfectly capable of carrying out the actual growing of the fruit but did not have the right grading and transport chain, managed and co-ordinated with the farmers' production.[6]

In other words, the identification of the new species is only the very beginning of a long process. It will involve many different efforts and disciplines, from the research worker at the beginning to the farmer in the field, the collector, storer and distributor. It may also require a processor who converts in a factory the commodity crop into the article that is actually consumed, whether it is edible fats from oil seeds or motor tyres from rubber. The chain will not be completed until there is an assured market at the end, in the sense that each of the links must add a value to each intermediate product.

To analyse in this way the problems that face a new discovery is to underline the fact that its full exploitation is no different in kind from the handling of an accepted commodity which already goes through these processes. What is lacking in the new is the vital confidence at each stage that the product is wanted at the next point and can arrive there on commercial terms. When this is not yet assured, the risks of loss and wasted effort over a period of years are great; it is not surprising to find that so many bright seeming opportunities are not adopted — or are only approached slowly and with some reluctance.

'Developed' Crops

The foregoing suggests that the immediate task should be to develop further those crops for which the prospects appear brighter in the longer term. Palm oil, rubber and sugar are three commodities whose production techniques have greatly advanced over the last 20 years — and much attention has been paid to them in this book. However, there are many others — such as coffee, tea, bananas, coconut palm and cocoa — which are grown successfully in plantations. In some cases it is possible to integrate them with basic subsistence crops.

Whether they wish to feed their people directly or to earn the foreign exchange with which to do so, Third World governments have a range of possibilities based on well-developed technologies. The plantation is the institution which can absorb and apply these technologies. Moreover, once its basic structure has been laid out — the ground cleared, roads built, labour housed and trained — it has a certain flexibility between commodities. Should world markets move against an export crop, for instance, it is possible within a few years to substitute some plantation crops for others, running down one crop while the other matures; so that over a period of say six to seven years a producer can go out of rubber and into palm oil or coconut oil or coffee or cocoa. The assets are the structure of the plantation and its labour force and management; it is the form of the institution that matters; it can be applied to many crops.

As has been said before, the constitution and ownership can be varied to suit national needs and political tastes; the test is that the institution should be capable of applying and operating with the international techniques that have proved themselves when they have been properly used. There is a wide variety of examples, ranging from the state plantations in Indonesia, publicly owned as to 100 per cent of their capital, through the mixture of privately owned and state-owned plantations in Malaysia and the flexible organisation of FELDA, to private and public plantations working side by side in Kenya and Cameroon. All are of a suitable size and constitution (neither too big nor too small) which enables them to operate according to management rather than bureaucratic criteria; this is an important element in their success. Most importantly of all, they have attained a standard of competence and scientific standing (sometimes by the use of expatriate managers initially) which enables them to be part of an international network of research and development. They publish their own discoveries and at the same time can use and carry forward in their own estates the advances that others in the international scene make reciprocally available, and their managements are insistent on such participation in the international networks.

Also available for growing all these crops is a form of plantation that has been specifically evolved to meet the needs of the developing country in educating its farmers and improving its cultivation of standardised crops — the nucleus plantation. This has been described in Chapter 6, with a case history in Chapter 7. It is essential that the nucleus itself be constituted strictly according to the best of available technology with experienced management. Outside the nucleus there is more room for manoeuvre. There is considerable scope for different organisation among the outworkers who are growing the crop for central collection and processing. They can be individual or family smallholders or a village or a co-operative. Provided the standards and the rules of the nucleus are maintained (and this must be the first priority), living patterns can be framed to meet social aims.

In other words the nucleus plantation can be a real and practical link between institutional management systems and the technology that they bring with them on the one hand and the wish of governments to provide for 'the small man' in their agricultural and social planning on the other. There may be a price to pay in terms of total production and returns per hectare of land under cultivation; but it may be felt by government that this is a price worth paying in return for its social values.[7]

Schemes for the Individual Farmer

Though plantation agriculture is a large employer of labour, its effects are usually very localised; indeed it often has to employ labour which is specially imported into the area; new plantations tend to be created out of clearing other types of growth, such as forests where previous inhabitants are scarce. To give the unemployed who are living in rural areas on the land — or the underemployed — work which will both increase productivity and provide them with a living is a very different exercise. It has strong attractions for planners both to prevent the drift to the towns and to cope at a basic level with the problem of unemployment which is often very serious.

Here, however, there should be pause for thought. The universal pattern is that, as countries advance further along the development path, their agriculture gets more productive and the number employed in it as a percentage of a population falls; so it could be represented that the single-minded pursuit of the employment of more people on the land runs contrary to what will be the eventual pattern of a much smaller percentage employed in agriculture.[8] Different countries have different patterns — but the trend is universal.

Nevertheless the problem of many developing countries is seen at the moment as one of employing more people productively on the land. This in its turn means installing systems which will make available the same technology as is used in intensively managed institutions in a form which can be applied to looser organisations. Can the techniques of the plantation be applied to a co-operative or to a regional project for smallholders?

The answer must be an unqualified yes; it has been done, as has been seen, in Mumias and elsewhere. What have been the secrets of their success and what are the obstacles that made other attempts fail?

Where there has been success, the common element has always been the effective application of technology. In other words there has been a change induced by new factors — whether these new factors are different methods of preparing the land, more detailed routines of care for the crops, the application of fertilisers or stricter requirements of processing. Even when claims are made of greater success with the old methods, it comes about by the better and more careful application of the old methods.

So there are two main factors which can be brought in from the outside: first, new strains of seed, new fertiliser, new processes; and, second, the improved application of what is already known — better and more regular irrigation, better planting, more regular weeding, harvesting at the crucial time, etc.

It has appeared throughout this book that what makes effective the application of all these factors is, in its most developed form, a management institution and, when the institution takes a looser form, a supervising management system. An experienced management providing the technology, the guidance as to how it is to be employed and the effective supervision of its implementation is a common feature in all the successes that have been quoted — whether they are recent developments in Africa (Chapters 6 and 7), established sugar plantations in the Dominican Republic or the pioneering smallholder sugar venture VIF in Swaziland (Chapter 9), or the path-breaking large cotton project in Gezira (Chapter 6, n. 7 and below). Management provides the skills and through them the organisation provides the machinery for application and the continuity.

Since the beginning of the 1970s, development literature has begun to take a very healthy and pragmatic interest in this subject. John R. Moris puts the problem and its solution very clearly:

the basic problem of getting effective agricultural performance from a field bureaucracy is general to most parts of the Third World. If the argument . . . is correct that the key hidden element which determines planning performance is the creation and continuous deployment of managerial resources within the field agencies then administrative structures which perform well under difficult circumstances in East Africa should prove equally effective elsewhere.[9]

It is possible to go further — if the 'key hidden element which determines planning performance' is indeed the creation and continued employment of managerial resources, it is possible to deploy a wider range of administrative structures adapted to different circumstances than those which are described by Moris. All that is mandatory is 'the creation and continuous deployment of managerial resources'. Thus 'there must be good local organisation to ensure the timely supply of inputs'. Similarly there must be 'an institutionalised transfer of modern skills coupled with various technical specialists in reach of each community'.[10] Provided these needs are recognised and accepted, the organisation to carry them out can be made to fit exactly the local circumstances — and it may not be the same in Africa as in Asia or anywhere else. What is required is the acceptance without prevarication of these needs; and it is failure to supply these needs efficiently which prevents a successful operation. The detailed tasks to be carried out (Moris gives cotton spraying as an example[11]) can only be expected to be carried out by an organisation formed for that and allied purposes — they do not lie within the nature of extension services or government departments and cannot be carried out by what Moris calls 'the hub and wheel' form of organisation used by government colonial and post-colonial services.[12] What is required is a hierarchical management structure which can function in many forms of organisation (Chapter 1). Moris himself quotes the example of the Kenya Tea Development Authority which 'relied heavily on the experience of commercial tea estates in drawing up a comprehensive programme for the expansion of smallholder tea in Kenya'. It has 'consistently met or exceeded its national production targets even though other attempts to sponsor smallholder tea in Asia have usually failed'.[13]

The Gezira is one of the most interesting and most consistently successful examples of a hierarchically managed institution which has over a period of more than 50 years provided both an income and food for a large number of Sudanese farmers and their families.[14] It is particularly interesting in the way in which the central managerial philosophy originally set up on a commercial model has lasted throughout successive changes in direction and ownership under both colonial and post-colonial governments. Because it is such a landmark it has also been criticised but, in terms of what has already been said in this chapter, for the wrong reasons. Yet even its detractors see its merits.

> It does not require social cost benefit analysis to indicate that without the scheme the people of the Gezira and probably of Sudan in general would have been less well off than they are at present . . . inasmuch as the scheme i) produces crops ii) supports a population iii) earns foreign exchange iv) continues to operate, it is a 'success'.[15]

It has produced for over 50 years a main cash crop — cotton — and fed a large number of people in the Sudan with subsidiary crops of millet, rice, wheat and groundnuts.

On the other side of Africa, in Nigeria, experience has been very different. With very few exceptions indeed the Nigerian government has insisted on large-scale — sometimes country-wide — attempts to influence agriculture. It has almost always worked through government departments and almost never introduced management-run agricultural institutions of a size that could be purposefully controlled. Recent very small experiments along these lines seem to have a chance of success but they are tiny in relation to the overall problem.[16] There is no sign that without a basic change of policy the more recent efforts are going to be any more successful than the government initiatives in the early 1900s.

Extension Services

Extension services by themselves do not seem to be sufficient to produce a marked and continuing change. They often have at their disposal all the necessary knowledge and technology, but the role of the extension officer is essentially an advisory one. He is not a supervisor and lacks the essential sanction available to the orthodox agricultural institution — whether it be of the FELDA or Gezira type, with penalties attached to insufficient performance by the smallholder, or the peasant farmer who is a member of a co-operative scheme, right through to the hierarchically managed commercial or parastatal corporate organisation. The shortfall in an extension service comes about through the failure to observe detailed routine rules and practices — to carry out meticulously the sort of duties listed by Jon Moris in his discussion of cotton procedures. He comments

> the organisational imperatives for effectiveness are clear. Somebody must keep the daily activities of distinct but vertically interlocked services under surveillance, must frame contingency plans in case the season or market shift prematurely, must indulge in bureaucratic politics in order to secure the commitments implied in an action programme and be prepared even to break the rules in an emergency.[17]

He calls this 'engaged planning', but in fact it is a description of the way in which a corporate management structure works.

He also goes on to dismiss the possibility of such activity — 'engaged planning' — being possible for a civil service. He says

> civil service rules prohibit the lateral communication so vital to the co-ordination of complex services. It is difficult for any other than the man at the top to request re-evalution of commitments because of changed circumstances. Civil service procedures almost never require the formulation of contingent plans; instead when a crisis strikes the organisation goes into immediate paralysis until orders are received from above. Many of the initiatives needed to realise long range objectives are in their immediate context technically illegal.[18]

Both because they are advisers and not managers, and also because they are subject to the same civil service bureaucracy, extension agents have a difficult and indeed impossible task.

When the farmer himself is motivated, extension officers can provide the technical advice and agricultural performance should thereby improve. But they do not and cannot provide regularly and efficiently the inputs that are necessary to enable a farmer to operate from day to day. These inputs vary from a tractor to seed to fuel for the tractor. If they are not supplied by an efficient organisation — which is executive in the sense that it takes these decisions and carries them out for itself — the whole of the work will stop regardless of the will to work or the degree of initiative of the individual farmer. It is this which tends to happen with the extension service. Leonard, a colleague of Moris, admits frankly that the Kenyan extension services have been disturbingly inefficient.[19] He produces a thorough and convincing examination of why this should be so and then passes on to recommend 'group extension services'. This is an institution under another name and, although the issue is not squarely faced, 'supervision' appears constantly as a very large part of the mixture. Thus he says 'staff at all levels respond best to non-authoritarian helpful styles of supervision'.[20] This is certainly true of many cultures, but the essential point is that 'supervision' is necessary to make the organisation work. It is well worth following the analysis in both these books in terms of organisation theory to understand the roots of the difficulty in dealing with smallholder cultivation of all kinds.

The Political Element in Agricultural Development

The reasons for choosing a particular location or a particular form or system of agriculture are frequently political, although with almost equal frequency they are not seen as such. Determining factors for the pattern chosen can be state policies (e.g. 'no foreign capital', or 'no expatriate management') or local politics which cause projects to be duplicated in order not to give a particular advantage to one region over the others, regardless of the viability of the project in the different regions.[21] Personal and private gain for sponsors or officials is another factor which frequently influences the choice of project or the allocation of credit funds.[22] It is not proposed to develop this further — it is a complicated subject which is examined fully by Bates. It is sufficient to point out that the price in efficiency is the same — sometimes more directly so — as in those cases where choices of agricultural systems are made for social reasons, for the sake of one type of community rather than another, or of one pattern of life rather than another.

A Summary

Agricultural production — especially of food — needs to grow faster. Traditional methods and larger areas cultivated produce a very slow increase which is not keeping pace with the growth of population. To feed their people adequately must be the prime objective of every state — for unless it can eat to live the population can enjoy no other benefits.

The basic ways of increasing productivity are now well understood as a result of a considerable advance in technology over the last 40–50 years. The technology itself needs and receives considerable development by researchers, experimenters and the producers of pilot and pioneering schemes but this technology has far outdistanced the ability to apply it effectively — particularly in the Third World.

The methods of applying the technology have been effectively studied only in one particular area — the plantation estate. This has become a corporate institution with its own specialised and highly developed techniques of management which enable it to turn the production of certain crops into a system which in some ways resembles an industrial process.

Industrial methods meet much prejudice when applied to agriculture. The standardisation of farming operations and the supervision which is needed to secure the regular and proper performance of agricultural tasks are alien to traditional ways of thinking. Moreover the institution which has done most to develop the system — the plantation — suffers from an accretion of prejudice in itself. The modern plantation estate is a very different entity from the forms of enterprise that used the name in the past. It is imperative that its new nature should be understood. The principles by which it is managed are clear and sufficiently broad to be capable of adaptation to meet most circumstances and a wider range of crops than those which are currently grown by plantation methods.

Once these principles are understood and the necessary adaptations made, the plantation estate is capable of much wider use. This extended use has been pioneered by some Third World governments to their great advantage. Elsewhere political attitudes are making slow progress. There is a strong case for rethinking, particularly by world organisations.

Where for any reason the plantation system is not acceptable, its principles and the system of the managerial corporate structure can be modified and applied over a wide range of different agricultural projects. There is a growing body of evidence that only the use of systematised management supervision and organisation can save the various types of loosely assembled communal efforts that are being used experimentally to tackle the problems of agriculture in the Third World today. This is the central message of this book.

Notes

1. The foregoing has been written with, of course, the standard principle of comparative advantage in mind. See pp. 13–14 above for an outline of how the principle may be applied to agricultural production by the LDCs.

2. T. Forrest, 'Agricultural Policies in Nigeria, 1900–1978' in J. Heyer, P. Roberts and G. Williams (eds.), *Rural Development in Tropical Africa* (St Martin's Press, New York, 1981), p. 224.

3. See C. MacAndrews, *Mobility and Modernisation: the Federal Land Development Authority and its Role in Modernising the Rural Malay* (Gadjah Mada University Press, Yogyakarta, 1977), pp. 80–5 for a detailed description of changes induced.

4. See National Academy of Sciences, *Underexploited Tropical Plants with Promising Economic Value* (National Academy of Sciences, Washington, 1975), pp. v, vi.

5. Ibid., p. 89.

6. An account of how vertical integration is an essential part of the banana industry — in this case in Cameroon — is to be found in B. Heinzen, 'The United Brands Company in Cameroon: a Study of the Tension between Local and International Imperatives', unpublished PhD thesis, School of Oriental and African Studies, London University, 1983.

7. See n. 27 in Chapter 7 for a comparison of estate and outgrower yields at Mumias; text and n. 27 of Chapter 9 for a description of outgrowers' performance at La Romana in the Dominican Republic.

8. In the *United Kingdom*, in 1981, out of a total working population of 25,435,000, only 333,700 (1.3%) were employed in agriculture. In the *USA*, in 1981, out of a total labour force of 110,812,000, 3.5 million (3.17%) worked in agriculture. In *Japan*, in 1981, out of a total labour force of 74.3 million, 6.68 million (9%) were employed in agriculture, forestry and fishing. In 1962 the proportion working in agriculture, forestry and fishing was 24.7% These statistics were taken from *The Statesman's Year Book 1983/84*. Similar statistics for *Malaysia* are less easy to come by, and the various surveys undertaken over the years are not strictly comparable. However, even in this developing country, the downward trend of the number employed in agriculture is apparent: in 1931, out of approximately 583,675 listed as engaged in various occupations, some 464,000 (80%) worked in agriculture and fishing; R. Emerson, *Malaysia: a Study in Direct and Indirect Rule* (University of Malaya Press, Kuala Lumpur, 1964), p. 183. By 1962, out of a total of 2,305,700 in employment, approximately 1,262,000 (55%) worked in agriculture, forestry, fishing and in the processing of agricultural products; Pierre R. Crosson, *Economic Growth in Malaysia: Projections of Gross National Product and of Production, Consumption and Net Imports of Agricultural Commodities* (National Planning Association, Washington DC, 1966), p 41. In 1979/80, out of a total labour force of 4,956,000, some 43% were employed in agriculture; Ministry of Finance, Malaysia, *Economic Report 1979/80* (Director General of Printing, Kuala Lumpur, 1979).

9. Jon R. Moris, 'Managerial Structures and Plan Implementation in Colonial and Modern Agricultural Extension: a Comparison of Cotton and Tea Programmes in Central Kenya' in D.K. Leonard, *Rural Administration in Kenya* (East African Literature Bureau, Nairobi, 1973), p. 98.

10. Ibid, p. 99.

11. Ibid., pp. 100–1.

12. Ibid., pp. 109–16.

13. Ibid., pp. 122–3.

14. For the definitive work on Gezira see A.G. Gaitskell, *Gezira: a Story of Development in the Sudan* (Faber and Faber, London, 1959). See also T. Barnett, 'Evaluating the Gezira Scheme: Black Box or Pandora's Box' in J. Heyer, P. Roberts and G. Williams (eds.), *Rural Development in Africa* (St Martin's Press, New York, 1981), pp. 306–24.

15. Barnett, 'Evaluating the Gezira Scheme', p. 313.

16. Small pockets of success are described in some detail in World Bank, *Accelerated Development in Sub-Saharan Africa* (Washington DC, 1981) — see n. 3 of Chapter 6 above.

17. Moris, 'Managerial Structures', p. 101.

18. Ibid., p. 102.

19. D.K. Leonard, *Reaching the Peasant Farmer: Organisation, Theory and Practice in Kenya* (University of Chicago Press, Chicago and London, 1977), p. xvi.

20. Ibid., p. 27.

21. R.H. Bates, *Markets and States in Tropical Africa: the Political Basis of Agricultural Policies* (University of California Press, Berkeley, 1981), p. 114.

22. See ibid., pp. 54–61, for an account of how the elite developed mechanised farming in the savannah region of Ghana at the expense of the smaller farmers.

BIBLIOGRAPHY

Alladin Hashim 'Land Development under FELDA: Some Socio-Economic Aspects' in B.A.R. Mokhzani (ed.) *Rural Development in Southeast Asia* (Vikas Publishing House, New Delhi, 1979)

Allen, G.R. 'Mumias Sugar Company', a paper presented to the Mohonk Conference, April 1980

Alleyne, D.H.N. *The International Sugar Industry and the Third World* (Third World Forum Occasional Paper no. 9, 1979)

Amara Pongsapich *et al. Chonburi Project: Institution and Human Resources Development in the Chonburi Region* (Chulalongkorn University Social Research Institute, Bangkok, 1970)

Amir Baharuddin 'FELDA Land Schemes' in Cheong Kee Cheok, Khoo Siew Mun and R. Thillainathan (eds.) *Malaysia: Some Comtemporary Issues in Sociological Development* (Persatuan Ekonomi Malaysia, Kuala Lumpur, 1979)

Ardener, E., Ardener, S. and Warmington, W.A *Plantation and Village in the Cameroons* (Oxford University Press, 1960)

Ariza, H.L. 'The Structure of the Sugar Sector in Cuba', Proceedings of the First World Sugar Farmers' Conference, International Federation of Agricultural Producers, Guadalajara, May 1981

Asian Productivity Organisation *Sugar Cane Production in Asia* (APO, Tokyo, 1980)

Attfield, M. 'Outlook for World Supply and Demand', *Sugar y Azucar*, April 1983

Awasthi, R.C. *Economics of Tea Industry in India* (United Publishers, Gauhati (Assam), 1975)

Baker, K.M. 'Problems of Food Production in West Africa: the Case of Rice in the Office du Niger, Mali', unpublished paper, School of Oriental and African Studies, London University, 1984

Baldwin, R.E. 'Patterns of Development in Newly Settled Regions', *Manchester School of Economic and Social Studies*, vol. 24, May 1956

Barnes, A.C *The Sugar Cane* (Interscience Publishers, New York, 1964)

Barnett, T. 'Evaluating the Gezira Scheme: Black Box or Pandora's Box' in J. Heyer, P. Roberts and G. Williams (eds.) *Rural Development in Africa* (St Martin's Press, New York, 1981)

Barlow, C. *The Natural Rubber Industry: its Development, Technology and Economy in Malaysia* (Oxford University Press, Kuala Lumpur, 1978)

Bates, R.H. *Markets and States in Tropical Africa: the Political Basis of Agricultural Policies* (University of California Press, Berkeley, 1981)

Bauer, P.T. *The Rubber Industry: a Study in Competition and Monopoly* (Longmans, Green and Co., London, 1948)

Beckford, G.E *Persistent Poverty: Underdevelopment in Plantation Economies of the Third World* (Oxford University Press, 1972)

Berg, E.J. 'The development of a labour force in Sub-Saharan Africa' in Z.A. and J.M. Konczacki (eds.) *An Economic History of Tropical Africa* (2 vols., Frank Cass, London, 1977)

Biswas, M.R. 'Agrarian reform and rural development', *Mazingira* (The world forum for environment and development), no. 12 (1979)

de Boer, A.J. 'Statistical Summary of the Sugar Industries in APO Member Countries' in Asian Productivity Organisation *Sugar Cane Production in Asia* (APO, Tokyo, 1980)

Bot, K. *Employment and Incomes in Sugar Cane Cultivation in Thailand* (ILO-ARTEP, Bangkok, November 1981)

Brook, E.M. and Nowicki, D. 'Sugar: Econometric Forecasting Model of the World Sugar Economy', The World Bank, Washington DC, March 1979
——and Ringlien, W.R. 'The Sugar Industry in the Dominican Republic', *F.O. Licht's International Sugar Report*, vol. 111, no. 34, November 1979
Bull, T.A. and Cullen, G.R. 'Chemical Products Applied to Sugar Cane Fields', *Sugar y Azucar 1981 Yearbook* (Palmer Publications, New York, 1981)
Carmichael, I. and Newton, B. 'Cost Economics of Production Capacity Expansion', a paper presented to the International Sweeteners and Alcohol Conference, The Future of Sugar, London, April 1980
Cheong Kee Cheok, Khoo Siew Mun and Thillainathan, R. (eds.) *Malaysia: Some Contemporary Issues in Sociological Development* (Persatuan Ekonomi Malaysia, Kuala Lumpur, 1979)
Chilvers, L. and Foster, R. *The International Sugar Market: Prospects for the 1980s*, Economist Intelligence Unit Special Report no. 106 (London, 1981)
Choeng H. Chung and Ezriel Brook 'The World Sugar Market: Review and Outlook for Bank Group Lending', World Bank Draft, 16 December 1976
Choomchai Atachinda and Prajuab Lewchalermvongs 'Thailand' in Asian Productivity Organisation *Sugar Cane Production in Asia* (APO, Tokyo, 1980)
Clowes, M.St.J. 'Ripening Activity of the glyphosate salts Mon 8000 and Roundup' in Proceedings of the ISSCT XVII Congress, Manila (3 vols., ISSCT, Manila, 1980), vol. 1, pp. 676-93
Colson, R.F. 'The Proalcool Programme: a Response to the Energy Crisis', *Bank of London and South American Review*, vol. 15, no. 11/81, May 1981
Courtenay, P.P. *Plantation Agriculture*, 2nd edn (Bell and Hyman, London, 1980)
Craton, M. and Walvin, J. *A Jamaican Plantation* (W.H. Allen, London, 1970)
Cromarty, W.A. *et al. World Sugar — Capacity, Cost and Policy* (Connell Rice and Sugar Co., New Jersey, 1977)
——'World Sugar Supply-Demand Outlook for Two to Five Years', *Sugar y Azucar*, April 1981
Crosson, P.R. *Economic Growth in Malaysia: Projections of Gross National Product and of Production, Consumption and Net Imports of Agricultural Commodities* (National Planning Association, Washington DC, 1966)
David, E. 'Sugar Production in Cuba', Sugar y Azucar, February 1983
de Wilde, J.C. *Experiences with Agricultural Development in Tropical Africa*, vol. 2, *The Case Studies* (Johns Hopkins Press, Baltimore, 1967)
Deerr, N. *Cane Sugar: a Textbook on the Agriculture of the Sugar Cane, the Manufacture of Cane Sugar, and the Analysis of Sugar House Products* (Norman Rodger, London, 1911)
——*The History of Sugar* (2 vols., Chapman and Hall, London, 1949 and 1950)
Drabble, J.H. *Rubber in Malaya 1876-1922: the Genesis of the Industry* (Oxford University Press, Kuala Lumpur, 1973)
Dunn, R.S. (University of Pennsylvania), unpublished seminar paper on plantation society, presented in Oxford (England) September 1981
Emerson, R. *Malaysia: a Study in Direct and Indirect Rule* (University of Malaya Press, Kuala Lumpur, 1964)
Emmanuel, A. *Appropriate or Underdeveloped Technology?* (John Wiley and Sons, Chichester, 1982).
Etherington, D.M. *An Econometric Analysis of Smallholder Tea Production in Kenya* (East African Literature Bureau, Nairobi, 1973)
Far Eastern Economic Review, published weekly
Fieldhouse, D.K. *Unilever Overseas: the Anatomy of a Multinational 1895-1965* (Croom Helm, London, 1978)
Fogel, R.W. and Engerman, S.L. *Time on the Cross: the Economics of American Negro Slavery* (Little, Brown and Co., Boston, 1974)
Food and Agriculture Organisation (FAO) *FAO Production Yearbook 1981*

Food and Agriculture Organisation *FAO Trade Yearbook 1981*

Forbes Munro, J. 'Monopolists and Speculators: British Investment in West African Rubber 1905-1914', *Journal of African History*, 22 (1981)

Forrest, T. 'Agricultural Policies in Nigeria 1900-1978' in J. Heyer, P. Roberts and G. Williams (eds.) *Rural Development in Tropical Africa* (St Martin's Press, New York, 1981)

Furnivall, J.S. *Netherlands India: a Study of Plural Economy* (Cambridge University Press, 1939, reprinted 1967)

Gaitskell, A.G. *Gezira: a Story of Development in the Sudan* (Faber and Faber, London, 1959)

Genovese, E.D. *The Political Economy of Slavery: Studies in the Economy and Society of the Slave South* (Vintage, New York, 1967)

Girwar, S.N. 'The Place of Government and Factory owned Plantations in the Sugar Industry', Proceedings of the First World Sugar Farmers' Conference, International Federation of Agricultural Producers, Guadalajara, May 1981

Godfrey, M. (ed.) 'Is Dependency Dead?' *Institute of Development Studies (IDS) Bulletin*, Sussex, vol. 12, no. 1, December 1980

Gunatilleke, G. (ed.) Special Issue on the Tea Trade, *Marga* (Colombo), vol. 3, no. 4, 1976

Hagelberg, G.B. *Outline of the World Sugar Economy* (Institut für Zuckerindustrie, Berlin, 1976), Forschungsbericht 3

——*Structural and Institutional Aspects of the Sugar Industry in Developing Countries* (Institut für Zuckerindustrie, Berlin, 1976), Forschungsbericht 5

——'Sugar and the Cuban Economy' in *F.O. Licht International Sugar Economic Year Book and Directory 1979*

Hance, W.A. *The Geography of Modern Africa* (Columbia University Press, New York and London, 1964)

Harris, S. 'The Development of Long Term Contracts in the International Sugar Trade', unpublished article for *World Sugar Journal*

Heinzen, B. 'The United Brands Company in Cameroon: a Study of the Tension between Local and International Imperatives', unpublished PhD thesis, School of Oriental and African Studies, London University, 1983

Helleiner, G.K. 'The fiscal role of the marketing boards in Nigerian economic development 1947-1961', *The Economic Journal*, vol. 74, no. 295, September 1964

Higgins, W. 'Worker Participation in Jamaican Sugar Production', *Rural Development Participation Review 1980* (United Sugar Workers' Co-operative council, Jamaica)

Hilton, H.W., Osgood, R.V. and Maretzki, A. 'Some Aspects of Mon 8000 as a Sugarcane Ripener to Replace Polaris' in Proceedings of the ISSCT XVII Congress, Manila (3 vols., ISSCT, Manila, 1980), vól. 1, pp. 652-61

Hirschman, A.O. 'A Generalised Linkage Approach to Development, with Special Reference to Staples', *Economic Development and Cultural Change*, 25 (1977), Supplement

Hojman, D.E. 'From Mexican plantations to Chilean mines: theoretical and empirical relevance of enclave theories in contemporary Latin-America', presented to a meeting of the Development Studies Association, Liverpool, March 1983

Hopkins, A.G. *An Economic History of West Africa* (Longman, London, 1973).

Hugill, A. *Sugar and All That: a History of Tate and Lyle* (Gentry Books, London, 1978)

——'Sucrose, a royal carbohydrate' in C.A.M. Hough, K.J. Parker and A.J. Vlitos (eds.) *Developments in Sweeteners* (Applied Science Publishers, London, 1979)

Ingram, J.C. *Economic Change in Thailand 1850-1970* (Stanford University Press, 1971)

International Labour Organisation *First Things First — Meeting the Basic Needs of the People of Nigeria* (ILO, 1981)

International Monetary Fund (IMF) *IMF Direction of Trade Statistics Yearbook 1983*

International Society of Sugar Cane Technologists (ISSCT) Proceedings of the XVII Congress in Manila, February 1980 (3 vols., ISSCT, Manila, 1980)

International Sugar Organisation (ISO) *Annual Report for the Year 1977* (ISO, London, 1978)

——*Statistical Bulletin*, published monthly

——*Sugar Year Book*, published annually

——*World Sugar Economy: Structure and Policies*, no. 6, *Argentina-Barbados-Jamaica* (ISO, London, 1980)

——*World Sugar Economy: Structure and Policies*, vol. 1, *Central and South America* (ISO, London, 1982)

——*World Sugar Economy: Structure and Policies*, vol. 2, *Africa* (ISO, London, 1983)

Jackson, J.C. *Planters and Speculators: Chinese and European Agricultural Enterprises in Malaya 1786-1921* (University of Malaya Press, Kuala Lumpur, 1968)

Jacquemot, P. (ed.) *Le Mali, le paysan et l'état* (Éditions L'Harmattan, Paris, 1981)

Jain, R.K. *South Indians on the Plantation Frontier In Malaysia* (Yale University Press, New Haven, 1970)

Jones, S., 'The Political Implications of Resettlement Policy in Malaysia', unpublished MA thesis, School of Oriental and African Studies, London University, 1980.

Kemp, J.H. 'Legal and Informal Land Tenures in Thailand', *Modern Asian Studies*, vol. 15, no. 1 (1981)

Knox, A.M. *Coming Clean* (Heinemann, London, 1976)

Leonard, D.K. (ed.) *Rural Administration in Kenya* (East African Literature Bureau, Nairobi, 1973)

——*Reaching the Peasant Farmer: Organisation, Theory and Practice in Kenya* (University of Chicago Press, Chicago and London, 1977)

F.O. Licht International Sugar Economic Year Book and Directory for the years 1979 and 1981

F.O. Licht's International Sugar Report, published 36 times a year, and generally referred to in the sugar trade as *Licht's*

F.O. Licht's International Sugar Report Special Edition, published as and when the need arises, and commonly referred to as *Licht's Special Report*

Little, I.M.D. and Mirrlees, J.A. *Project Appraisal and Planning for Developing Countries* (Heinemann, London, 1974)

——and Scott, M.FG. *Using Shadow Pricing* (Heinemann, London, 1976)

——and Tipping, D.G. *A Social Cost Benefit Analysis of the Kulai Oil Palm Estate, West Malaysia* (OECD Development Centre, Paris, 1972)

MacAndrews, C. *Mobility and Modernisation: the Federal Land Development Authority and its Role in Modernising the Rural Malay* (Gadjah Mada University Press, Yogyakarta, 1977)

McCatty, T. 'A Review of Sucrose Enhancer Trials in Jamaica in 1974-78' in Proceedings of the ISSCT XVII Congress, Manila (3 vols., ISSCT, Manila, 1980) vol. 1, pp. 630-43

Manual of Industrial Project Analysis in Developing Countries, vol. 1, *Methodology and Case Studies* (OECD Development Centre, Paris, 1968); vol. 2, Little, I.M.D. and Mirrlees, J.A. *Social Cost Benefit Analysis* (OECD Development Centre, Paris, 1969)

Martineau, G. and Eastick, F.C. *Sugar* 7th edn (Pitman and Sons, London, 1938)

Martinez-Alier, J. *Haciendas, Plantations and Collective Farms*, Library of Peasant Studies No. 2 (Frank Cass, London, 1977)

Mason, G.F. 'Chemical Ripening of Variety B41227 in Trinidad' in Proceedings of the ISSCT XVII Congress, Manila (3 vols., ISSCT, Manila 1980) vol. 1, pp. 663-74

Messineo, J. 'Thailand's Proverbial Sugar Problem', *Sugar y Azucar*, October 1981

Miller, W.K. 'The International Sugar Agreement: a Status Report', presented to the Conference of the Queensland Cane Growers' Council in Brisbane, March 1982 (ISO, London, 1982)

Million Baht Business Information Thailand 1980-1981 (Pan Siam Communications, Bangkok, 1980)

Ministry of Finance, Malaysia *Economic Report 1974/5* (The Treasury, Kuala Lumpur, 1974)

——*Economic Report 1979/80* (Director General of Printing, Kuala Lumpur, 1979).

Morgan, D.J. *The Official History of Colonial Development*, vol. 2, *Developing British Colonial Resources 1945-1951* (5 vols., Macmillan, London, 1980)

Moris, J.R. 'Managerial Structures and Plan Implementation in Colonial and Modern Agricultural Extension: a Comparison of Cotton and Tea Programmes in Central Kenya' in D.K. Leonard (ed.) *Rural Administration in Kenya* (East African Literature Bureau, Nairobi, 1973)

Muscat, R.J. *Development Strategy in Thailand: a Study of Economic Growth* (Praeger, New York, 1966)

National Academy of Sciences, *Underexploited Tropical Plants with Promising Economic Value* (National Academy of Sciences, Washington, 1975)

National Council of Applied Economic Research, *Techno-economic Survey of Darjeeling Tea Industry* (NCAER, New Delhi, 1977)

Office du Niger, 'The Niger Development Corporation 1932-1982', unpublished document, Ségou, Mali, December 1982

Olayide, S. and Olatunbosun, D. *Trends and Prospects of Nigeria's Agricultural Exports* (Nigerian Institute of Social and Economic Research, Ibadan, 1972)

Paisal Sricharatcharya, 'Thailand tries to iron out the production bumps', *Far Eastern Economic Review*, 5 November 1982

Pantin, D. 'The Plantation Economy Model and the Caribbean', *Bulletin of the Institute of Development Studies* (Sussex University), vol. 12, no. 1, December 1980

Persi, A.E. 'Colombia expands palm oil output', *Foreign Agriculture*, 9 January 1978

Quarterly Economic Review of Malaysia, Singapore and Brunei (Economist Intelligence Unit, London)

Rendell, Sir William *The History of the Commonwealth Development Corporation 1948-1972* (Heinemann Educational Books, London, 1976)

Reuter Sugar Newsletter, published daily Monday to Friday

Rodriguez, H.D. 'Cuba: Development and Building of New Sugar Mills', *World Sugar Journal* (Special Edition, Cuban Sugar Industry at a Glance), February 1982

Rothman, H., Greenshields, R. and Callé, F.R. *The Alcohol Economy* (Frances Pinter, London, 1983)

Sacerdoti, G. 'Cracks in the Coconut Shell', *Far Eastern Economic Review*, 8-14 January 1982

Scott, B. 'The Organisation Network: a Strategy Perspective for Development', unpublished PhD thesis, Harvard University Graduate School of Business Administration, 1979

Scott, C.D. *Tecnologia, Empleo y Distribucion de Ingresos en la Industria Azucarera de La Republica Dominicana* (Organizacion Internacional del Trabajo, Programa Regional del Empleo para America Latina y El Caribe, PREALC/158, Septiembre 1978)

Scott, M.FG., MacArthur, J.D. and Newbery, D.M.G. *Project Appraisal in Practice: the Little-Mirrlees Method applied in Kenya* (Heinemann, London, 1976)

Shamsul Bahrin, Tunku and Perera, P.D.A. *FELDA: 21 Years of Land Development* (FELDA, Kuala Lumpur, 1977)

Smith, D. *Cane Sugar World* (Palmer Publications, New York, 1978)

Smith, I. 'Can the West Indies' Sugar Industry Survive?' *Oxford Bulletin of Economics and Statistics*, 1976, part 2

Standard Chartered Review, published monthly

Steiner, S.J. *Vassouras, A Brazilian Coffee Country 1780–1900* (Harvard University Press, 1957)

Sugar World (GATT-Fly, Toronto), vol. 4, no. 5, December 1981

Sugar y Azucar, published monthly

Sugar y Azucar 1980 Yearbook (Palmer Publications, New York, 1980)

Sugar y Azucar 1981 Yearbook (Palmer Publications, New York, 1981)

Sullivan, J.D. 'The US Sugar Market 1983–1985', *Sugar y Azucar*, April 1983

Suret-Canale, J. *French Colonialism in Tropical Africa 1900–1945* (Hurst, London, 1971)

Thillainathan, R. 'Public Policies and Programmes for Redressing Poverty in Malaysia — a Critical Review' in B.A.R Mokhzani and Khoo Siew Mun (eds.) *Poverty in Malaysia* (Persatuan Ekonomi Malaysia, Kuala Lumpur, 1977)

Third Malaysia Plan 1976–80 (Government Printer, Kuala Lumpur, 1976)

Thoburn, J.T. *Primary Commodity Exports and Economic Development: Theory Evidence and a Study of Malaysia* (J. Wiley, London, 1977)

Unilever Report and Accounts 1981

United Nations Conference on Trade and Development (UNCTAD) Secretariat Report, 'Marketing and Processing of Sugar: Areas for International Co-operation', Ref. TD/B/C.1/PSC/29, Geneva, 9 December 1982

UN National Account Statistics 1979

Vuilleumier, S. 'World Corn Sweetener Outlook', *F.O. Licht's International Sugar Report*, vol. 113, no. 12, 15 April 1981

Ward, B. *Progress for a Small Planet* (Penguin Books, Harmondsworth, 1979)

Ware-Austin, W.D. 'Report on a Visit to the Mumias Sugar and Mumias Outgrowers' Companies, 1978', CDC mimeograph, July 1978

——'Report on a Visit to the Mumias Sugar and Outgrowers' Companies, 1979', CDC mimeograph, September 1979

——'Report on a Visit to the Mumias Sugar Company and the Mumias Outgrowers' Company, 1980', CDC mimeograph, August 1980

——'Mumias Sugar Company and Mumias Outgrowers' Company: a Brief History and Description', CDC mimeograph, February 1981

Wikkramatileke, R. 'Federal Land Development in West Malaysia 1957–1971', *Pacific Viewpoint*, vol. 13, no. 1, May 1972

Winn, S.J.F. 'An Introduction to Simunye Sugar Estate', *Proceedings of the South African Sugar Technologists' Association*, June 1979

Wohlmuth, K. 'Der Staat in peripheren Okonomien und die Transnationalen Konzerne: Interaktionen am Beispiel der Kenana Sugar Corporation, Sudan', Research Report No. 7, October 1979, University of Bremen

World Bank *Accelerated Development in Sub-Saharan Africa* (Washington DC, 1981)

——*World Development Report 1981* (Oxford University Press, 1981)

——*World Development Report 1982* (Oxford University Press, 1982)

World Sugar — Capacity, Cost and Policy (Connell Rice and Sugar Company, New Jersey, 1977)

'World Sugar Economy: Review and Outlook for Bank Group Lending', Report no. 1894, World Bank, Washington DC, 2 February 1978

World Sugar Journal, published monthly

INDEX

Printed in the United States
by Baker & Taylor Publisher Services